Railwaymen in the War

Also by Kazuo Tamayama:

BURMA 1942, JAPANESE INVASION
TALES BY JAPANESE SOLDIERS OF THE BURMA CAMPAIGN 1942–45

Railwaymen in the War

Tales by Japanese Railway Soldiers in Burma and Thailand 1941–47

Kazuo Tamayama

First published 2005 by
PALGRAVE MACMILLAN
Houndmills, Basingstoke, Hampshire RG21 6XS and
175 Fifth Avenue, New York, N.Y. 10010
Companies and representatives throughout the world

PALGRAVE MACMILLAN is the global academic imprint of the Palgrave Macmillan division of St. Martin's Press, LLC and of Palgrave Macmillan Ltd. Macmillan® is a registered trademark in the United States, United Kingdom and other countries. Palgrave is a registered trademark in the European Union and other countries.

ISBN 1–4039–3224–7 hardback

This book is printed on paper suitable for recycling and made from fully managed and sustained forest sources.

A catalogue record for this book is available from the British Library.

Library of Congress Cataloging-in-Publication Data
Railwaymen in the war : tales by Japanese railway soldiers in Burma and
    Thailand, 1941–1947 / [edited by] Kazuo Tamayama.
        p.   cm.
    Includes bibliographical references and index.
    ISBN 1–4039–3224–7 (cloth)
    1. Burma—Siam Railroad—History.   2. Japan. Rikugun—Military
    construction operations.   3. Japan. Rikugun—Biography.   4. Nihon
    Kokuyu Tetsudo—Employees—Biography.   5. World War, 1939–1945—
    Regimental histories—Japan.   6. World War, 1939–1945—Personal
    narratives, Japanese.   7. Oral history.   I. Tamayama, Kazuo.
    D767.47.R35 2004
    940.54'2591—dc22

                                                            2004048578

10   9   8   7   6   5   4   3   2   1
14   13   12   11   10   09   08   07   06   05

Printed and bound in Great Britain by
Antony Rowe Ltd, Chippenham and Eastbourne

Contents

List of Maps and Illustrations

Preface

This book tells the stories of a group of men who were devoted to their duty of moving the trains and constructing the railways even under the hardest conditions of war. They were the Japanese railway soldiers, a unique branch of the army that specialised in the operation and construction of railways, and the employees of the Japanese National Railways conscripted into the army.

The first Japanese army unit of railway engineers was established in 1896, as the result of the bitter experiences in the Sino-Japanese war (1894–5) of supplying the fronts in the vast expanse of Manchuria all by inefficient horse-drawn cart. During the Russo-Japanese war (1904–5), a Japanese railway battalion built a narrow-gauge railway between Antung on the Yalu River and Mukden (296 kilometres) following the advancing Japanese army. In 1918 two railway regiments were formed, and during the war with China (1937–1945) four more railway regiments were added. When Japan attacked Pearl Harbor and Malaya on 8 December 1941, she had seven railway regiments, of which two (the 5th and 9th) went to Malaya and then to Burma.

The 5th Railway Regiment was formed at Chiba in April 1938, and went to China, and to French Indo-China. When the war broke out in December 1941, it moved to Malaya via Thailand, together with the 9th Railway Regiment which had been mobilized two months before.

Five thousand employees of the Japanese National Railways (JNR) were conscripted and were sent to Burma as the 4th and 5th Special JNR groups. The JNR had an outstanding performance record, as the employees had received strict training emphasizing obedience to regulations, responsibility and discipline. JNR employees performed their difficult duties as faithfully as the soldiers of the railway regiments.

The two railway regiments then moved to Burma and repaired the railways that had been demolished by the retreating British. After the Special JNR units were transferred to the operations in Burma, the two regiments played the key role in the construction of the Burma–Thailand railway, a very arduous task deep in rugged mountains where cholera, malaria and tropical diseases were rife. The 415 kilometre railway was built within 15 months, which was a remarkable engineering achievement, but one accomplished at the cost of the deaths of 12,626 prisoners of war (British, Dutch and Australian), more than 15,000 local workers (Burmese,

Thais, Tamils etc.) and 1,000 Japanese. The extreme hardships of the PoWs engaged in the construction work, which resulted in the high death rate of 25 per cent, have been well documented in various publications.

After its completion, the two regiments worked to keep the trains running on the Myitkyina line and on the Burma–Thailand line in the face of the persistent demolition of the bridges and facilities by British and US war planes, and to transport Japanese troops and their essential supplies to the terminal stations. After the devastating defeat of the Japanese 15th Army in the Imphal area, the 5th Railway Regiment retreated from the Myitkyina line to Mandalay and then south to the Sittang River, fighting rearguard actions.

After the Japanese surrender on 15 August 1945, the railway regiments restored the badly damaged railways in Burma, working under British orders as 'Japanese Surrendered Personnel' (JSP) – not as prisoners of war under the Geneva convention – and operated the Thailand–Burma railway. Then more than one thousand railway officers and soldiers were arrested on suspicion of being war criminals and were put in prison at Changi and Rangoon, where they were treated harshly with starvation rations for a year. Seven railway officers and eight JNR men were prosecuted in the military war crimes courts, and Major-General Sasa, who commanded the construction of the railway, and Captain Hirota, a platoon leader, were hanged. Also 89 officers, guards and military police in charge of PoW camps were prosecuted and 43 of them were hanged. Apart from those who were sentenced to imprisonment, most of the men of the railway regiments had been sent back to Japan by October 1947.

This book tells the stories of the railway soldiers and JNR men during their training, their working experiences in Burma, their brave engagements with the allied armies, and their life as JSP after the surrender. Readers will understand that they were people who really liked the railways and carried out their duties faithfully at all costs. From another viewpoint, the book tells the history of the two railway regiments and two Special JNR units from their formation until their official termination. As the book takes the form of an oral history, it was not possible to get stories from those guards and soldiers who were extremely cruel to PoWs, since these had either been sentenced to death in the war crimes courts, committed suicide, or escaped to become Burmese residents in anticipation of their arrest. The extreme sufferings of the prisoners who were subjected to hunger and to cruel torture by the Korean guards and Japanese soldiers have been recorded in many writings of ex-PoWs, so only the titles of these records and a summary of an official report are given in this book.

Acknowledgements

Much of the material in the book is based on soldiers' recollections recorded in battalion or regimental memoirs or other publications. Some stories were abstracted from interviews. Details of these sources are given below. I am grateful to Mr Masanari Tazawa of the former 5th Railway Regiment, and Mr Ren-ichi Sugano of the former 9th Railway Regiment, who kindly agreed to let us use various parts of the relevant memoirs and photographs, and gave us various kinds of information on the railway engineers.

I would also like to acknowledge the extensive help and advice of Dr Caroline Rose in the writing of the introduction. My warm thanks are extended to Major-General Ian H. Lyall Grant for advice on the British view, contributing three chapters; to Mr John Nunneley, Mr Peter Dekkers, Mr Tatsuo Morohoshi, Mr Kazuya Tsukamoto and Mr Satoru Inazawa for their useful advice in many fields; to Mr Hugh E. Wilkinson for editing and revising my English writing; and to my wife Sazanami for the untiring support and encouragement she has given me.

Photo credits

Illustrations 1.1.1, 5.1.1 and 5.1.2 were offered by Mr Masanori Tazawa representative of veterans association of the 5th railway regiment. Illustration 3.16.1 was prepared by the author. Cover photography of the railway was taken by the author near Arrowhill in 1999 (see also page 23). All other illustrations were offered by Mr Ren-ichi Sugano who brought back the photographs hidden between the backplate of his waistbag smuggling through the rigid inspection of the Allied forces. After the surrender, Japanese were not allowed to take back any papers nor photographs by the order of the Allied forces. Thus all valuable records were destroyed.

Sources used

R indicates Railway Regiment, Bn battalion, J Special JNR unit; for example: 2Bn9R is the second battalion of the 9th Railway Regiment.

A. Publishing committee 2Bn5R, '2daitai kakutatakaeri' (memoir 2Bn5R) Taimenkai, Tokyo 1953

B. Publishing committee 4Bn5R, 'Tetsu5 dai4daitai Tatakainoato' (memoir 4Bn5R), Senshi-henshu-jimukyoku, Tokyo, 1956

C. Yoshikawa Takao, 'Miitokiina boueisen ni okeru Tetsudoutai' (Railway unit at the defence of Myitokyina), 51kai, Tokyo 1977

D. Publishing Committee 4Bn9R, 'Zanshou' (The afterglow), 4Bn9R Senyukai, Tokyo, 1958

E. Publishing Committee 4Bn9R, 'Hikari to Kage' (Light and Shadow) 4Bn9R Senyukai, Tokyo, 1969

F. Tetsurin kai, 'Tetsurin' (Steel wheels, memoir 9R), Tetsurin kai, Tokyo, 1975

G. Publishing Committee 5J, 'Dai5 Tokusetu Tetsudou Kousakutai' (The 5th Special JNR Engineering Group), Harashobo, Tokyo, 1976

H. Tarumoto Juji, 'Arusenpan no Shuki' (Note of a War Criminal), Gendaishiryoshuppan, Tokyo, 1999

I. Ishida Eiichi, 'Ishida Eikuma Ikoshu' (posthumous manuscript of Eikuma Ishii), E. Ishida, Kagoshima, 1999

J. Tetsu5 Ireikai, 'Eikouno Tetsudoubutai shashinshu', (Photographs of the glorious railway unit, 5R), Tetu5kai, Tokyo, 1956

K. Hasegawa Saburo, 'Tetsudouhei no Oitachi' (Growth of Railway soldiers), Sankousha, Tokyo, 1984

L. 'Isho-shu' (last Notes) hand written by Honryu Tanaka, Yasukuni-kaiko Library, Tokyo, (1946)

M. Futmatsu Norihiko (ed), 'Taimen-tetsudou kensetsuki' (memoir of construction of the Burma-Thailand Railway), Hanazono-shobo, Tokyo, 1955

N. Interview by the author, 2001 & 2002

O. Shimizu Sekito, 'Tooi Kiteki' (Distant Whistle), Asao-sha, Takasaki, 1978

P. SEATIC Bulletin No. 246 8 October 1946, (Singapore)

Q. Iwai Ken, 'C56 Nanposensen wo Yuku' (C56 runs in southern battlefields), Jijitsushinsha, Tokyo, 1978

R. Tsukamoto Kazuya, 'Miyanma saigono C56' (The last C56 in Myanmar), Tetsudo fuan No 466,467, Tokyo, 2000

S. Takaichi Shozou, 'Biruma sensen no Kiseki' (Traces of Burma frontline), supplement, private publication, Kure, 1989

Supplementary references

The following materials were also used.

a. Ando Toshiro, 'Keonoi no nagareni', (On the river Kwai) Nihon Art Centre, Tokyo, 1987

b. Kenmochi Yasuharu, 'Shito Gunzoku Tetsudoutai' (Struggle of JNR unit) 5Jotu7, Tokyo, 1958

c. 5Jotu4, 'Tatakau Biruma Tetsudoutai' (Fighting railway unit), Otsu3birumakai, Tokyo, 1962

d. Hiroike Toshio, 'Taimenntetsudo – Senjoni nokoru Hashi' (Burma-Thailand railway, The Bridge remaining in the battalefield), Yomiuri Shinbunsha, Tokyo, 1971

e. Takahashi Hiroshi, 'Uingeto teisintai tono tatakai' (Fight against Wingate force), Kaiko No 111, 1998 p. 24

f. Kamenaga Kentaro, 'Dai5 Tokusetu Tetudoutai Shimatuki' (Composition of J5), Kaishi Biruma no.45, ABVAJ, 2001

g. Kamenaga Kentaro, 'Michinasen Mooruno omoide' (Recolletion of Mawlu on Myitokyina line), Kaishi Biruma no 49, ABVAJ, 20

References for sections in the book are given in the table below. The number after the letter indicates the page in which the related matter or the major event are described. Supplementary references are listed without the numbers.

Section	Source & page no.
1.1	A89, K114, 134
1.2	H6, f
2.1	F101, E82
2.2	F111
2.3	A185
2.4	A170
2.5	A185
2.6	A124
2.7	A205
3.1	E110, M
3.2	O42
3.3	I119, G, d
3.4	F167
3.5	E115
3.6	F147
3.7	E149
3.8	F147
3.9	K419
3.10	B292
3.11	I174, G
3.12	K453
3.13	F105
3.14	F163

(*Continued*)

Section	Source & page no.
3.15	N
3.18	P
4.1	K461
4.2	K475, e, g
4.3	K485, J
4.4	K488
4.5	K508
4.6	C
4.7	K560
4.8	B369
5.1	K535
5.2	B223
5.3	K530, 560, c
5.4	K572
5.5	H235, R102
5.6	H213, R100
5.7	H240, b
5.8	F172
5.9	N
6.1	Q216
6.2	N
6.3	I231, S164
6.4	N, L
6.5	L
6.7	S

Introduction

The origins of Japan's railway regiments and the onset of war

Japan's first unit of railway engineers was created in the wake of the first Sino-Japanese war (1894–95) when the Japanese army's supply lines serviced by horse-drawn cart proved too inefficient to support the six divisions in Manchuria. In 1900, one company of Japanese railway engineers took part in restoring and operating the badly damaged railway between Beijing and Tianjin during the Boxer rebellion, and the performance of the Japanese railway company was highly regarded by the allied armies. Japan's railway construction on the continent developed further during the early twentieth century as Japan's empire expanded. During the Russo-Japanese war (1904–5), one railway battalion composed of three companies moved to Korea and surveyed and supervised construction of a standard-gauge (1435 mm) railway between Seoul and Uiju on the Yalu river and then built a light railway from Antung (Andong) towards Mukden (Shenyang) following the advance of the Japanese army. The construction of the Antung railway through rugged terrain involved a work-force of three railway companies (800 men), two transport corps (400 men), 500 Japanese civilian craftsmen and about 1,000 local workers (coolies). By early February 1905, approximately 172 kilometres of track had been completed, close to the front line, and ammunition and food were forwarded by train eight times a day.

In 1918 as a part of the modernization of the army, the 1st and 2nd Railway Regiments were formed at Chiba and Tsudanuma respectively (illustrations on pages 28 and 29). The standard number of men for a railway regiment was 1,300, to be expanded to 2,500 during wartime. These barracks were later used to train soldiers for new regiments. The 1st Railway Regiment was stationed in China in 1931 when the Kwantung Army took over Manchuria. The rail-tractor developed by Japanese, which could run on rails of different gauge and on land, proved very efficient. As the railways built by the Soviet Union had a wider gauge (1524 mm) than the standard (1435 mm), the rail-tractor was useful in combat as it could run on the wider gauge at 40 km/hour pulling four wagons (also with a changeable gauge). Furthermore, the rail-tractors were armour-plated to protect them from enemy attack. The Soviet wide gauge was converted to the standard gauge as the Japanese advanced.

By 1932, the Japanese had established the puppet-state Manchukuo, and from that point on the Kwantung Army pushed ever further into north China. In 1934 the newly formed 3rd Railway Regiment replaced the 1st Regiment which returned to Japan. They were soon joined by the 4th Railway Regiment, formed in 1938, underscoring the import-ance of these units to maintaining Japan's position in the area. At that time, the Japanese army was preparing for war with Soviet Union. Each regiment had two light armoured trains covered with 10 mm steel plate, which had two 75 mm guns on turrets usable for anti-aircraft, and one heavy armoured train with two 105 mm cannons (maximum range: 18,000 metres), two 75 mm anti-aircraft guns and turrets for medium machine guns. All the armoured trains were convertible to the Soviet gauge, and one light armoured train per regiment was always put on the Soviet gauge ready to advance into Russia. There were also one hundred armoured cars in Manchuria which could run on rails, in addition to several 240 mm cannons (maximum range 50,000 metres). When war war broke out between China and Japan in 1937, the 1st and 2nd Rail-way Regiments were moved to north China, followed by a newly estab-lished 6th Regiment and a supply depot. These were administered by the Railway Command Group (equivalent to a brigade in the Japanese army). The armoured train or rail-tractor often spearheaded the advance of the infantry, as the roads in China were unsuitable for lor-ries. A new armoured rail-tractor which could be fitted with caterpillars, thus doubling as a tank, proved effective since the Chinese armies had no cannons or anti-tank guns.

The origins and activities of the 5th Railway Regiment up to their involvement in the construction of the Burma–Thailand railway are worth discussing in detail here since the stories of these railway soldiers form a central part of this book. In the early morning of 12 April 1938, an NCO in charge of mobilization at the headquarters of the Imperial Guard Division came on a sidecar to the headquarters of the 1st Railway Regiment training unit in Chiba and produced orders for the mobilization of the 5th Railway Regiment to the officer of the week. This was the most important order among many issued in the army. The officer alerted the men in the barracks by bugler, and sent messengers to those living outside the barracks.

As the war in China had expanded and a crucial battle was to come, it became urgent to send one more railway regiment to China. So far the 1st, 2nd, 3rd and 4th Railway Regiments were in China. When the mobilization was decided it was relayed to the division and the headquarters of regimental district in charge of the unit. The call-up sheets (so-called 'red paper') of the men in reserve were sent to the village or town office, from where they were delivered to each person by the quickest method.

Approximately one fifth of the men of the 5th Regiment were soldiers on active service, and the remainder were those who had been trained for two years or more in the army. So the 5th Regiment was a capable unit, ready for the battlefield, on a par with the existing four regiments. Later, as the number of railway regiments was increased, untrained new conscripts had to be drafted which lowered the capability. From day four of the mobilization, the called-up men started to arrive. If a man was from the nearby area he was escorted by many neighbours who carried flags and cried 'Banzai' at the gate of the barracks to pray for good luck in war. He was then taken to the medical room and those who were found unfit for military service were ordered to return home immediately. Names of those sent home were immediately sent by telegram to the regimental district, who then sent out a call-up sheet for a replacement. If this replacement was also found unfit, a man from the training unit was transferred to the regiment, because of the time limitation.

On days seven and eight, many visitors came to the barracks from early in the morning. For the families this could be the last chance to see their beloved husbands, brothers or sons, to whom they presented the *senninbari* (a good-luck belt embroidered with a thousand stitches).

On 23 April every man assembled in the yard fully armed, and the new regiment was formally organised, as follows. Under the regimental commander Colonel Tsunejiro Aomura, there were

1. *Regimental Headquarters*: adjutant (major), four officers, eight non-commissioned officers (NCOs) and eight soldiers (privates and lance corporals): Total 22 men.
2. *Four battalions*, each commanded by a Major: one battalion consisted of headquarters[1] and two companies.[2] The companies were numbered consecutively within the regiment. So the 4th battalion contained the 7th and 8th companies.

3. *Supply and machine shop*, commanded by a Major: four officers, one
   quartermaster officer, two warrant officers, fifteen NCOs including
   one quartermaster, one medical officer and 125 soldiers: Total 148
   men.

In total the regiment had 2,235 men.

On 24 April, the regiment, led by buglers, marched to Chiba station
cheered on by people who lined the way. They went by train to Osaka
and arrived in Shantung (Shandong) province in eastern China on
29 April where they immediately took part in Operation Hsuchow
(Xuzhou). The Japanese army captured Hsuchow on 19 May, but the
fighting continued until 16 June when the Chinese demolished the bank
of the Yellow River, flooding more than a thousand square kilometres
of the plain. It was the task of the railway regiment to transport the
Japanese army through the flooded area. The regiment built a bridge of
4,256 metres long over the Yellow River, completed on 11 April 1939,
before being moved to south China in November 1939, and north
Indo-China in September 1940.

With 22 divisions, 13 mixed brigades[3] and others, the Japanese soon
occupied the major cities in north and central China and the railways
linking the cities. The Japanese had reasoned that the deployment of
850,000 troops, the superiority of their own equipment and the acute
shortage of Chinese equipment would before long oblige the Chinese to
sue for peace. But it soon became clear that the struggle would continue
for some time. Chiang Kai-shek and his forces had retreated into the
mountainous region around Chungking (Chongqing), some 1,500
miles west of Nanking (Nanjing). Here the United States and other
countries were supplying them with modern equipment and other supplies. The Japanese estimated that in July 1940 China was receiving the
following tonnage monthly: 6,000 tons via Hong Kong, 15,000 tons via
French Indo-China and 10,000 tons via Rangoon, Burma. The coastal
route, via Hong Kong, was closed by the Japanese navy, and the Indo-
China route through negotiations with France and French Indo-China.
As a result the Burma route took on increasing significance. By the end
of the year, the supplies along this route were estimated to have risen to
15,000 tons a month. Burma had suddenly become a very important
country to Japan.

In 1940 the surrender of France and Holland, and Britain's defeats on
the continent, left the European colonies in Southeast Asia weakly
protected. The Japanese moved into French Indo-China with the aim of
closing the supply route to China via Saigon, and later in 1941 into

southern Indo-China to prepare airfields to support a possible invasion across the Gulf of Siam (Thailand). German pressure on Vichy France ensured compliance in Indo-China with Japanese wishes. In July, however, the United States froze all Japanese assets in the United States. The British and Dutch governments followed suit. By August the United States had placed a complete embargo on oil and aviation fuel. These actions effectively cut Japan's supply of oil and other resources. By the end of 1941 Japan would run out of oil and would be forced to withdraw from China, as battleships, aircraft and tanks would be useless. Also scrap iron was essential in Japanese steel production because of the poor quality of her iron ore. Negotiations between the United States and Japanese governments took place in the latter part of 1941. The United States requested, after consultation with Britain, China and Holland, among other things, the withdrawal of all Japanese military and police forces from China (including Manchukuo) and Indo-China, and the settlement of the 'China Incident'. In return, the United States would restore trade and help Japan to secure the resources it required. Demands were met with countermands, but no compromise was reached. The attack on Pearl Harbor on 7 December was swiftly followed by a series of successful Japanese operations against American, British and Dutch bases in China and Southeast Asia, the primary aim being to secure oil and other resources.

The railway regiments in Burma

On 20 January 1942, when the Japanese were advancing towards Singapore, the Japanese 55th Division, followed by 33 Division and the 2nd Battalion of the 5th Railway Regiment, crossed the Burma–Thailand border and captured Moulmein on 30 January (see part 2, section 4). The Japanese defeated the British and captured Rangoon on 7 March, seizing the port and cutting off the last supply route of the military equipment bound for China (see part 2, section 5).

The Japanese had captured all of Burma by the end of May 1942, thus cutting the potential supply route from north-east India to Kunming in China, later called Ledo Road. The two railway regiments (the existing 5th and the newly-formed 9th) followed the advancing infantry and supplied ammunition and essential materials by trains (see part 2, sections 6 and 7). Their tasks involved a great deal of repair work, and they were moved around. For example the 5th Regiment, except the 4th Battalion which had stayed in south China, had landed at Saigon on 20 August 1941 and was engaged in repairing the railway around the

Thailand–Indo-China border, before moving to Bangkok and then going southwards along the Malaya mainline. They repaired the bridge over the Perak River, the largest river in Malaya with a width of 400 metres. As there was not enough material for major repairs, the bridge was first rebuilt for combined use for light trains and lorries (see part 2, section 3). The wagons pulled by a heavy engine were divided into units of less than 60 tons pulled by a rail-tractor, and after crossing the bridge the wagons were re-coupled and were hauled by another engine towards Singapore. In this way the heavy trains could be mobilized to carry essential supplies. The regiment's advance train arrived at Johore Bahru station on 31 January and Singapore station on 16 February, the day after the British surrender. The regiment embarked at Singapore and arrived at Rangoon on 25 March 1942.

Meanwhile the 2nd Battalion turned around at Taipin on 22 January and went to Kanchanaburi in Thailand. They crossed the rugged mountains and reached Tavoy and Moulmein (see part 2, section 4). At the River Sittang they operated combined-boats to ferry tanks and guns. They then captured the Rangoon freight yard on 9 March, and started train operations (see part 2, section 5). The regiment went north repairing the railway to Mandalay and then to Myitkyina.

The 9th Railway Regiment was officially formed in September 1941 (see part 2, section 1). The regiment was organized along the same lines as the 5th Regiment, but about 15 per cent of its men were untrained new recruits, unlike the 5th Regiment. The regiment landed at Haiphon in Indo-China in October. The majority of the 4th Battalion moved to Hainan island, landed at Singora on 8 August 1941 and then advanced southward (see part 2, section 1), repairing and operating the main line between Bangkok and Singapore. The 1st Battalion were in Sumatra from March to June 1942, while the major part of the regiment landed at Rangoon on 12 April, where it was involved in repairing and operating the Mandalay line. After Burma was occupied, the regiment arrived at Bangkok in July by boat from Rangoon.

In addition to the 5th and 9th Railway Regiments, special JNR units played an important role in the maintenance and operation of imperial Japan's expanding railway network. The 4th Special JNR Unit and 5th Special JNR Unit (see part 1, section 2) were officially formed on 18 October 1941 at Kuriyama field barracks in Chiba prefecture. Each unit was commanded by a Colonel and consisted of about 300 army men and about 2,200 conscripted employees of Japanese National Railways. Both units left Osaka on 27 October in a convoy of eight ships, and landed at Haiphon on 7 November. They gradually moved to Phnom Penh, and on 9 December to Thailand to help operate the southbound trains. The 4th Special Machine Unit remodelled the C56 engines sent from Japan to suit the local standards. The 5th Special JNR Unit left Bangkok on 2 April, embarked at Singapore and arrived at Rangoon on 20 April, and assembled and modified C56 engines at the Insein factory. The unit took over operation of all railways in Burma from the 9th Railway Regiment on 10 June 1942, by which time plans were under way for the construction of a new railway linking Burma and Thailand. The two railway regiments started surveying the railway line, the 5th Regiment on the Burma side, the 9th on the Thailand side.

Planning of the Burma–Thailand railway

When Japan planned its advance into Burma, the troops and supplies were sent ahead by ship under the cover of the Japanese navy. However in order to maintain the army in Burma and to prepare for the inevitable counter-attack to come, a large quantity of supplies and reinforcements had to be moved. Moreover any action such as the proposed invasion of India would double or triple those requirements.[4] The long sea haul from Singapore to Rangoon via the Bay of Bengal was close to India and was liable to attack by British air and naval forces. The burden of sea transport would be greatly reduced by using ships for the journey from Japan to Saigon and then trains to Burma. This also reduced the time needed for the transportation, and the railway was a more reliable method as the trains could be safely hidden in the sheltered sidings, whereas ships were more vulnerable to attack. As a road across the border mountains did not exist, the Japanese army initially built a single-lane unpaved road to advance into Burma, but it could not be used in the rainy season and had limited capacity. Since the construction costs of a good paved road were equal to that of a railway, and the Japanese did not have enough lorries to move large amounts of supplies to Burma, a Burma–Thailand railway was judged to be the best choice.

The staff of 2nd Railway Command Group led by Lt Colonel Toshio Hiroike investigated the route of a railway linking Burma and Thailand, and compared the following five routes (see Map 1):

1. Chiang Mai to Toungoo
2. Phitsanok to Moulmein via Rahaeng (the route along which the 55th division advanced)

3. Kanchanaburi to Thanbyuzayat
4. Kanchanaburi to Tavoy (the route along which the Oki branch advanced, see part 2, section 4)
5. Chumphon to Mergui

Routes 1 and 2 would involve crossing big rivers (Salween and Menam respectively) and tunnels might be needed to cross the mountains at the border. Route 4 would need tunnels and a railway between Tavoy and Ye. Route 5 was short and the landscape was easy, but would require the use of ships from Mergui to Moulmein. Thus, it was felt that route 3 would be the least problematic.

On 12 March 1942, the Command Group issued the first order to prepare for the construction of the railway linking Burma and Thailand. Based on this, staff officer Major Irie surveyed the entire line of the route on elephant-back, which took two weeks, and concluded that the construction of the railway was possible. Within two weeks, scale maps, covering the whole line at a width of 10 kilometres (five kilometres both sides from the proposed line), were prepared from aerial photographs by an ordnance detachment which happened to be in Bangkok. With these, a detailed construction plan was prepared based on the use of C56 engines. The C56 engine was considered appropriate for the railway, as it was a lightweight engine designed for use in Japanese local lines, 37.67 tons in operating condition, and with a tender for long-distance operation and the facility to move in reverse.

By the end of May 1942, the 1st Battalion of the 9th Regiment moved from Sumatra to Banpong in Thailand, and the 3rd Battalion of the 5th Regiment to Thanbyuzayat, and started to survey and prepare for construction. On 7 June 1942, the Southern Army issued the formal instructions for the construction of the Burma–Thailand railway, based on a directive from the Imperial General Headquarters.5 The railway was expected to be completed by the end of 1943, using mainly local materials. The order advised that 50,000 PoWs in addition to Asian labourers should be used for the construction, although the 2nd Command Group had planned to use local workers only. Although figures vary widely, it is generally acknowledged that approximately 60,000–64,000 PoWs and over 200,000 Asian labourers were used during the construction of the railway. It is estimated that approximately 12,626 PoWs and perhaps between 15,000 and 90,000 labourers died.[6] It should be noted that this order was issued only four days after the defeat of the Japanese navy at Midway where she lost four key aircraft carriers. It

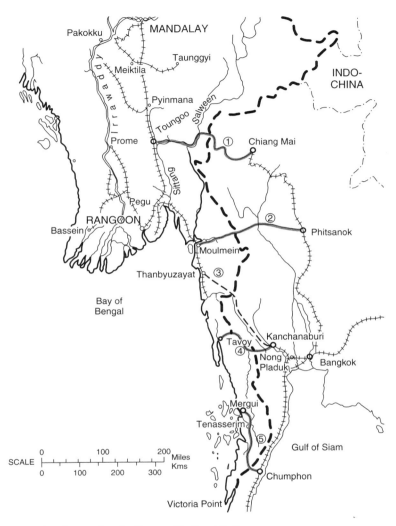

Map 1 Five Routes for the Burma–Thailand Railway

seemed that the Japanese would no longer be able to protect the sea lane from Singapore to Rangoon, and the further success or even survival of the Japanese army in Burma depended on the speedy completion of the railway.

Construction of the railway

The route was to connect the railway systems of Thailand and Burma. The Thai railway went to Indo-China and was to be connected across China to Korea, and by ferry to the Japanese mainland. The starting point of the Burma–Thailand railway was a small station, Nong Pladuk, about 80 kilometres west of Bangkok on the southern line. The line would go north-west over a plain for 51 kilometres to Kanchanaburi, cross the Mac Khlong river and then follow the Kwai river continuing across the frontier to the Three Pagodas Pass, the Burma–Thailand border, the highest point being 300 metres above sea level (see Illustration I.1 and Map 2, pp. 19 and 20–1). In Burma the line would descend from the Pass to Thanbyuzayat, in a fairly straight line as there was no river suitable for transportation. Just 36 kilometres from Thanbyuzayat on the Ye line was Moulmein, connected by ferry via Salween to the Burmese main line. The route would shorten the Japanese line of communications by almost 1,000 kilometres, as formerly all supplies to Burma had to be shipped around the Malay peninsula. But the route traversed laterally the formidable Bilauk Taung range of mountains which formed the natural boundary between the two countries. The area was for the most part completely undeveloped with very heavy monsoon rainfall in the two rainy seasons. Seventy per cent of the route passed though thick jungle infested with malaria, cholera and tropical diseases.[7]

The Japanese received permission from the Thai government for the construction of the railway on the condition that the portion between Nong Pladuk and Kanchanaburi (51 km) should be the property of the Thai national railway company (RSR). That portion was built urgently with the help of the 9th Railway Regiment as Kanchanaburi was to be the base of their construction work.

The 5th Railway Regiment was in charge of construction from Burma, while its 4th Battalion was still in China. The 3rd Battalion arrived at Thanbyuzayat via boat from Rangoon, drove in the 'zero mile post' on 23 June 1942, and started to survey the route. As there was no river which could be used for transportation of supplies, its 5th Company started to build a road along the route. The 1st Battalion removed the rails from the double-track Mandalay line, and the 2nd Battalion moved to Thanbyuzayat and started to build the rail foundations. As the railway between the Sittang and Thanbyuzayat had been demolished and abandoned, the 1st Battalion worked on recovering this section of the railway, building many wooden bridges. On 28 November the survey was completed up to Nihke, and the road was completed up to the border. The wooden bridge over the Sittang (length 1,996 metres) was completed by the 1st Battalion and the 4th Special JNR Bridging Unit on 23 April 1943 after four-and-a-half months of hard work. All the engines, rails and other materials were sent to the construction site in 35 trains (see illustration 2.3.10, page 159), but two weeks later the bridge was washed away by floods. The engines were heavy and could not be landed at Moulmein harbour, so the bridge played an essential role in the construction.

On their arrival from south China in March 1943, the 4th Battalion of the 5th Regiment and then the Imperial Guard's engineering regiment, started to build the rail foundations between Nikhe (282 km) and Tamuron (244 km) from 23 March (see part 3, section 10). In April, the Burmese Labour Service Corps started to arrive at the construction sites. As smallpox sufferers were found among them, all the workers were inoculated at Moulmein before going on to the site. In the middle of April the rainy season started one month earlier than the usual. By early May a cholera outbreak at Nikhe soon spread in both directions.

On 12 June Thanbyuzayat station was attacked by four B24 bombers, damaging some rails. The bombing was repeated on 18 and 27 June, and then regularly every week or ten days, but as the station was converted to mere passing rails the damage was not heavy. On 15 June many bridges were washed away by heavy rain and roads became impassable, thus the transportation of rations was stopped, endangering the work units in the mountains. In mid-July the supply communications opened from the Thailand side by boat, and a part of the 5th Regiment was supplied by them. When the heavy rain in Burma eased and the cholera infection came under control, construction work was resumed. On 25 August almost all working parties gathered at the border area to carry out the last phase of the work.

The 9th Railway Regiment was responsible for the construction of the railway on the Thailand side from Nong Pladuk towards Nikhe (later to Konkoita). The zero mile post was driven in on 5 July 1942 at Nong Pladuk station, and the Mouri team began its survey (see part 3, section 1). The main part of the 9th Regiment arrived at Bangkok on 29 July and the 3rd Battalion started building both a permanent (steel) bridge and a wooden bridge at Tamarkan (see part 3, section 2). In late September, the track was laid up to Kanchanaburi. Construction was started along the river at several points between Kanchanaburi (51 km) and Wang Yai (124 km). By the end of the year, the wooden bridge over the Mac Khlong was completed. During January 1943 the construction had reached Takunun (218 km). In February, the 4th JNR Unit moved to Kanchanaburi to take part in the construction, and in March an engineering regiment, four field hospitals and others were added to the construction (see note in Illustration 3.16.1, page 162).

In March, the 1st and 3rd battalions moved west of Kinsaiyok, and the steel bridge over Mac Khlong was completed in early May. From late June, British scout planes frequently flew over the line. This, along with the fear of contracting cholera, caused many local workers to flee. The rock blasting at Hintok was completed on 2 July (see part 3, section 8). The cholera epidemic spread to most of the work sites in June (see part 3, section 7) but was under control in August. In mid-August the track was laid up to Takunun (218 km). The line reached Konkoita (262 km) from both the Burma and Thailand sides on 17 October, and the ceremony celebrating the completion of the railway was held on 25 October (see part 3, section 12).

The operation of the railways

After completion, the 9th Railway Regiment and the 4th Special JNR Unit operated and maintained the railway. During the course of construction, the design capacity of the Burma–Thailand railway was reduced to 1,000 tons per day (from an original 3,000 tons per day) in order to complete the construction by October 1943. In fact the maximum transportation achieved was 500 tons per day, but this was enough to carry materials destined for Burma. Because of the shortage of ships and disruption by US submarines, there was not much material to transport. Burma produced enough rice and petrol, so ammunition and reinforcement troops were the major transport. By the end of 1943, in the first two months of operation, 12,000 tons of essential supplies were transported by railway to Burma, of which 5,000 tons went to the Myitkyina line to supply the three divisions which were to advance towards Imphal, before the operation started on 8 March 1944.[8]

The 5th Railway Regiment was operating the Myitkyina line, carrying 500 tons per day of supplies including food to the terminal stations despite constant bombardment by the British airforce (see part 4, sections 1 and 4). The 5th Regiment built, at all key bridges, a detour wooden bridge and also foundations for the bridge under water on which a pre-assembled truss could be quickly put in place when needed. This underwater foundation was never demolished by the British and at least one train went through nightly. However the transportation from the terminal stations, Yeu and Meza, to the front lines by lorries was frequently disrupted by the British airforce, often by fighter planes carrying bombs, and many of the supplies were destroyed at the crossing points of the Chindwin. Thus only a small amount of supplies reached the front lines. In May, the 5th Regiment broke through the Chindit line north of Mawlu and transported 800 tons of supplies in four trains to the starving 18th Division, stretched north of Myitkyina, under cover of Japanese fighter planes (see part 4, section 4).

As the Japanese 15th Army retreated from Imphal, many patients and starving soldiers were carried back by train towards Mandalay (see part 4, section 5). The Japanese then planned to halt the advance of the British on the banks of Irrawaddy, but the British 255 Armoured Brigade broke through the Japanese defences and captured Meiktila in a surprise attack. The Japanese counter-attacked and after bitter fighting decided to retreat on 28 March 1945. The 5th Railway Regiment fought a difficult rearguard action and retreated to the Sittang (see part 5, section 3). The 5th JNR Unit transported many Japanese civilians and JNR men from Rangoon to the Sittang (see part 5, sections 5 and 6). Then they moved, first on foot and then by the Burma–Thailand railway, to Malaya (part 5, section 7). In 1945 the railway was used to carry patients and troops from Burma to Thailand under severe air attacks. The train ran only during the night when the demolished wooden bridges were repaired quickly using pre-cut timbers.

The Trans-Sumatra Railway

After the completion of the Burma–Thailand railway, the 4th Battalion of the 9th Railway Regiment moved to Kra Ismuth and built the Kra railway which linked Chumphon, on the Malaya main line on the east coast, and Kra Buri and Kophagu on the west coast whence boats went to Mergui (see Map 1, page 9). The 91-km railway was completed on 25 December 1943. The battalion then moved to Sumatra, arriving at Pekanbaru on 17 April 1944. The Trans-Sumatra Railway which linked Muara, on the existing line, and Pekanbaru, an inland port on the northern coast of Sumatra, had been planned, and some construction work begun, in early 1943 by civilian construction companies, and the battalion was sent to expedite the completion of the railway. The railway was needed to carry Sumatran and Javan goods first to Singapore and then to Japan, and to move troops from Singapore to Sumatra and Java when needed. In February 1944 the Rogas branch line was completed and coke from Rogas coal mine was sent by rail to Pekanbaru and then to Singapore. The whole line was completed on 15 August 1945, the day that Japan surrendered. Hence the Trans-Sumatra Railway was never used and no longer exists.

The Japanese surrender

When Japan surrendered on 15 August 1945, the 5th Railway Regiment was on the Thai southern line. On 25 September all weapons were delivered to the British, except one rifle per five men which was returned to the regiment for safe keeping. The regiment was moved to the Burma–Thailand railway by the end of October, and maintained and operated the line. From February 1946, ex-PoWs or local workers attended by military police came to look for those who had been cruel to them during the construction. No suspects were found as the 5th Regiment was not in Thailand during the construction. On 10 October 1946 the railway was turned over to Thailand and the regiment was transported to Bangkok for repatriation. In Bangkok, 58 men were retained on suspicion of war crimes, and were transferred to Changi Prison in Singapore. The rest of the regiment disembarked at Uraga in Japan on 6 November 1946.

The 9th Railway Regiment, except the 4th Battalion, was on the Burma side of the Burma–Thailand railway at the end of the war. Lt Tarumoto and two other officers were summoned and imprisoned (see part 6, section 3). The regiment was moved to Mandalay in July 1946 and repaired the Myitkyina line. In January 1947, a total of 267 men of the regiment including all officers were imprisoned in Rangoon. But most were released by the end of June. The regiment, along with the 4th Battalion of the 5th Regiment, was repatriated on 8 August 1947, when both the 5th and 9th Railway Regiments were officially disbanded. Most men belonging to the 4th and 5th Special JNR Units had been repatriated by May 1946.

Those surrendered to the Allies in south-east Asia were referred to as 'Japanese Surrendered Personnel' or JSP, and it was decided that Japanese military organization should be maintained, under the command of the Allied forces. Japanese officers remained responsible for the maintenance and discipline of their own men. The Japanese (approximately 783,000

men) were gradually accommodated in JSP camps, pressed into hard
labour, or used for peacekeeping purposes by the European powers whose
intention it was to reassert power in the region. As Dower points out,
the British (and the Dutch) insisted on keeping over 100,000 Japanese
personnel in the Dutch East Indies, Malaya and Burma until October
1947.[9] Conditions for JSP were uncomfortable, rations were low, and
the incidence of disease high (see Appendix 2).[10]

The task of identifying, locating and apprehending suspected Japanese
war criminals was carried out mainly by the British and American military authorities. The investigation and trials of those who had committed
war crimes against British nationals became the responsibility of General
Headquarters, Allied Land Force, South-East Asia. Military courts were
held in ten locations in the British territories including Singapore and
Rangoon, where the majority of railwaymen held on suspicion of war
crimes were put on trial.[11] Approximately 15 members of the 5th and
9th regiments and the 4th JNR Unit were prosecuted; of these two were
sentenced to death and ten received a prison sentence. Staff of PoW
camps were prosecuted and sentenced more severely than those of the
railway regiments.[12] Forty-three men from PoW camps were hanged
compared to two from the railway regiments. As for Korean guards
at the PoW camps, ten were hanged, 12 got life imprisonment and
39 others received a prison sentence. In the Dutch courts, four men of
the 5th Regiment and an officer of the Thai PoW camp received prison
sentences. Regarding the Trans-Sumatra Railway, PoW camp commander
Captain Rohei Miyazaki was hanged, one officer got life imprisonment
and another officer a prison sentence. Eleven Korean guards received
between five and 14 years' imprisonment. Two railway unit commanders (colonels) received life and eight years' imprisonment respectively.
It was felt that the Dutch courts delivered more severe sentences than
the British ones. The British trials came in for criticism on the one
hand, by those who felt that the treatment of Japanese war criminals
was too lenient, and on the other, by those who argued that treatment
was too harsh and sentences too arbitrary. Some of the JSPs felt that
they did not receive a fair hearing because the trials were too rushed or
were viewed as a means of exacting revenge.[13]

The Burma–Thailand Railway after the war

The Burma–Thailand Railway continued to be operated and maintained
on a small scale until the rails of the Burma side were removed on
26 January 1946 by order of the British. Thus the Burma–Thailand Railway

Table 1   Distribution of all railway units at 7 December 1941

Unit name			HQ
Eastern Army (Japan mainland)		1st Regiment Training Unit	Chiba
		2nd Regiment Training Unit	Tsudanuma
Kwantung Army (Manchuria)	1st Command Group	2nd Regiment	Harbin
		2nd Supply Depot	Harbin
	3rd Command Group	3rd Regiment	Harbin
		4th Regiment[c]	Mutankiang (Mudanjiang)
		3rd Supply Depot	Mutankiang
China Army	North-China area army	11th Armoured Train Unit	near Beijing
	Mid-China area army	1st Regiment	Hankow (Hankou)
Southern Army	Philippine area army	6th Regiment[a]	Manila
	2nd Command Group	5th Regiment (4th Battalion in Canton)	Cambodia[d]
		9th Regiment[b]	Haiphon[d,e]
		1st Supply Depot	Saigon
		4th Special JNR Unit	Saigon[f]
		5th Special JNR Unit	Cambodia[d]

Notes

a) Two platoons of the 6th Regiment took part in the Java operation from February to June 1942.
b) The 1st Battalion of the 9th Regiment took part in the Sumatra operation from March to June 1942.
c) The 4th Regiment took part in the Sekkan operation in mid-China from June 1942 to January 1943.
d) Moved to Malaya and to Burma in March/April 1942.
e) 4th Battalion was off Singora, Thailand.
f) Moved to Malaya.

came to an end after 27 months, although the passenger operation between Nikhe and Kanchanaburi was continued.

On 10 October 1946, the 5th Railway Regiment transferred all railway facilities to the Royal State Railway of Thailand. In 1950, the RSR removed the rails north of Namtok (128 km), but today two to four trains per day run between Kanchanaburi and Namtok attracting sightseers and those interested in the history of the railway. Two C56 engines used on the railway are on display, one near the bridge at Tamarkan, Kanchanaburi, and another two kilometres north of Namtok.

General description of the Burma–Thailand Railway[14]

The Burma–Thailand Railway was completed in October 1943, and transported up to 500 tons of cargo and passengers a day during the war.

The railway connected the railway systems of Burma (Myanmar) and Thailand (Siam) at Thanbyuzayat and Nong Pladuk, and so provided a direct route to Moulmein from Bangkok and Indo-China. At Moulmein there was connection by ferry across the Salween to Martaban and so to the rest of the Burma system. The railway thus shortened the Japanese lines of communication by many hundreds of miles, since formerly all supplies for Burma had to be shipped for Rangoon (Yangon) by way of Singapore, where boats were frequently attacked by the British.

The line was about 415 kilometres (262 miles) long. It was built by the Japanese between November 1942 and October 1943, by which latter date the track was completed and traffic operating. In this period of one year, clearing had to be made for almost the whole distance through dense forest, many large cuttings and embankments constructed to negotiate hilly country, and 688 bridges (as well as a number of culverts) built over rivers and chaungs.

From Thanbyuzayat in Burma the line runs south-eastward for 110 km (70 miles) up to the Burma–Thailand frontier at the 'Three Pagodas Pass' (273 metres or 897 feet above sea level). In its course through Burma it follows in turn the valleys of several different streams, and crosses several low divides between these valleys. From the frontier for the whole way to its junction with the old southern line at Nong Pladuk, it descends undulating along the east (left) bank of the Kwai and then along the Mac Khlong. The country is, for the most part, completely undeveloped. There is a very heavy monsoon rainfall on most of the line, though it is more torrential on the Burma side.

Length: 414.916 km (257.9 miles), all single track
Track gauge: 1 metre

Loading gauge: corresponds with Burmese and Thai railways with which this line connects.

(a) *Type and weight of rail*: Rails were mostly old rails (flat bottomed) from lines in Burma and Malaya dismantled by the Japanese. The Malayan rails (used for the southern part of the line) were mostly 60 lb/yd (29.8 kg/m), in 30-foot lengths; the Burma rails were mostly 60 or 75 lb/yd (29.8 or 37.2 kg/m), in lengths of 30 to 39 feet. (A quarter of rails were brought from Japan.)

(b) *Type of rail-fastening*: Rails were spiked direct to sleepers, with four spikes to each sleeper.

(c) *Sleepers*: Hardwood, 25 by 15 cm (10×6 inches) in section. The number to a kilometre was about 1400 (2200 to a mile).

(d) *Ballast*: Broken stone from local quarries and river-bed gravel. It was generally laid to a width of 1.5 m (5 feet), and where construction was best, to a depth of 25 to 30 cm (10 to 12 inches).

(e) *Maximum axle-load*: About ten tons; this is indicated by the weight of the Japanese C56 locomotives which were running on the line. A rail of 60–75 lb/yd would bear a maximum axle load of 13–17 tons; but weak formations and bridges would reduce this figure. Many of the bridges were of unstable construction and were crossed at 'dead slow' speeds.

(f) *Gradients*: The highest point on the line is 273.72 km (897 feet) above sea-level, at 300.72 km at Three Pagodas Pass (see Illustration I.1). The steepest gradient is also at this point, being 29/1000. The second highest point is 266.6 metres at 147.52 km (Tampi). The steepest gradients are in the section comprising ascent to the pass located at the following points: 306.00 km – 27.5/1000, 317.70 km – 27/1000, 318.00 km – 29/1000. It was customary in these areas to use two locomotives, one pushing and one pulling.

(g) *Bridges*: There were 688 bridges on this line. Most bridges were of standard design, and 680 bridges were constructed out of locally-cut timber. The Japanese engineers responsible for the design gave full consideration to such matters as strength of material, load-carrying capacity, and so on, adapting the American Merriman-Wiggin standard practice for timber structure.

The construction policy, however, sacrificed the factor of safety in favour of speed, exemplified by the almost entire use of softwood throughout when hardwood was readily available. In this connection the Japanese had abundant labour at their disposal (Japanese and PoW) and were in a position to effect rapid renewals when

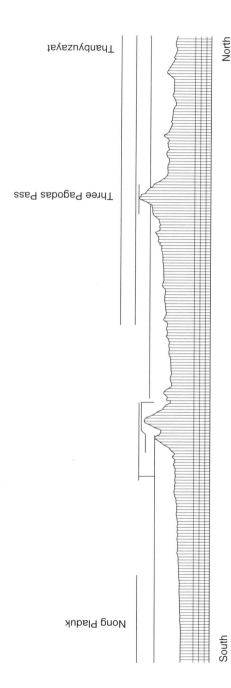

Illustration 1.1   Gradient profile of the Burma–Thailand Railway, drawn from the elevation diagram prepared by Mr Kazuya Tsukamoto and based on the map obtained by Mr Peter Tyler (Professor of Deakin University, Australia) from RTR archive in Thailand

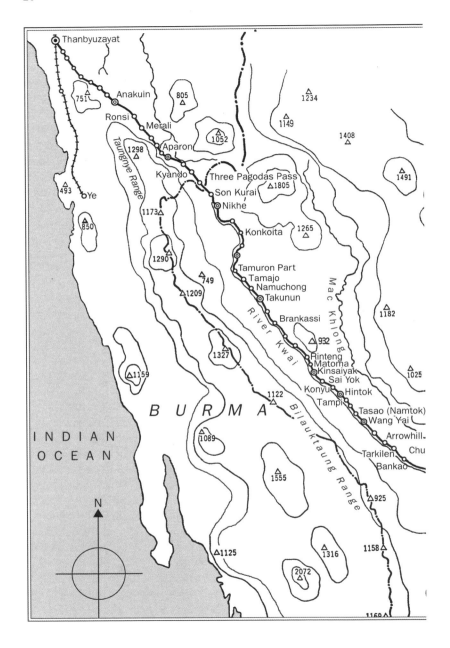

The Burma–Thailand Railway
LENGTH 414.916 km

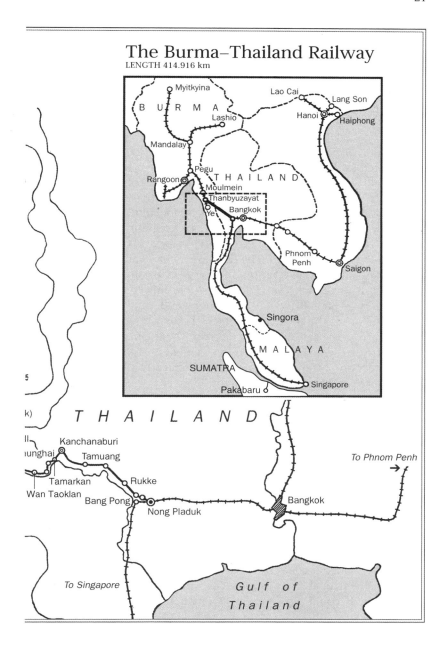

necessary. Due to Allied bombings many bridges had to be rebuilt as often as six times. On such bridges the wooden components were bound together using cramps instead of bolts. Thus the bridge disintegrated under the bomb-blast, and undamaged components were collected and quickly assembled as before.

(h) *Stations*: The line was not intended for civilian traffic (although there was some civilian traffic after the surrender). The stations were not, generally speaking, stations in the usual sense of the word. Points on the line where there were passing loops or sidings were treated as stations, and given arbitrary names taken from the nearest village or physical feature on the map; at 57 of these there are few facilities other than the passing loops or sidings, though at six key stations there were various facilities for locomotives etc.

(i) *Telegraphic communication*: There was a telegraph line alongside the track with two or more pairs of wires (one wire 200-lb copper, the rest 200-lb galvanized iron). The poles were cut locally and untreated.

(j) *Passing loops*: The average distance between passing loops or so-called stations was about seven kilometres (four miles). Most passing loops were between 350 and 450 metres long and some were shorter.

(k) *Spur tracks*: Thirty-one spur tracks branched off into the jungle, mostly on the east side of the railroad. These spurs average about 500 metres in length; they were an expedient adopted for daytime protection of trains from air-attack from early 1944 onwards when all movement took place at night.

(l) *Standard of maintenance*: The early construction at either end of the railway was done reasonably well; cuttings were wide and the roadbed was sound. As construction progressed this standard noticeably deteriorated; cuttings became so narrow as barely to permit a train to pass through, and other faults, in consequence, developed: for example sleepers sank flush into the formation, collapses occurred, and there were landslides in cuttings. Bridges deteriorated particularly on the Burma side.

(m) *Workshops*: There was an excellent railway workshop at Kanchanaburi, reputed to be the best equipped in Southeast Asia. The total capacity of this workshop exceeded the normal needs of the line provided it could be adequately staffed, its requirements being 1,100 men, apart from labour. The workshop could handle 500 cars a year. It could also handle 12 engines simultaneously. It was a completely independent unit and included, among other things, three forges, three engine shops, one foundry, three power stations, one sawmill, one water conduit and an installation for refining crude oil, spread across a wide area to reduce damage by air-raid.

Illustration 1.2 The remains of the Burma–Thailand Railway. This photo, taken near Arrowhill in 1999, shows most of the original features of the railway

Notes

1. Battalion headquarters had one adjutant, one officer, one medical doctor, one quartermaster officer, five NCOs (including one each of medical and quartermaster), and 22 soldiers: Total 32 men.
2. A company consisted of four platoons and a small 'command unit'. A company commanded by a captain or lieutenant had four lieutenants or second lieutenants, each of whom commanded a platoon, and a warrant officer who supervised the command unit, 15 NCOs, two medics and 234 soldiers, a total of 257 men. A platoon consisted of four sections, each led by a sergeant or corporal, and a section had about 14 soldiers.
3. A mixed brigade consisted of four to five independent battalions, each with one 75-mm mountain gun, two medium machine guns and three to four infantry companies. A company consisted of three platoons, each with three light machine guns and two 50 mm mortars.
4. The joint meeting of the Imperial General Headquarters and the Japanese government held on 15 November 1941 agreed that one means of defeating Britain would be to invade India, and so the Imperial General Headquarters issued an order on 22 August 1942 (operation number 21) to the Southern Army to prepare for an attack on north-east India (Bōeichō, *Biruma kōryaku sakusen* [Advance into Burma], (History Section, War Ministry) 1967, p. 558). But this operation was postponed as the divisional commanders in Burma did not like to venture into India partly as the health of their soldiers had not recovered from the hard fighting.
5. Hiroike Toshio, *Taimen Tetsudo* (The Burma–Thailand Railway), (Tokyo, Yomiuri Shinbunsha, 1971), pp. 111–12.
6. The figures for numbers of PoWs are available from military records, but the statistics relating to Asian labourers were either destroyed at surrender or never fully documented. The figure of 15,000 deaths is the author's own. See also Sibylla Jane Flower, 'Captors and captives on the Burma–Thailand Railway', in Bob Moore and Kent Fedorowich (eds), *Prisoners of War and their Captors in World War II* (Oxford, Washington DC: Berg, 1996), Clifford Kinvig, 'Allied PoWs and the Burma–Thailand Railway' in P. Towle, M. Kosuge and Y. Kibata (eds), *Japanese Prisoners of War* (London and New York: Hambledon and London 2000).
7. The route happened to be almost the same as the one which a British company had surveyed several years before, and their old survey posts were found during the course of construction. According to Kinvig, the British rejected the plan because of engineering problems, the terrain and economic reasons. Kinvig, 'Allied PoWs and the Burma–Thailand Railway'.
8. When the Imphal operation began, the 5th Regiment studied the plan to connect Burma and India by railway, and proposed a rough plan to connect Indaw on the Myitkyina line and Dimapur on the Assam Railway, via Banmauk, Tamanti and Kohima. As the operation failed the plan was scrapped.
9. John Dower, *Embracing Defeat: Japan in the Wake of World War II* (Harmondsworth: Penguin, 1999), p. 51.
10. A distinction must be made between JSP, the treatment they received, and Japanese prisoners of war captured during the war. See Hata Ikuhiko 'From consideration to contempt: The changing nature of Japanese military and

popular perceptions of prisoners of war through the ages', in Moore and Fedorowich (eds), *Prisoners of War and their Captors in World War II*.

11. For the official account of the machinery set up to bring war criminals to trial, see *The History of the United Nations War Crimes Commission* (HMSO, 1948).

12. Allied PoWs who were forced to work on the Burma–Thailand Railway were temporarily under the command of the railway regiments until October 1942. Thereafter the Thailand PoW Administration (which reported to the commander of the Southern Army) administered the PoW camps, and supplied PoWs to construction sites on a daily basis in accordance with requests from the railway units. PoWs were taken to the sites by men from the railway platoons and the PoW Administration issued notices about the treatment of PoWs (see part 3, sections 2 and 3). The PoW camps and the railway regiments belonged to separate administrative organizations, and railway regiments had to negotiate with PoW camp NCOs (see part 6, section 3). Flower notes that at the start of the construction of the railway, the PoW Administration comprised 40 officers, 85 NCOs, and 1,280 Korean guards. Considering the number of camps and the distances between them, this 'had the effect of devolving considerable authority on individuals of lowly rank' (Flower, 'Captors and Captives', p. 236). See Flower for a more detailed outline of the way the administration of PoW camps worked. The verdicts of some of the war crimes trials showed that those in charge of the PoW camps rather than the railway soldiers tended to be held responsible for the illtreatment of the PoWs.

13. See Philip R. Piccigallo, *The Japanese on Trial: Allied War Crimes Operations in the East, 1945–1951* (Austin, Texas and London: University of Texas Press, 1979) and Azuma Kunihiko (ed.), *Senpan Saiban no Jisso* [The Truth about the War Crimes Trials] (Tokyo: Maki shobo, 1952) for examples of these views.

14. See SEATIC Bulletin No. 246, 8 October 1946 (Singapore).

Part 1   The Training of Railway Soldiers

1.1   A new conscript

Private Eiji Shibata, 3rd Company, 2nd Battalion, 5th Railway Regiment

In September 1939, the Nazi army invaded Poland, an event which marked the beginning of World War II. The following year, 1940, the big celebration of the 2,600th anniversary of the foundation of Japan was held throughout Japan, while she was fighting with China.

It was at the end of 1940 that I received my call-up notice as a conscript. 'You are ordered to be a Railway Soldier.'

I had never heard of the railway soldier. I guessed that railway units must be a part of the engineer organization. When I passed the conscript physical examination, the conscription officer, a Colonel, asked me, 'Which branch of service do you want to join?' I had answered 'Tank corps.' But now, 'Railway soldier!'

To find out more I visited an army veteran, who told me, 'What a serious soldier you are going to be! It may be difficult for your loosely-built body to keep up with the hard military training. I sympathise with you. I believe that the central body of the railway unit is in Chiba.'

So I was deeply worried by the expectation of the hardship that I had to suffer. However I had no choice of the branch of service, so I made up my mind to strengthen my body as much as I could, and to change my life for the better by the military service.

While Hitler's army continued to win and Japan as a whole was becoming more militaristic, the year 1941 and then my day of entering barracks came. On 20 March, when cherry blossoms started to bloom under the spring sunshine, I went to 37th Regiment in Osaka where I passed the physical examination and was given my military outfit.

Nothing there fitted my small body. The only thing to fit me exactly were military socks while my uniform was baggy. I looked around hoping to find shoes to fit me. But all the shoes there were too big. As I was still wandering around, an elderly soldier caught me and barked at me, 'Don't fit the shoes to your feet, you should adjust your feet to the shoes!' I was shaken up by his stern voice. I came to know that the army was a terrible place where you were not allowed to complain. Anyhow a new Junior Private was born wearing a shoulder ensign with a star on a red background.

Wearing the full military outfit, we walked to a Japanese-style hotel where we stayed one week waiting for the boat. At the hotel we were treated really as guests, breakfast and supper were served by maids and meeting with visitors was freely allowed. We did basic military drill every day at a primary school ground while we received none of the slapping that we had been told was very common.

I felt at ease as time passed and I learnt what kind of men my comrades were, from a variety of backgrounds. All of them were well built and would be true railway soldiers. I felt pity for my poor body but I felt better as I made up my mind firmly that army life was a good chance to test my strength.

On the day of departure, we marched along the streets of Osaka where a lot of men on both sides were waving Japanese flags and sending us off with hearty cheers. While walking to the harbour, I could not help feeling lonely as it might be the last chance to see Osaka, where I lived for twenty years from my birth. We were told that we were going to the south but we did not know where. At that time the south, where palm and rubber trees grow, was a place that most men yearned after. As I was sensitive to cold, I felt the south was much better than cold Manchuria and north China. I put rice-straw rope around my shoes and climbed up the gang-plank of the boat. I had a lot of charms (amulets) on my body. Also I wrapped around my body a thousand-stitch belt that the ladies of the local Women's National Defence Society had prepared for me, and a Japanese flag on which many of my friends wrote a short note for me.

Fortunately the sea was very quiet throughout the voyage. We lived in a tight space. As our deck was divided into three layers, we could not stand upright and walked with our body bending low. Three of us slept on a straw mat, where we could not move even an inch. We were given about 2 pints of water per day. We could just wipe our faces, without any chance of taking a bath. An NCO who escorted us mentioned, 'You have been treated as guests in the homeland, but we

Illustration 1.1.1A Barracks of 5th Railway Regiment (aerial photo)

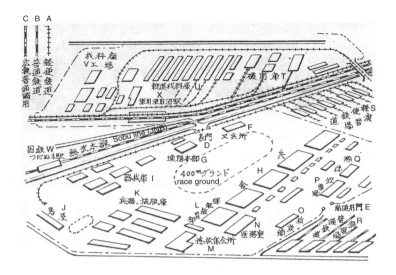

Barracks of 5th Railway Regiment. This was originally the barracks for 2nd Railway Regiment and men of 5th Regiment were trained here before they moved to South China.

Key

A	light railway (600mm)	M	officers' club
B	narrow gauge (1067mm)	N	medical room
C	combined narrow and standard gauge (1423mm)	O	coal-throwing yard
D	main gate	P	kitchen
E	south (rear) gate	Q	PX (army canteen)
F	guard house	R	training ground for railway
G	regimental HQ	S	training ground for light railway
H	barracks for other ranks	T	engine shed
I	tool storage	U	storage for rail materials
J	stable	V	machine shop
K	weapons and clothes store	W	Tsudanuma station of JNR
L	engine drivers' training department	X	station for military use

Illustration 1.1.1B Barracks of 5th Railway Regiment (plan)

cannot afford to keep you useless. Be prepared well for the hard military life!'

That was what we had been expecting. We had to be ready to receive the slapping at any time. But time passed while nothing like this happened, and the boat was going up the river and arrived at Huangpu harbour where I took my first step on the China mainland.

We got on a wide-gauge train, went north, passed through Canton and arrived at Sekihai. There was no platform and we had to jump off the high train. There the new conscript training unit was eagerly waiting for our arrival, and we were to be slapped and trained to our limit. It was isolated far from the regiment, which was in a vast pineapple field with no house to be seen. It was unique and spectacular to me who was brought up in a city. The vast landscape of China was very impressive as well as tranquil which let me forget for a while that I was in a land at war.

At the barracks, our battalion commander and company commander addressed us, and we reaffirmed that we were army privates. This was the beginning of a hard time of suffering for new conscripts, day and night. As a preparation for the hard time I had brought two extra pairs of glasses, but these were broken in the first four months. The daily schedule at the barracks was as follows:

Get up 5:00–6:00 (a few minutes before sunrise)
Morning roll call, soon after getting up, inside our room, or outside
Breakfast 6:30–7:30
Practice 10:00–16:00 (lunch 12:00–13:00)
Bath 16:00–19:00 take bath every day
Supper 17:00–18:00
Free time 18:00–20:00 studying, washing, go to PX (canteen)
Evening roll call 20:00
Lights off 20:30–21:30 (All go to sleep except night watches)
Studying allowed in company office.

All the above activities started and ended with a bugle call, the only music in army life. In the morning we were woken up by the wake-up bugle, and after roll call by the duty officer, we returned to our room, cleaned it and prepared for breakfast. One hour after the wake-up, the meal bugle was sounded. After one hour we assembled ready for military training. A little before noon, the training was finished and we returned to our room to eat. At 13:00 training started again and finished around 16:00. End of training and supper time varied depending on the season. At all meals rice was served mixed with wheat; wheat was added as a precaution to avoid beriberi. At the beginning I could not take this mixture as wheat felt unfamiliar to me. However as training got tougher I ate all the mix served to me because of hunger. To railway soldiers who do hard physical labour, 975 gms of rice was fed, which was 10 per cent more than normal soldiers' ration. As a side dish, fish and meat were often served, together with soup. About twice a week, fruit or a sweet were served as well. Evening roll call was held at 20:00 all through the year, and the number of men was counted in the presence of the duty officer. Then orders, assignment of duties and matters to be attended to were promulgated. After a while the lights-out bugle was sounded on a slow tempo as if to comfort troops for the day's hard work.

On the third day each of us was personally handed a type-38 cavalry rifle by the company commander in a ceremony. This rifle was to be kept as the most important item next to our life, and should be given the utmost care. When the rifle became dusty during combat training, we cleaned it throughly. However if a senior soldier found even a tiny uncleaned part, we were forced to apologise to the rifle. We had to 'present arms' and shout loudly 'Cavalry rifle, sir! I regret that I did not clean you enough!' Often the senior soldier said for his amusement, 'Your voice is low. The rifle cannot hear it.' The man had to repeat it several times in a loud voice which could be heard all through the company.

After training with rifles in firing positions, and in unit movement, miniature rifle practices were done twice in the barracks, where small bullets were fired at a target 15 metres away. Later we went out of the barracks to a shooting range five times. It was nice to go out on fine days. After a week in the barracks, new conscripts were allowed to go to the PX, after supper until five minutes before the evening roll call. As new conscripts got hungry, we enjoyed this the most. However as we were really busy taking care of weapons and washing, including the clothes for senior soldiers, we could not dawdle. Squeezing a short time between duties, we ran to the PX and came back while eating. On Sunday, as the PX was open from nine in the morning until supper time, we went there after lunch with good friends, and ate red-bean soup with rice cake, noodles, and rice cake stuffed with sweet bean paste, while talking with each other. It was the most enjoyable time, eating and chatting, and I still remember it with nostalgia.

From the tenth day, the training for laying rails was started, which is the basic work of railway soldiers. The first step was to move a rail carrying it with our hands or on our shoulders, and to hit a point on an old sleeper or a tree root several hundred times with a spiking hammer, in order to make us capable of track-spiking, fixing a rail on a sleeper. Also we were trained how to drop a rail from piled rails on the laying-wagon by six men as a team. The rail had to be dropped within 30 cm from the existing rail ends so that the connection could be made efficiently. Then we were trained how to connect rails using a fish plate (joint bar) and six bolts.

We were trained how to work on wood, using axes, various types of saw, screw-cutters and chisels. I had done no work with wood so it was hard for me to master, but at the end of a four-month period, I was able to cut the top of piles flat, or drill holes. As a basic training for building bridges, piling work was done using hand-pulled movable monkeys and scaffolding. As earth work was essential for building embankments or trenches, we were trained how to dig using a shovel or beater as well as how to carry earth in straw-baskets on our shoulders, or by wheelbarrow.

At the end of four months, we went through the first-stage inspection by the regimental commander for four days, ranging from military exercise with rifles, rail laying, and building a wooden bridge to building an embankment. At every step the commander commented on our performance. After the inspection we were given a one-day holiday, and then our new assignments were published. In the second stage of training, we 70 men in the 3rd company were assigned to diversified special skill training as follows:

Work on the railways

Engine driver 8
Wagon checker 2
Communication 6
Rail-truck driver 8

Work at the regimental machine shop

Assembler 2
Carpenter 4
Lathe operator 2
Machine adjuster 2
Canning 2
Electrician 1
Finisher/fitter 2
Photographer 1
Hammer-smith 2
Watch repair 1
Iron casting 1

Work in the barracks

Armourer 1
Diver 1
Sewing work/tailor 1
Trumpeter 1
Shoe repair 1
Proper 21*

After the first stage inspection, the order (grade) of new conscripts was made known. This encouraged the soldiers to work hard together under keen competition, as well as under a private punishment of slapping for careless mistake or for disobedience. Graduates of university, college and middle schools could become officers from ordinary soldiers if they passed the test for officer cadets. They would become second lieutenants in two years if their performance was good. An alternative way was to become an NCO then apply to be an officer, but this took much longer.

In the army one had to do 'reporting' and 'salutation' which is done at one's promotion, transfer or despatch. Most of these are pleasant occasions. When I passed the test for an officer cadet, I went to my company commander, officers, and Master Sergeant to report it. Then five of us from the company went together to the kitchen for greeting, where we got an unexpected souvenir. 'We were ordered to be officer cadets. We hereby beg to greet you!'

As soon as we finished saying the salutation, heavy punches hit our faces, with the word 'Congratulations!' Though we had been slapped many times and hence we should have resistance to this storm of slapping, I can never forget the pain of those punches. This I had to accept, trying to take it in a favourable sense, as a warning not to be satisfied with one success but to keep endeavouring to be a good officer.

The organisation of a railway regiment was as follows:

Command headquarters
1st battalion: 1st company – 4 platoons; 2nd company – 4 platoons
2nd, 3rd and 4th battalion – each with two companies
Store and machine shop
One platoon consisted of four sections with about 15 men each.

---

* The 'proper' is the major stream of railway soldiers, who will be the assistant in training the next intake of conscripts. Some of the proper soldiers (about five each) went through varied special training for about three weeks each as survey assistants, blasting assistants and rowers.

Illustration 1.1.2 New recruits laying rails

Illustration 1.1.3   Bridge-building exercise

1.2   A military civilian

Sanzou Tomii, 5th Special JNR Machine-work (Miya 5824) Unit, 5th Special JNR Railway Group

I had been working at the Ooi factory of the Japan National Railway (JNR) located in a suburb of Tokyo. On 17 September 1941, I was told to report to the factory manager, and eight men from the electric appliance shop, including myself, were conscripted as military employees who would be sent out of the country. After a simple physical examination, we were allowed to go home, taking with us our personal items.

As we were to assemble at the club house of the Ooi factory secretly on 12 October, I had a simple dinner with a stirrup cup attended only by my family and a sister of my wife. I had three children: aged five years, three years, and a baby. Various thoughts arose in my mind as I saw the baby sleeping soundly. This could be the last time I would see them. I left my house feeling lonely. At the club house many men had already assembled. After all of us had spent a sleepless night with many thoughts, we had breakfast of miso soup with soy-beans and got on a train to Tsudanuma station, where guide soldiers led us on rail-trucks to Narashino field camp.

At the camp, we went through a physical examination and those who passed it were told of their assignment and were led to the big camp building, which was dusty as it had not used for some time. We cleaned the floor, laid rice straw and straw mats, and settled down in a space designated to each team.

We were given clothing, blankets and many other items. As the clothing was all for summer, we guessed that we were going to a southern district, though our destination was confidential and we had no idea where it would be. We were kept busy keeping up with army life and with inoculations, paperwork for the secondment officer back home, and the organization of personal items. All of us were ordered to cut our hair short.

On 18 October, the 5th Special JNR Railway Group was formed officially under command of Colonel Iwasaki and Railway official Hibi. It was composed of Headquarters (5895) Unit; 11th Special Train operation (5822) Unit; 8th Special Railway construction (5827) Unit; 5th Special Bridge (5894) Unit; and 5th Special Railway Machining (5824) Unit. (Numbers in brackets are the code numbers of units which are used in public and as a mail address.)

The Machining (5824) Unit to which I belonged had 32 army men and 285 JNR employees, and consisted of the following sub-units: adjutant department (merit, personnel, general office & recording sections); weapons department (weapon and material sections); accounting department; medical department; and clerical, technical (equipment, survey, engine and wagon sections), and shops (engine, canning, forging, lathe, cast iron, wagon, machining and supply warehouse).

Then we did combat training for ten days, running around the big camp area, and got sunburnt. Once someone lost his bayonet and all of us had to look for it. Fortunately the lost bayonet was found caught in a tree branch, to everybody's relief.

It became cooler day by day, and it was not easy to sleep even with the four blankets which had been issued. After lights-out, men were smoking here and there. When the duty officer discovered this he got angry about it. In the day time we queued at the PX and bought bean-jam buns. The only enjoyment we had was to sleep and to eat.

On 27 October we fell-in in full uniform but without rifle, heard the address of our commander, Colonel Okamoto, and walked to the Tsudanuma station. Though we were instructed to close all the wooden blinds of the coach, when our train passed Shinagawa I opened the left side window and looked at the Ooi factory where I had been working. I saw many men waving hands, probably they knew that we were passing by. The train then moved onto a freight line and passed Tsurumi where I lived. Though I looked around I could not see anyone I knew.

Our train ran through the night and arrived at Osaka the next morning. We walked for an hour and a half and arrived at a primary school where we stayed overnight. Ladies of the Women's National Defence Society worked like beavers to feed us tea and help us settle down.

Next morning I went to Osaka harbour and loaded our machines and equipment onto a 7,000-ton freighter, the *Yae-maru*. All of us embarked and the boat left at 15:00 while we said good-bye to our homeland.

1.3   The British view: Railways in the Burma campaign

Ian Lyall Grant

When in the late nineteenth century, Japan became a modern industrial country, a Japanese rail network was constructed. In a climate of national discipline and obedience to authority, the railways flourished and were very efficiently run. They had the great advantage of using coal, a fuel which was available both in Japan and from Korea. Oil, essential for the army and navy air forces, and for the modern ships in the navy and merchant navy, could only be obtained from the West, notably from the oilfields in the Dutch East Indies. The use of motor vehicles was therefore kept to a minimum and, except in the large industrial towns, there were few modern roads in Japan. When considering a possible advance into Southeast Asia, Japanese planners quickly noted that the rail networks of French Indo-China, Thailand and Malaya were compatible and interconnected. There was, therefore, ready to hand a splendid all-weather communication system, fuelled not by oil but by wooden logs, economical in manpower, and one which they were particularly adept at using. Provided they could occupy one or more of these countries without fighting, locomotives and rolling stock would be available. Consequently from the beginning of 1941 they began to call up conscripts and to form and train a number of new railway operating and construction battalions. They placed so much importance on the railways that their plans envisaged railway companies landing over the beaches in the early waves of an assault.

In contrast to this, British armies relied much more on motor transport in the forward areas. Indeed the Indian Army, when World War II started, had no military railway, and no docks-operating or inland-water transport companies at all. There was therefore no nucleus of trained personnel for expansion. Gradually, during late 1940 and 1941, a number of units were raised from scratch and trained, but all were dispatched to the Middle East, GHQ India having no responsibility for the defence of Burma at that time, So when the Japanese invaded Burma in December 1941 and January 1942, the British were obliged to rely, for bulk transportation, initially on such organizations as the Port of Rangoon Authority, the Burma State Railways and the Irrawaddy Flotilla Company, which were all manned entirely by civilians.

After the air raids on Rangoon in December 1941, much of the civilian dock labour vanished, and many Burmese railway workers also started to leave, although the Anglo-Indians and Anglo-Burmese stayed staunchly at their posts. It was now realized that it was highly desirable to militarize the railways and docks, but with the battle starting it was felt to be too late to make the change. However, two senior transportation officers and some small units from the Middle East were rushed to Burma, arriving in February. This was just as well, for General Mutton had decided to transfer three-quarters of all the reserves in Rangoon to the Mandalay area. Without these reinforcements there would have been a complete breakdown in the docks and on the railways.

On 24 February 1942, after the disaster at the Sittang River, the Chief Railway Commissioner declared that it was impossible, due to staff shortages, to run any more trains from Rangoon. The Governor now stepped in. The Commissioner and his three senior assistants were dispatched to run the railways in north Burma, and the army took over the running of the railways from Rangoon up to Prome and Toungoo, the civilian staff being made subject to military discipline. A few more engine-drivers and signalmen were flown in from India. Military control was later extended to north Burma. On the whole this ad hoc system worked well in British-controlled areas. However, it ran into trouble where the Chinese were in control. Ill-disciplined Chinese troops hijacked trains at the point of the bayonet and, ignoring schedules and safety, forced drivers to obey their orders. As a result there were some horrendous accidents, and the morale of the railway staff plummeted in Chinese areas.

Part 2   Advance in Burma

2.1   Assault landing on Singora

Sergeant Jiro Sakai, 7th Company, 4th Battalion, 9th Railway Regiment

On 16 September 1941, I was called up again for the second time for military service and went to Tsudanuma barracks in a relaxed mood as I had had a good drink of *sake* at lunch with a friend. At the entrance gate the chief guard who was a corporal called out 'Salute!' and I was abashed and realized that I was a civilian no more. A soldier with a blue armband came running up to me, asked who I was, carried my suitcase and led me to the physical examination. There I saw Dr Konuma, who had been with me in the 1st Railway Regiment and was drafted this time. I asked him repeatedly 'Please let me return home', but he said 'I am also going. You cannot be helped.' So I passed the physical test and went to a room where there were about ten men. Captain Kusuda told me, 'You are to be assigned to battalion headquarters.' But as I told him that I would rather be excused from the headquarters, I was assigned to 7th Company. Guided by a soldier, I went out of the gate and came to the railway warehouse which was to be the barrack for the 9th Railway Regiment, a new regiment being formed. As I was amazed that there was nothing in the vast warehouse, the guide soldier left saying, 'After a while soldiers on active service will come from the second regiment.' This put me in a bad frame of mind. What a treatment for an experienced draftee like me! As I sat down in the warehouse I fell to sleep from the effect of the lunchtime drink.

After an hour or so, I was woken by the sound of footsteps, and found a lieutenant standing beside me. He asked me, 'May I ask your name?'

I was amazed by his polite expression and sensed that he was also drafted from civilian life.

'I am Sergeant Sakai who is assigned to 7th Company.'

'I am company commander Mino. Thanks for your trouble. As active servicemen will come from the remaining troop after a while, please command them and engage in the mobilization work.' And he walked out immediately. I went to sleep again.

I did not know how long I slept, but I was awakened by the stirring sound of military boots. They were on the feet of about forty regular soldiers led by Master Sergeant Ueki, who was in charge of the command unit of the company. Corporal Kashiwagi reported to me in a voice full of vigour, which reminded me that I was in the army. By the systematic work of the corporal and his men, a telephone was installed and desks and other articles were brought in, a temporary office was opened, and I started to live in army style. More draftees, new and experienced, came in the next day.

On 23 September the 9th Railway Regiment was officially formed, commanded by Colonel Itaru Imai. The regiment left Tsudanuma, battalion by battalion at three-day intervals, and we, the 4th battalion, left on 12 October in train coaches with wooden blinds closed for anti-espionage, and boarded the *Victoria-maru* at Osaka. In the train we could peep at the outer world from the slits of the blinds, but in a big ship we were separated from the outside by a black steel plate. We were not allowed to go on deck even at night. We did not know where we were going. As it was cold in the cabin, blankets were issued for everyone, but after a few days it became very hot.

On 29 October we landed at Haiphon in French Indo-China. We were trained how to run the local trains in Haiphon. Some of the engine drivers went on local engines to the Chinese border regularly, wearing local drivers' uniform. So some guessed that we would be attacking China from the south. On 19 November, most of 4th Battalion, with a part of the supply depot, left Haiphon in a shabby transport ship, where we were served only pumpkin and rice at each meal, so we called the ship *Pumpkin-maru*. We arrived at San-a on Hainan island, but as there were no other ships there we had to wait two more days in the ship eating pumpkin. Each of us was given a pocket-size handbook entitled 'Read this and we will win' (how to fight in a tropical area). We read it carefully as we had nothing else to do in the ship.

On the island we slept in a big tropical tent with mosquito nets, and undertook training in transferring from actual transport ship to steel boats by rope ladders. On 3 December we were separated and boarded three separate ships, in case of a loss, and were notified of the order by the army commander Lt General Yamashita, 'The army is to board on *x* day, and intend to land at *x* (place) on *x* plus *x* day. Our enemy is the British!' The figures at *x* were to be filled in later.

We got up early and loaded our vehicles first, and boarded the *Kansai-maru* in the evening. We were placed in the bottom hold which was unbearably hot.

Next morning I went up on deck. The sky was clear blue and the voyage was quiet. We were in a very big convoy. I tried to count the number of ships which were moving in two long files. I counted several times but did not get the same number as both far ends were hard to see. I could count up to 55. Outside the convoy a cruiser and several destroyers were escorting us and a seaplane was circling overhead. The ships were sailing in good order and quietly, so it was hard to believe that we were going to an enemy land.

On 5 December, Sergeant Kanematsu and I were called to company commander Mino, and received the order: 'Hirota leader and nine men will land at Singora in the first group.' We were ordered, in case we had to fight against the Thai army, to land in the night and secure Singora station and the 06:24 train for Malaya with its engine driver. Infantry and other troops had received their orders and were to move in good order. It was an important time for our country, whether we succeeded or failed. I told this to the selected men who were also excited and wanted to march to Singapore. I could not sleep that night owing to the heavy responsibility.

About noon on 7 December, an air raid alarm was sounded; a British patrol plane came close to our convoy but nothing happened and it left soon. Surely we were discovered by the enemy and our commanders must have been deeply worried. But we were not attacked by British planes and we arrived off the coast of Singora and started landing at 1:00 on 8 October. The sea was rough and the boat was floating up and down. I had to go down the rope ladder which was old and some wooden steps were missing. The boat was moving up and down like a branch of a tree, and appeared quite different to what it looked like from the deck. When the boat went down it was too far to jump, so I jumped when it came up. I landed well and gave a sigh of relief. As I looked up, a man missed the opportunity to jump and was shouted at by the boat crew. Thus we were delayed but the boat started off as soon as it was full. The transport ship that we were on looked as big as a mountain. The waves were high but the engine of the boat sounded in good condition. However the sound it made when it raced on top of a wave made us feel uneasy. When the boat was on top of a high wave we could see the dark forest of Singora, then it fell down into the trough. We were tossed about at the mercy of the sea, and I kept low and abandoned myself to despair. When the boat came to about 100 metres from the coast, I raised my head to look, but suddenly vomited. Some of the mountain gun soldiers in the boat were also sick.

When we came close to the beach, the anchor was cast out and the boat dashed towards the beach, then a crew member pulled a rope from the boat to the beach. I jumped out into the water. The sea was deeper than I thought, above my waist, and I nearly tumbled down, pushed by a big wave. Being fully armed, I struggled to walk in the water and reach the land. I had no time to rest as our party of ten, with a leader, had to find the railway station. We ran on the paved road in the dark. After a while I saw several figures running towards us. Private Shimoyama put his finger on the trigger of his rifle. I cried, 'They are natives! Wait!' So the disaster was avoided. As we advanced a little more, our leader cried in an excited voice, 'Here are rails! The station is over there!'

So we ran towards the station. Suddenly the front lamp of an engine, which had not been lit, shone on us. Aiming the lamp, one infantry section of the 5th Division was setting up a machine gun. We cried, 'We are railway soldiers. Wait!' We ran and jumped on the engine. We were the first to occupy the station and engine, without any damage. Our mission was completed. We were very pleased with ourselves, and tears of joy came from our eyes. Immediately we got hold of the Thai driver to run the engine, and passengers on the train were moved to the station buildings with their luggage. At that time the Japanese consul at Singora came with his wife and was deeply impressed to see us. He said, 'How I longed for today!' When we put down our knapsacks and guarded the station for ten minutes, about thirty soldiers of Asai platoon with white bands across their chests came from the side of the station. As we challenged 'Who goes there?' they seemed to be disappointed to know that Hirota platoon had already occupied the station.

We checked the station yard and found that the switches were locked, so we had the Thai station men unlock them and start shunting the wagons. A train which consisted of five wagons in front of the engine followed by twenty wagons behind it, was formed in order to carry Miyamoto Battalion, the advance unit of 5 Division.

As I was running around the station in preparation, Miyamoto Battalion, for which we were waiting, arrived, but they mistook us for Thai army and charged towards us. I cried 'Friendly army' and managed to avoid a clash. As soon as all of them had gathered, they wanted the train to start immediately, but engine and wagons had not been inspected and water had to be fed into the engine. Water was carried to the engine by a long line of men with buckets of water, and the train was ready to move by dusk. Platoon leader Hirota himself rode on the engine, and the first train left Singora. We were in the front part of the train. We took off our knapsacks and ate breakfast from the transport ship.

After the train had been running for an hour or so, at about 07:00, the sentry reported urgently, 'Men who look like a patrol with an officer of the Thai army have jumped off the track.' Then the Thai army opened fire on us. Later we were to discover that the negotiation between Thailand and Japan lasted until early morning of 8 December, so the cease-fire order from Thai headquarters had not reached the men at the front by that time.

We jumped off the train and lay flat wherever we could find cover. The Thais continued to shoot. It was almost unbearable to do nothing under the severe firing. Then suddenly Private Uzaki cried, 'Commander, show us the target!' But our company commander who was close to me did not allow us to shoot. We were irritated as our infantry was shooting back. 'An order is heavier than a mountain', but we soldiers could never get along in our present situation without shooting. If we were to shoot, our minds would be calmed. I felt immoderately thirsty. The reflection from the strong sunshine was painful to my eyes. A very long time seemed to have passed.

I wanted to see the situation on the other side of the train, so I climbed up on it and found that the enemy was also firing from that direction. As plenty of bullets were coming, I had to lie low behind the embankment. Our infantry were not firing strongly at the beginning, but now they could not stay where they were and started to advance.

Under the circumstances our engine returned to Singora to replenish ammunition. But the fighting ceased after we left for Singora. This was the first battle in which our battalion took part, recorded as the Battle of Nahmnoi.

Our train continued to move on the Singora branch line which was then peaceful, but there were several places where rails had been removed or demolished. It took until 16:00 to repair them, and the train arrived at Hat Yai before getting dark. From there the infantry advanced on foot, and we stayed at the station overnight.

Next day, 9 December, 23 men of Hirota platoon left Hat Yai on bicycles towards Sadao, and stayed the night at a primary school. Next day we arrived at the Thailand–Malaya border almost at the same time as the infantry. We arrived at Pattanbessar at 17:00 and after a short rest I was ordered to go on a reconnaisance of demolished bridges with five men, and we left on bicycles. We went along the railway, and it became dark after an hour when torrential rain came down. The lamp of the bicycle did not work and lighters or matches were not usable. We slipped down many times in the dark and travelled 28 km with utmost difficulty, arriving at the demolished bridge at 02:00. There Senior Private Iwase was exhausted and said, 'Please leave me here as I am not able to walk.' I could never forget his words. So we left our bicycles there and travelled light to Klong station where we reported the situation by telephone.

From there, we moved south as an advance unit and captured many wagons on the way. We advanced 1,200 km, finally arriving at Johore Bahru at 10:00 on 12 February 1942, and our eyes saw Singapore island which we had been looking for.

2.2   The first battle

Senior Private Toru Hozomi, 7th Company, 4th Battalion, 9th Railway Regiment

On 8 December 1941, we landed on the beach of Singora in the second group, completely soaked with sea water. Our section gathered 100 metres inland and headed for Singora station. As we advanced, shells came from the direction we were heading. One exploded close to us though not a big one. As we had only rifles, we retreated a little into a house. Meanwhile our tanks which had just landed advanced towards the gun and the shelling stopped. So we advanced again and arrived at the station, where Hirota platoon was preparing a train. We helped to feed water into the engine, and got on the train together with infantry soldiers.

When the train had been travelling for about an hour, we were fired on from the front. I jumped out of the train and, eager to find a shelter, tumbled like a ball down the right-hand slope of the embankment. I lay down with my face on the marshland, which smelled strongly of grass. For a while I just heard the sound of firing and could not move. I felt that the bullets were raining down close to me. I had a desire to pass water, but I could not urinate lying down flat. As my heartbeat was calming down, I decided to look for a safer place and to reconnoitre the enemy situation. As I turned my head, I saw the bullets were focusing on the engine, and logs in the tender were making popping sounds. I saw Apprentice Officer (equivalent to British 2nd lieutenant) Hirota climb up on to the engine despite the heavy shooting. I prayed for his safety with my eyes closed; I could not bear to see him hit. After what felt like a long time, I heard the sound of steam. As I opened my eyes, the engine started to move backward with black smoke coming out of the chimney. The gunfire concentrated on the engine more persistently. I felt relieved to see the train gradually increase speed and move outside of the range of firing. It was a marvel that the Apprentice Officer was not hurt at all.

As the train left, the firing concentrated on us who were spread out. The bullets hit the right bank of the embankment and earth spattered on me. As I lifted my head a little and looked around, I saw that the enemy was shooting in several directions from the mid-slope of the hill where bushes had been cut open. I was right in the firing line. 'This place is no good at all. If I stay here, I am sure to be hit,' I thought.

I decided I had better cross over the embankment and find a place to hide. I thought I ought to crawl up the embankment in a slack moment of the firing, but I was too frightened to do it. Then the brave and quick action of leader Hirota which I had seen a little time before strongly inspired me. I thought, 'Here I go', and jumped over the embankment, and some of my comrades followed me.

As I rushed down the steep slope as though rolling down it, I saw a comrade was holding on to the bank of a rice field. I could not stop myself and dropped into the rice field. It was deeper than I thought. Somebody shouted loudly, 'Keep your head down! Head down!'

I clung to the bank with my body under water up to my chest. My bladder, which was really too full, reacted to the cold water and warm liquid flowed in my pants and crept up to the navel. 'Put mud on your helmets!' So I smeared mud all over my helmet.

The enemy positions were about 200 metres in front of us, on the hill just behind the crossing of railway and road. The enemy could see us clearly, just as in my last position. One relief was that the thin bank was some help in hiding me. It was better than when I was in the open field with nothing to hide me from the enemy's sights. Gradually more bullets approached me. I was worried that the bank was gradually falling down, and looked for a sturdier bank and moved there for my safety.

After some time, the infantry started to advance while we railwaymen stayed where we were. Machine guns of the infantry advanced on the road and started firing. Then the infantry formed the front line and railway soldiers were on the second line at their back, so to say as a reserve. Enemy firing concentrated on the front line and a few bullets came around us. But as we were in unfavourable ground, the fighting did not proceed well. Then a young infantry officer dashed forward with a section in order to destroy the enemy machine gun on the hill. But the section led by that brave lieutenant met concentrated gunfire, some men were wounded and they could neither advance nor retreat. The advance was halted.

Seeing such a critical situation, Lieutenant Asai sprang up in a rage to help his classmate in the military academy who was in danger. Pointing to soldiers around him, he ordered, 'Men up to there and the NCO, follow me!'

We had not been spread out in an orderly fashion as in our training. It was a mixed skirmish line formed in confusion as each man eagerly looked for a place to shelter. I thought it was advantageous to be a bit away from the leader in such a situation. The section advanced some way, but they were also brought to a halt between the enemy and us. Lieutenant Asai was hit through his upper arm and shoulder, and Private Honda was hit through his waist and was immersed in water. Company commander Mino lay in a curve of embankment serenely smoking a cigarette. He seemed to be either bold or self-possessed in the unfavourable situation. I admired him as an experienced man who had fought with the army in China.

Around noon the bearer of a flag of truce came from the Thai army proposing to end the fighting without further bloodshed. The fighting ended and one officer stopped a Thai automobile which came by and asked the driver to take Lieutenant Asai to the field hospital. Private Honda on the other hand was carried lying face downward on a door plate and sent to Singora station on a wagon. He was seriously wounded, with his abdomen distended due to internal bleeding. Why was he not given priority? Human life should be respected equally in lieutenant and private. It is a contradiction that the lightly wounded lieutenant got priority rather than the seriously wounded private. Were we in a society where rank counts most even in a critical situation? When the lieutenant was wounded, the commander ordered him to retreat. The officer came back walking boldly in a dignified manner, while being advised, 'Asai, it's dangerous! Lie down, lie down,' which became a nice topic of conversation for us for a long time. But why could not such a great officer say, 'Don't mind me. Send Honda first'? Did he not have any such idea in the confusion of the fighting?

If one regards human beings as a war machine, the country spent a long time and a great deal of money to train a lieutenant. His importance is beyond comparison with a private. Is it true that in every society those whose value lies in their rare and important skills are given priority for medical treatment?

2.3   Advance to Malaya

Private Yoshiharu Ukai, 3rd Company, 2nd Battalion, 5th Railway Regiment

We left south China, and landed at Saigon peacefully on 18 September 1941 and later moved to Phnom Penh in Cambodia. There I learned how to operate the local engines which use wooden logs as fuel, and the use of vacuum brakes or steam pressure brakes, my speciality being that of engine driver. All soldiers who were enrolled in March, including myself, were promoted to private from junior private, to our delight.

In December, officers moved around busily, though we new recruits did not understand what was going on. Meanwhile the company commander gave a lecture to all of us and told us to write our wills, as we were going on an important operation. I only wrote thanks to my parents, as in the army death should come inevitably.

I was selected as a member of the advance party led by 2nd Lieutenant Aso, which consisted of 30 men who had various speciality skills. On 30 November we left our company in three lorries and came to a place near the world-famous temple of Angkor Wat, where we joined with an infantry group. While we were waiting we went around the grand temple but regrettably we could not take souvenir photos as film was not available.

From the morning of 7 December orders were issued one after another and we prepared busily for the move. Our team loaded dry rations and tools on our three lorries and started in the evening. Many lorries appeared. We were placed around 60th from the front, and there were more to follow. A total of 160 lorries advanced towards the south with their headlights off, on the relatively good paved road in the dark night. On the right-hand side of the convoy, sidecars were running constantly back and forward to give us order and information. After we drove about three hours, while we could not see anything around us because of the dark night, a message was relayed: 'Put on steel helmet. Load bullets. Prepare for combat!' I loaded my rifle, released the safety catch and stood ready to fight. I felt especially strained as it was the first time I had taken part in a fight, and similarly the eyes of all comrades around me were brightened. Suddenly I heard the sounds of firing to the front and also a sound similar to that made by tanks. At that moment I felt a strong tension as if my heart was freezing. I listened carefully again but now there was no sound, it was very quiet.

After a while, a message was relayed from the front, 'Put on safety catches!' So we put down our rifles and relaxed. The lorries advanced again. This was 01:00 on 8 December 1941, the day Japan entered the Great East Asia War (as we called it), as we found out later. The main part of our railway regiment went into Thailand in a big group of rail-trucks after repairing the damaged rails.

We heard the whirr of planes in the air, and heard a message from the sidecar: 'We will now cross the border and go into Thailand. We are going into Thailand peacefully, but be careful how you act, so that you do not spoil the dignity of the Japanese army.' The lorries advanced slowly, and at a small river which marked the border, we saw unarmed Thai soldiers holding hands up and welcoming us in a dim mist. We continued our advance on the dusty road while our planes were circling over us. As our lorries were old we had to do maintenance work and fix burst tyres often, so we had no time to have a good rest. We ran day and night, eating dry biscuits and being welcomed by the cheering villagers on the way.

We arrived at the central park of Bangkok, capital of Thailand, on 10 December, where we heard that Japan had entered the war against Britain and the USA, and that our navy had attacked Pearl Harbor. As our bodies were dusty all over, we jumped into the pond in the park completely naked and refreshed ourselves, despite the surprise of Thai people around the pond. East Asian people never take off their underwear even while bathing, so they must have been surprised by our nudity and must have thought that we were barbarians. We had to queue for the toll toilets in the park, where we tried not to close the opened door, as we did not have Thai money. We slept in the park that night and the next morning, 11 December, our main party arrived on rail-trucks. We engine drivers were immediately despatched to Bangkok engine shed, and rode on the engines of the military transport trains bound for the Thailand–Malaya border, which were operated by Thais, as guard/escort.

When I returned to Bangkok after two days' escort duty, our company had already left for the front, so I hurriedly followed and caught them up at a town called Hat Yai which was close to the border. While I was relaxing back in my company, I saw a plane coming which I thought might be ours. But the plane started to circle and suddenly dived and fired machine guns three times. It was a British plane but fortunately there were no casualties among us. I was quite shaken by the first air-raid I had experienced, and felt that we were close to the battlefield.

We asked some local men to let us have lorries which we badly needed for the transportation of repair materials. Our 3rd platoon went to a small town called Kangar. We acquired ten lorries but their quality was poor, only just usable, as the British had requisitioned the good

Illustration 2.3.1 Perak bridge supported by sleepers piled crosswise

Illustration 2.3.2 Temporary walkway attached to demolished Perak bridge

Illustration 2.3.3 Derailed train left by the British

Illustration 2.3.4   A part of the repaired Perak bridge

Illustration 2.3.5   Gemas bridge demolished

Illustration 2.3.6 Japanese soldiers crossing the demolished bridge carrying bicycles

Illustration 2.3.7 Japanese trains arriving at Johore Bahru. In the background, burning oil tanks in Singapore

Illustration 2.3.8   First train to cross the repaired causeway into Singapore

Illustration 2.3.9 Rail-tractor type 100 at Ipoh, January 1942

Illustration 2.3.10 Wooden bridge over the River Sittang

ones. Loading supplies on these lorries we went on to the bad road which had been destroyed when the British retreated. Despite the destruction we advanced about 40 km a day, and came to the Perak River, the biggest river in Malaya, where a crowd of our heavy vehicles was waiting to cross.

Looking at the railway bridge, I saw that one girder 47 metres long had been blasted in the middle and hung down in a V-shape. The bridge was more than ten metres above river level. We were told that the battalion must urgently repair the bridge which was critically important for the Malaya operation. We stayed in a primary school located south of the bridge and started 24 hour working from 28 December. We got plenty of coffee, milk and sugar from a nearby British warehouse, which refreshed us in the hard work.

On 1 January 1942, we had nothing with which to celebrate New Year's Day, no *sake* (rice wine), no *mochi* (rice cake), and no time to rest. We just assembled to salute in the direction of our homeland. After our exhausting work, the repair was completed by noon on 4 January, and we were happy to see hundreds of military vehicles cross the river and advance to the front.

We advanced following the front-line infantry, repairing many bridges and facilities, and arrived at Johore Bahru in early February. A lot of ammunition and aviation fuel that was needed for the attack on Singapore was carried on the rail line we repaired. Singapore was captured on 15 February and the main part of our regiment left Singapore on boats to Rangoon in Burma on 25 February.

2.4   Advance to Moulmein

Senior Private Tadao Fujihashi, 3rd Company, 2nd Battalion,
5th Railway Regiment

We had been moving towards Singapore along the Malaya main line repairing railway bridges. When we arrived at Ipoh, our 2nd Battalion was ordered to assemble at Bangkok to take part in the Burma operation. Our 3rd Company was to advance to Burma by marching through trackless jungle and steep mountain ranges, while 4th Company and our vehicles were to go on the road which was still under construction by the army to advance into Burma.

With the preparation of our rations and other supplies for the hard march almost finished, leader Sekimoto ordered me to go to the company headquarters. There I was told to go to Burma by plane as a member of the advance party of eight men led by battalion commander Major Tsushima. All the members had special-skills training, for example as mechanics and engine drivers.

I came back to my platoon, rearranged my gear, and bade farewell to my friends over a drink of *sake*, as the mission could be dangerous, we being few in an enemy land.

In the early morning of 28 January 1942 we went to Bangkok airport and after having our weight checked, we boarded a transport plane and took off at about 9 o'clock. Soon we saw the mountain ranges of the Burma–Thailand border, steep mountains covered by jungle. The commander told us that our 3rd Company was to march over this mountain. We were amazed that our friends would have to walk through such a terrible jungle which must be very hard work, and felt that we should apologise to them for taking an easy flight.

As we were flying over the enemy territory we looked out the windows in case we were attacked by enemy fighters. After a while we saw the Indian Ocean and the plane arrived safely at Tavoy airport in about a one-hour flight. Tavoy had been occupied nine days ago by Oki branch.

Men of the Japanese Special Service Unit took us to a house and we bought fresh fish for supper. That evening the commander told us: 'We alone will advance to Moulmein to secure the station, engine shed, locomotives and wagons. Then we will occupy the Ye–Moulmein line and run trains between Ye and Moulmein.' We felt that our responsibility was large and were high-spirited.

The special service found one sedan and two small lorries for us. We loaded enough petrol and food on them and left Tavoy early next morning. The road went through the mountains, with valleys and steep slopes, and often we had to tow our cars with the commander in the lead. Once we had help from an elephant. When we came close to Ye, one lorry broke down beyond repair. So I moved to the sedan of the commander. This overloaded the sedan, but we could still advance as it was the dry season, the streams were shallow and the slopes were not slippery. After the hard drive, we arrived at Thanbyuzayat where we had an early supper. As soon as we had eaten, the commander ordered us to depart immediately in order to arrive at Moulmein before sunset.

The two vehicles ran at a good speed on the paved road. The lorry gradually dropped back and we lost sight of it. But our sedan ran at full speed, and came close to Moulmein with pagodas on the hill. We saw no inhabitants – all must have dispersed because of the battle. Moulmein had just been captured by the infantry of 55 Division, and smelled of corpses. We four arrived at Moulmein station, got out of the car without waiting for the four men on the truck and ran towards the engine shed. To our delight we found four engines undamaged: 'Hurrah! (*banzai*)' we shouted. The machine tools were also left intact. So 2nd Lieutenant Muto and I started to check the engines. I came across a fuse line, which indicated a serious problem. The fuse led to the four engines, all machine tools and the water feed tower. We cut the fuse in a hurry and looked into the fire beds of the engine-boilers where we saw a bundle of dynamite sticks. The two of us took them out quietly with utmost care. After finishing the nervous work we looked at each other with a sigh of relief. After a while the four men from our truck came running, and seemed relieved to met us. They had been further delayed due to engine trouble.

If our occupation of the station had been delayed, all of the locomotives would have been destroyed – a great hindrance to the transportation of our main party and further operations of the army. We said, 'The god of Burma supported us. We were blessed.' We all looked around the engine shed and water tower, and took off the remaining dynamite. Then we checked the passenger coaches and freight wagons, and found sand pushed inside the axle-bearings of about half of the coaches and wagons to make them unusable. However we were unperturbed as there were enough wagons which we could use to carry our 3rd Company. The commander was delighted to know it, and sent a wireless message to the headquarters: 'We have captured four engines, about thirty coaches and wagons at Moulmein station and engine shed.' Then he wanted us to make ready one engine with one wagon so that we could go out to survey the condition of the rail track next morning. We checked the amount of water left in the engines, and found that only one engine had a small amount of water while the other three had none at all. The water tank was empty and it was not possible to fill the engine with water as the feed pump had been broken. But it seemed that the engine alone might be able to go to Mudon on the remaining water.

Next morning five of us got on the engine and just managed to arrive at Mudon station. After filling the engine with water we went to the town, where to our delight we found all the inhabitants. Mudon is a big town near Moulmein. We went to the county (district) office in the town. There were many Burmese officials, and all of them were pro-Japanese. The commander met the county headman, explained to him our situation and asked for cooperation which he offered willingly. He called for the head of track maintenance, whom we asked to collect line-men and coolies, and load timber for fuel for our engine.

We advanced southwards smoothly but the bridge near Ye was demolished. The commander wanted to repair the bridge before the arrival of our main party, who were to come up from Tavoy, so we went back to Moulmein immediately. Next morning we made a train of three coaches and three wagons, loaded with sleepers, timbers, tools and many local coolies for repairing the bridge at Mudon and arrived at the site. One section of infantry from Oki branch came to guard our work. We called the maintenance headman and told him, in a mixture of English, Burmese and sign language, to build a saddle of sleepers at the destroyed pier. He said, 'Agree, very good' and shook hands with us. The Burmese coolies worked very well, unlike the workers of French Indo-china. The work proceeded smoothly and the bridge repair was completed several days before the arrival of our main party. The local villagers brought three ducks and about twenty eggs and (using sign language) told the commander to eat them, probably to celebrate the completion. We prepared a 'bowl of rice with chicken and egg' with them and ate fully. We also gave some of it to the coolies, who were delighted and gave many thanks.

From that night four of us stayed to guard the bridge. Corporal Machida and three men stayed at Moulmein; they kept two engines in running order and did various maintenance work on wagons, tools and the station facilities. One regret was that we could not repair the water pump as spare parts were not available. Our mission, the transportation of our main party from Ye to Moulmein, was completed on time.

2.5 Advance to Rangoon

Private Yoshiharu Ugai, 3rd Company, 2nd Battalion, 5th Railway Regiment

We moved from Ipoh in Malaya to Ban Pong in Thailand, where we were ordered to reduce our belongings to helmet, gas mask, rain coat, portable tent, mess kit, underwear and a few necessities for living. In addition we were allocated some portable tools for railway soldiers which we tied to our knapsacks.

On 1 February 1942 we went to Kanchanaburi by truck, and then started the long march towards Tavoy. We carried as many rations as we could and the rest was carried by local porters. At first we were nervous of the porters as they each carried a woodman's hatchet with a 50-cm blade. But as we went into the jungle we realized the merit of the hatchet. It was essential for cutting bushes and vines and for cooking.

At Wang Po we joined with an infantry battalion of 55 Division, and went into deep jungle walking step by step on a narrow path that the advance engineers had cleared. I dragged my tired feet, trying not to lag behind; if I dropped out I might be a prey for wild tigers. We lived on dry rations, so we were eager to reach the Burmese plain where we expected to eat plenty of good fresh meals. Sometimes we sliced the soft core of the banana tree and put it in a soup of dried *miso* (bean curd) trying to get a taste of vegetables just for a change, but the core was tasteless. We went through dense bamboo forest and were scratched all over our bodies by the sharp thorns.

Finally we crossed the jungle-covered mountains and came to the plain, and arrived at a small village with several simple palm and bamboo huts with raised floors. However there was nothing in the poor little village, despite our expectation of getting food, and we were all really disappointed. Some of my comrades were so discouraged that they developed a fever. Next morning we started our march towards Tavoy which was 20 kilometres ahead. Though the road was roughly paved, the hard surface made our legs tired after a long walk in the mountains, and we lay down flat in the middle of the road whenever a short rest was allowed. At the evening of 13 February 1942 we arrived at Tavoy dragging our tired legs. We were proud that none of us railway soldiers had dropped out during the hard march, though we heard substantial numbers of infantry men could not keep up with the march.

Next day we rested in Tavoy. We ate a lot of fish, vegetable and boiled rice and were given black sugar and Burmese cigars as luxuries. The Burmese cigars wrapped in tree leaves were unique and made our smokers happy. We were refreshed when we left Tavoy, and walked to Ye next day. From there we went to Moulmein on trucks and trains arranged by the advance party led by the battalion commander. Moulmein smelled of battle, but being only a private I could not tell what had happened there. I was assigned to collecting rations from the crowded pier. Next night we crossed the River Salween in a civilian ferry and came to Martaban. The consignment of ammunitions, rations and other goods was at the pier area in jumbled confusion and it smelt bad. Nearby the pontoon (floating dock) for transferring railway vehicles seemed undamaged. After a short rest I was put in a scout team of five men and walked on the railway leading to Pegu. At Thaton station (24 miles from Martaban) we saw several abandoned corpses of Indian soldiers and felt that we were on a battlefield. We picked up a light truck and moved again pushing it on the rail. On the way we found vegetables and put them on the truck. We kept advancing and came to a river about

50 metres wide. The arched railway bridge with two spans had been demolished. At the approach to the bridge we saw a helmet and puttees hanging on a telephone pole, and under it were scattered several cavalry rifles, bags, gas masks and telephone supplies. On the other side of the river was a red-brick building with few windows. It looked like a factory. The area was quiet, and we saw no sign of men. We thought something must have happened and loaded the scattered Japanese rifles and fittings on to our truck to take them back. Suddenly we were assailed by sweeping fire from the windows of the red-brick building. We five jumped and fell down two metres from the top of the embankment to the ground.

Some dust kicked up in front of us. We were panic-stricken. As there was no place to hide ourselves, we ran up the embankment with desperate courage and lay down on the other side. But as we could not win with our five rifles against the machine guns, and since the terrain was unfavourable, our leader ordered us to retreat, and we ran for dear life into the bushes and long grass trying to hide ourselves, pursued meanwhile by the firing noises.

We ran for about two kilometres and came to a road. My throat was burning dry and my feet were moving as if floating on air. Then suddenly we were challenged 'Who goes there?' Seeing the friendly army in front of us, we all fell down with relief.

We rejoiced at our safety, and the water from the canteen tasted so sweet. My body was covered with scratches made by the thorns. The sentry told us that we were in the front line, and he was surprised that we had dared to go there with our light arms and had come back alive; but we had not known the situation. After we had rested at our house until the evening, our whole platoon went to the bridge hoping to recover the arms of our friend, and food. Unfortunately the moon was shining brightly and we had to be careful not to make a noise or emerge from the shadow, but to our disappointment at the approach to the bridge not only the rifles but our fully loaded truck had disappeared.

Two days later our company went to the river and worked on repairing the road bridge which had been demolished, and we also ferried our advancing troops in folding boats. We were told that, as the locomotives could not be moved from Moulmein to Martaban, our battalion had no railway operation to do, so we were doing the field engineer's work vital for the current operation.

We ferried many lorries fully loaded with soldiers, ammunition and rations, while hearing the roar of guns from the front line. We seldom saw Japanese planes, but British planes came around several times. So the lorries moved only during night when enemy planes did not come. However we continued to build the wooden road bridge in daytime while sentries carefully watched the sky. One day we were suddenly fired on by a British bomber. As we were in the dry river-bed, there was no place to shelter. We lay flat on the ground and I thought that it could be the end of my life when sand kicked up by bullets came close to my feet. The plane came around three times and shot around us, but fortunately none of us was hurt. The bridge under construction was not damaged either. After the bridge was completed, we enjoyed eating water melons and peanuts from the nearby farms and talked of our lucky experience in the air-raid.

On the evening of 22 February, the company commander with several men went ahead to check the possibility of securing the big bridge over the River Sittang. We followed them after a while. We were held up at Kyaikto as heavy fighting was going on ahead of us. When the sun rose, gunfire almost died out. So we advanced though we were advised to watch out for enemy soldiers still around. An infantry soldier told us that the Sittang bridge was demolished by the British. When we came closer to the bridge, it was very hot as many enemy vehicles were still burning on the roadsides and in level places. There were many corpses of Indian soldiers scattered around the river beach. The big Sittang bridge for both railway and road had been demolished, and two spans had fallen down in the water in a V shape. We saw here and there something like human bodies caught on the girders. The company commander went out in a small boat to survey the bridge. We were worried that the boat might be attacked by enemy planes, but they came back safely and told us that the damage was too big for our railway battalion to fix, even for temporary use. We crossed the river following the main part of the infantry on the steel boats of the field engineers during the night, and advanced on lorries along a dusty road crowded with vehicles. We saw abandoned corpses, and then tanks with Japanese flags destroyed near Waw station. We prayed in silence for the tank crews. At a station near Pegu we captured a small engine undamaged; this was our first capture.

As Japanese forces captured Rangoon on 8 March without fighting in the city, we rushed to Maragon marshalling yard. Though we found ten or more engines, all their power transmission parts, such as connecting rods, were missing. We had to try hard to find a way of making some of the engines workable. We found a lot of supplies in the store, and after a lot of tedious trial and repair work, we made two engines usable and ready for rail transport from Rangoon to Pegu.

2.6   Start the train service

Captain Shigehiro Asakura, Commander 3rd Company, 2nd Battalion, 5th Railway Regiment

The road over the Burma–Thailand border was opened for motor traffic on 20 February 1942, and our vehicles as well as the 4th Company arrived at Sittang. Our battalion crossed the River Sittang on 6 March 1942, and advanced on lorries via Waw and Pegu. My company went south on the Mandalay–Rangoon road while a part of the battalion went on patrol along the railway.

Flames and dark smoke covered the pier area when we came to Rangoon in the evening of 9 March. My company went to secure Maragon marshalling yard. There were about 15 engines but all of them had been made unusable by removing the left-hand parts of the driving mechanism. Nonaka platoon from the regimental supply depot, who came with us, went to secure Insein railway workshop which had not been demolished.

From 10 March we started to secure engines, organize station yards, repair demolished rails, open stations as far as Pegu, and repair telephone lines. I went with a platoon on a light train to check the rail track and found that the railway bridge over the Pazundaung creek, 11 miles from Rangoon, had been demolished. It was a double-track bridge over an inlet-like creek of the Rangoon River. The bridge consisted of a 130-metre truss in the centre with a steel beam on each end. It seemed that the British had tried to blast the central truss with a massive charge of explosives, but only some of the charges had exploded, while most failed to go off. So the truss did not collapse. The lower beam of the truss on the downstream side was damaged, but fortunately it was not completely cut. We checked whether the bridge was capable of allowing trains to cross. Though the demolished lower beam did need to be reinforced in the future (which could not be done using the tools our company had), we judged that the trains could pass through on a single track of the bridge. We replaced and repaired three rails on the bridge, and called a YD engine with three heavy wagons and made them pass over the bridge. This confirmed that the bridge was passable on a single track. While we were working on the bridge, the patrol from Pegu arrived and confirmed that the rail track between Pegu and Rangoon was usable.

It was not easy to secure usable locomotives. According to the former local employees, the enemy had taken away all the parts on the left side of the engines, which they said would be sent to Prome to be dumped in the River Irrawaddy, or in Rangoon harbour. As the engines were not destroyed by explosives, we tried hard to swap parts between engines, and to use makeshift parts, and in this way succeeded in repairing four engines. We heard from the field engineers* that there were two engines in good condition on the demolished bridge at Wanetchaung, 30 miles from Rangoon. In fact the engines had gone on to the demolished bridge slowly and had fallen down into the river. I went there with two platoons on a heavy train pulled by a YD engine carrying sleepers, a jack for lifting, wire rope and necessary tools. We lifted the engines with saddles of sleepers, and then the YD pulled them up from the fallen bridge (1.5 metres), and put them back on the rails. After repairing the bridge also, we brought the two engines to Insein factory where minor repairing was done. We were happy to have acquired two good engines in a day.

With seven engines, including one small tender MC engine, we started to run trains between Rangoon and Pegu (46 miles) and carried 55 Division and then 56 Division who had landed at Rangoon. The difficulty was that the seven engines had to be used continuously day and night, and when their fusable plugs were melted down they were plugged by a rifle bullet as an emergency measure. Because of the lack of a water-gauge, the driver could not tell when he ran out of water. So usually he asked the troops who were passengers to fill up the engine with water by relaying buckets from a nearby stream or pond. Because of the shortage of engines, 100 empty wagons were pulled by an engine across the flat terrain, which was a spectacularly long train. When an engine broke down we sent it to Insein factory where our railway soldiers with local employees repaired it promptly.

Insein factory had been secured without any destruction. Some of the machines had been packaged ready for shipment to Prome, but none had been sent. Most of the Burmese employees came back to work, and the factory was operating in good order, which was a big help for our railway operation. At that time we were told that C56 engines brought from Japan, which had been adjusted to run on one-metre gauge, had been landed at Rangoon pier. We rejoiced to hear that reinforcements were coming. But they did not come to our front. Then we were told that because their overall width was bigger than the Burmese loading gauge, many parts had to be cut off or remodelled which took a long time.

---

* Engineers of 33 Division attacked the last train from Rangoon at Wanetchaung.

As the army advanced north, our supply depot acquired more MC engines at Toungoo and Pyinmana, and the shortage of engines was lessened. During the time we were busy transporting the newly arrived 56th and 18th divisions to the front, the C56 engines did not reach us. On 23 March, the major part of 5th Regiment, 1st and 3rd Battalions, landed at Rangoon. The newly arrived battalions were in charge of repairing the tracks in front; our 2nd Battalion did the transportation service; while the supply depot secured materials and undertook maintenance work.

2.6 Diary of a company commander (extract)

Lieutenant Zyoichi Saito, Commander 4th Company, 2nd Battalion, 5th Railway Regiment

10 March 1942: The company crossed the River Sittang at 16:00, and went along a bad road littered with enemy bodies and disabled tanks. On the way we were shot at but we moved through quickly and arrived at Pegu at 22:00.

15 March: I received the following order at the battalion headquarters in Rangoon.

(1) The battalion will follow the advance of the front line, and will be in charge of developing train operation between Pegu and Toungoo.

(2) The 3rd Company will continue its present duties, and also repair the rail track between Rangoon and Pyuntaza (88 miles), and have train operation between Waw and Pegu transferred from the 4th Company at noon 17th.

(3) 4th Company will advance promptly to Pyuntaza area and repair the rail track up to Toungoo.

23 March: Repair of the bridge over the River Kun was completed at 18:00 today. The 4th Platoon moved to Pyu (134 miles) in the early morning and repaired the Pyu bridge. The company headquarters left Kanikuin (124 miles) at 18:00 and moved to Zeyawaddi (138 miles). Zeyawaddi is a small village where there is a big sugar factory. When the enemy retreated two trains collided head on and were destroyed. These trains were fully loaded with sugar and military supplies. Enemy corpses were scattered everywhere and sugar bags, which were used instead of sand bags, were left here and there – a miserable sight.

26 March: According to a report of our patrol, both railway and road bridges at Toungoo were demolished by the enemy this morning. The Japanese army seems to have surrounded Toungoo and is fighting with the Chinese who resist stubbornly.

30 March: The strongly resisting enemy retreated in face of our fierce attack and Toungoo was captured. Field guns and mountain guns that we transported were rushed to Toungoo. In the afternoon three officers from 3rd Battalion came to us. They had arrived few days ago from Singapore and are going to take over from us the development of the rail track ahead.

4 April: Repaired the railway bridge south of Toungoo (166 miles), and the test run was completed satisfactorily. The company advanced to the terminal station at Toungoo and started to run trains between Toungoo and Pyuntaza. Major Tsushima, our battalion commander, was transferred to the commander of the reserve unit of 1st Railway Regiment by an order put out yesterday. The battalion commanders held a simple farewell party at regimental headquarters at Pegu, where I also had the honour of being present in the lowest seat. It seems that the rainy season is coming to Burma; it rained yesterday and today.

7 April: The company is operating military transport trains between Toungoo and Rangoon. This also sends back patients wounded at the battle of Toungoo, making use of returning empty wagons. So far 192 patients have been sent back to Rangoon. Kyuboe station (149 miles), which is in our area, was suddenly attacked by the enemy at 23:30. After fighting for about thirty minutes, the enemy retreated. None of us was injured. The station master is Sergeant Shimada.

10 April: New battalion commander, Captain Masaji Saito, made his first tour of the unit. I went to meet him at Pyuntaza to show him around my operating area. At 14:50 train no. 13 was derailed and over-turned (one engine and ten wagons overlapped upon one another) at Oktwin, owing to the opening of a switch (point) which seemed to be the result of sabotage by enemy soldiers. I went to the site promptly, made arrangements for recovery and adjusted train timings. It was fortunate that there was no damage to aviation fuel or bombs.

12 April: The recovery of the derailed engine was more difficult than expected, and it will take all day tomorrow. The work did not progress as planned as the maintenance team led by Sergeant Okada has only ten men. At 12:00 the regimental commander came to inspect the site. The battalion commander urged us to recover the engine as soon as possible. I reported that the track will be open by 24:00 tomorrow night.

13 April: Second Lieutenant Shibata and 25 men who were doing transportation on the Martaban line returned to the company at 21:30. The derailed engine at Oktwin was put back on the rails at 19:10 today.

1 May: Arrived at Thazi (306 miles) at 14:00. My company has been in charge of the operation of both Thazi and Thedou (322 miles). Mandalay was occupied by our army at 22:00 today. Lashio was occupied by 56 Division on 29 April. The enemy is retreating from Mandalay towards Myitkyina.

2 May: Reported to battalion commander in the morning and received order. In the afternoon I went to Palei (374 miles) with Sergeant Nakata and his men and opened the station. Soon afterward I crossed the River Myitnge to see the situation at Mandalay. Two trusses, each of one hundred feet span, of the Myitnge bridge have been demolished and as it is difficult to build a detour route, 18 Division is transferring vehicles and guns across the river on a raft. I took my first step into Mandalay at 20:00, a memorable moment.

3 May: The company was ordered to cross the Irrawaddy and occupy and develop Myitkyina line from the south together with the 1st Battalion. Asakura 3rd Company of the 2nd Battalion is to advance to Myitkyina going around via Lashio and will develop the Myitkyina line from the north. The main part of 3rd Battalion is to repair Myintage bridge urgently. We have to advance quickly.

10 May: 98 men of the Company moved to Shwebo (64 miles from Mandalay) in three groups: heavy train, light train and automobile. 33 Division had captured Tangon (101 miles) and expected to arrive at Kanbalu (110 miles).

11 May: Fine day. The balance of the company led by 2nd Lieutenant Takizawa arrived at Shwebo at 14:00. Three cholera patients were reported in Mizuno unit. Circulated sanitary notice. Three bridges around Tangon were destroyed, the repair will be done by 1st Battalion.

13 May: Opened Kanbalu station. While repairing damaged rails in the station yard and the water-feed system, prepared the first train at the request of the army. Quite busy. Two teams of engine drivers who left Shwebo urgently last night arrived at 05:00. Though they had not slept at all, they repaired and prepared the train of the 1st Battalion, which left in the morning. A part of the maintenance team built a tank for water-feed system at Tantabin (90 miles).

14 May: The repair train and troop train arrived at Kolin (156 miles). The repaired water-feed pump at Kanbalu broke down and it became impossible to fill the locomotives with water. The water-feed system is vital for operating the trains. We used a hand-operated pump while

repairing the existing one. Went to bed late, but could not sleep owing to heat and persistent cicadas.

15 May: Received telephone message that Shibata platoon left Shwebo at 5:00 for Kanbalu. The pump started to move in the morning as a result of the overnight work of four men led by 2nd Lieutenant Kamasawa, with special thanks to the effort of Senior Private Kajihara.

16 May: The repair train of the company arrived at Wuntho (156 miles) at 06:00. When the Chinese army left Wuntho, they set fire to a train fully loaded with ammunition. So station building and facility had all disappeared, and pieces of shells and deformed rails were scattered all over around there. A Burmese ox-cart happened to pass by the station and touched a mortar shell which remained from the burning, and was blown to pieces while I was watching.

18 May: Connected the company repair train to a troop train of 33 Division and left for Naba (210 miles). Naba station had been opened by Sergeant Kotaku's team. However there are 60 wagons and 10 burned wagons on the main line between Seiwa (202 miles) and Indaw (206 miles) and it is not possible for the train to pass through. All stations around here are fully occupied by wagons loaded with supplies for China or the household goods of fleeing families.

19 May: The wagons left between Seiwa and Indaw were removed at 17:30. The work was hard as the inclination of the track around the area is the steepest on the Myitkyina line, and the track runs through jungle. Immediately started to advance and arrived at Naba at 23:00. Naba was the end of our responsibility. The 3rd Company, who detoured and came down from north, had advanced smoothly, but were delayed by the derailed engine nine miles north of Naba. Because of this our 4th Company arrived at the target before the 3rd Company. All lines in Naba station were filled with loaded wagons and burnt wagons, and many rails were destroyed. So it is not possible to move trains.

23 May: The derailed engine nine miles north of Naba was put back on the rail, but the crane used for the work tumbled down and it will take some more time to recover it. Sent ten men, led by an officer, to help the recovery work.

24 May: Through overnight work, the repair of the derailed site was completed at 05:30. Now it is possible to run through trains from Sagaing to Myitkyina for the length of 343 miles.

1 June: Opened Katha station today. Arai telephone line repair team worked overnight and fixed the branch line to Katha (15 miles). Today we received the memorial badges celebrating the 2,600th anniversary of the country.

2 June: The company was requested to despatch three NCOs and five soldiers for the survey of the Burma–Thailand railway line. Selected men for it. Transportation of 55 Division was completed by today. Handed 400 yen to Sergeant Inoue to be put in my savings deposit. 4 June: Today is my birthday. I wonder if anyone remembers it? Sergeant Yoshikawa and seven men left for the Burma–Thailand border. 8 June: It seems that the rainy season has come. It rained every day and is cool. I felt cold in the morning. Received orders for the promotion of men to Lance Corporal and Senior Private.

9 June: Reported our situation to battalion commander who was on his way to regimental headquarters at Iwatan on train no. 14. Lance Corporal Kokubo who was injured at Pinta arrived on a motor car. The wound was smaller than expected but he has to have a finger cut off.

10 June: We are definitely in the rainy season. Troops are loading wagons drenched in the rain. News of today tells us that our army captured an American fortress in the Aleutian islands.

11 June: As replacement for this year, eight new apprentice officers arrived at regimental headquarters at Iwatan, and among them Morita is assigned to 4th Company and is coming on train no. 13. The new Privates we trained at Kwangtung last year come back to us as officers.

13 June: Despatched Lance Corporal Fukumoto to Mandalay to put in order the supplies we left at Mandalay. It was reported that Corporal Hatayama has died on duty in an automobile accident. He had been suspected of deserting while on duty watching personal belongings.

14 June: Second Lieutenant Hashimoto who was injured in the Mandalay operation is missing as his ship was sunk by an enemy submarine while he was on his way back to Japan. Men's fortune is hard to tell. Prayed for the repose of his soul.

20 June: At 00:24 Pita station was attacked by a guerrilla group of 25–26 men who retreated at 01:05 repulsed by our station men.

22 June: Troop transportation of 33 and 55 Divisions was completed by the full effort of all platoons. From today the train schedule of Myitkyina line was changed and four to five through trains will be run in a day. The bridge south of Tangon was washed away at 19:00.

25 June: The heavy rain which fell from last night onwards destroyed railways at many places throughout the main line.

28 June: Senior Private Gen-ichi Ookawa and 14 men arrived as replacements. Surveyed their career and allocated them to platoons. Six Burmese and Indian thieves were arrested at Meza station.

26 July: Entertainments will be held at Sagaing for three days from today. Soldiers are allowed to attend on a rotation basis.

27 July: Mandalay and Sagaing area was bombed at 13:00. One man of the supply depot was killed by a bomb. To our disappointment, we see only a few of our planes these days.

28 July: Two men of the special JNR unit visited us to arrange for the transfer of train operation from us. At 15:00 Naba was attacked by enemy planes but we suffered no damage.

2 August: Started to prepare for move to our new assignment, the construction of Burma–Thailand railway.

10 August: Left Iwatan at 8:00 and crossed the River Irrawaddy, which we had crossed northbound on 2 May, about three months ago. Left Mandalay by special train to Rangoon.

22 August: Left Rangoon pier no. 17 on board a 900-ton freighter to Moulmein.

23 August: Arrived at Moulmein at 13:00. Left for Thanbyuzayat on 30 lorries. We had crossed the border on foot and had arrived at Moulmein on 17 February – a memorable place.

25 August: Duties of the company on the construction of the new railway are to build bridges between zero and forty kilometres, and build road and barracks needed for it. Went to the planned road together with platoon leaders.

2.8   The British view: British railway demolitions in Burma, 1942

Ian Lyall Grant

The metre-gauge Burma Railway system was not connected to that in Thailand. Hence, when invading Burma, it was very important for the Japanese to capture some locomotives intact. Now the demolitions by the British in Burma as they retreated were carried out by the newly-raised Burmese and Indian field engineer companies, often at very short notice. Many of these were tactical demolitions aimed at slowing the immediate Japanese follow-up along the roads. Except at the pass at the Thai frontier near Mae Sot, these were not very effective until after the capture of Rangoon. Japanese equipment then included field artillery, tanks and vehicles and became more dependent on the roads.

The destruction of the railway system and its locomotives was regarded as strategic demolitions. The British were, of course, reluctant to accept that they were being driven out of Burma, and so were loath to destroy railway bridges until the last minute, by which time rearguard commanders were more interested in tactical demolitions. Again, field engineers would have preferred to destroy locomotives by blowing the boilers to pieces. However a policy of removing various parts from the left-hand drive was ordered, no doubt because if fortunes changed the locomotives could be quickly made serviceable again. South of Moulmein only a few railway bridges were destroyed, while the decision to evacuate the town was taken in such haste that the small party of engineers, who had prepared the four locomotives there for demolition, had to be diverted to other tasks, and did not destroy them. North of the unbridged Salween, however, demolitions were more effective. The rail ferry across the river was damaged and several substantial railway bridges were demolished. The section from Martaban to Kyaikto was not repaired for some weeks. Finally, the great rail bridge across the Sittang river was demolished, at the cost of many lives, and this was never repaired. An alternative bridge was built in 1943 four miles upstream (see page 1 and Illustration 2.3.10, page 59).

A special demolition plan was made for the evacuation of Rangoon. The oil refineries were destroyed and much damage was done to the docks. Two serious errors were, however, made with regard to the railways. The first was the failure to demolish the 450-foot span of the big rail bridge over the Pazundaung Creek. This bridge, a few miles from Rangoon on the mainline from the docks to Mandalay and the north, had long been prepared for demolition. Insufficient attention was paid to this highly important task, and when the demolition failed on the afternoon of 7 March, there were neither time nor materials available for another attempt.

The second serious failure was at the railway workshops at Insein. The plan was to remove its most important machinery to Mandalay, and this had been boxed accordingly. Something went wrong, and it was never moved, being soon re-installed by the Japanese in its previous position, and proving to be a most useful asset.

All locomotives except two had been withdrawn to Prome or Toungoo. These last two left Rangoon at 19:30 on 7 March, pulling the last train loaded with military police. At Wanetchaung they encountered a damaged bridge which was part of a Japanese ambush. Both locomotives toppled off the bridge. The military police drove off their attackers but the engines were abandoned, and the Japanese later succeeded in recovering them both.

The main British forces now retreated to Prome. A number of large railway bridges were blown on this line, as well as one at Gamonzeik on the branch line to Henzada, and two on the west bank of the Irrawaddy on the line connecting the port of Bassein with the river-ports at Henzada and Myanaung.

A part of the British forces had been covering the routes which entered Burma from Thailand through the Shan States. They now retreated up the main line to Mandalay from Pyuntaza towards Toungoo, demolishing several rail bridges en route. However at Toungoo, they handed over command to the Chinese, and crossed the hills to join the rest of the British forces north of Prome. The British did not meet a railway again until they reached Taungdwingyi and the branch line to Kyaukpadaung. There were a number of large bridges on this route but no attempt was made to demolish them, although it would have been easy to do so, as they were apparently considered of insufficient importance.

With the collapse of Chinese resistance in the Shan States, it became apparent that withdrawal across the Irrawaddy was esssntial. There was only one bridge over the river, the great Ava bridge. To cover the withdrawal, the British fought a battle at Kyaukse and three railway bridges were blown up around that town. This was followed by the demolition of the two big bridges, one rail and one road, over the River Myitnge. Finally, in the evening of 30 April, the order was given to destroy the great Ava bridge across the Irrawaddy. This bridge carried two railtracks and two roads, and it would not be repaired until 1955. Its destruction isolated the rail system west of the river, and was the last rail demolition carried out by the British in this campaign.

Part 3   Construction of the Burma–Thailand Railway

3.1   The zero mile post

Norihiko Futamatu, engineer (JNR), 5th Special Railway Unit, Southern Army

On the morning of 5 July 1942, I was walking from Ban Pong to Nong Pladuk station under a blue sky with two assistant engineers. I was sweating as I had on the khaki uniform of an army civilian employee, with a sword and leather gaiters. Nong Pladuk is a small station on the Southern Siam main line which runs from Bangkok to the Malaya border.

I had been despatched from my unit located in Malaya to Ban Pong to work with the 1st Battalion of the 9th Railway Regiment who were to construct the eastern half of the long railway linking Burma and Thailand through the rugged and uninhabited mountain ranges. I had been given a series of 1:20,000-scale maps which had been hurriedly prepared from aerial photographs, but they did not show the surface conditions. So the first step in the construction work was to survey the land and then decide the route of the railway. My first assignment was technical guidance on the land survey which was to be carried out by a team headed by 2nd Lieutenant Mouri of the railway regiment. At the station many soldiers and Thai workers were unloading rails and sleepers from wagons, preparing for the major construction work. I was met by survey leader Mouri and then went to establish the starting-point of the railway (the zero mile post). Following the custom of the Japanese railways, a 4-inch-square wooden pile was driven into the ground in the centre of the station. The four sides of the post were marked with large zeroes, indicating that it was the starting point of the important railway line.

Leader Mouri straightened himself and saluted me with the words, 'Engineer Futamatsu, this is the start of the operation. Please give us your guidance all the way.' I encouraged him, saying 'Put all you have into it as this will be a really hard job.' As he was a graduate of Kyoto university, who had specialized in civil engineering as I had, it was a strange stroke of chance that had brought us together. We were both full of emotion, and looked forward to the completion of the unprecedentedly difficult work.

In peacetime the start of such major railway construction work would have been celebrated by a big ceremony attended by many persons. But as this was a military railway in a remote area, and its planning had to be confidential, only a few people attended this impressive occasion.

The survey team headed by Mouri started their work. He had been training his staff during the past month helped by our assistant engineer Ikegami. The staff were soldiers selected from within the railway regiment who had three months' training in surveying, but they needed intensive training. I went into the field of operations to guide the work every day.

The team started from the zero mile post at Nong Pladuk station and marked the centre line of the Burma–Thailand railway on the ground. The country was mostly flat but there were big tall trees, dense undergrowth, bushes and paddy fields deep in mud, which made the going very hard for the team. They built bamboo platforms 20 metres high at 4-kilometre intervals to provide good viewing points for the transit theodolite, a key item of surveying equipment.

As we advanced we came to dense forest – the so-called jungle, where it was only with difficulty that the trees and dense undergrowth of bamboo were cut down, using hatchets, axes or saws. Sometimes we had to blast their roots out with dynamite. After we had set the centre line on the ground, 20 metres both sides of the line were cleared of trees and other obstacles by the cutting team, and this operation was then followed by the construction of the track bed.

One day I stood on the top of a platform and watched the operations. The platform was strongly built using long bamboos, but it still swayed even in a mild wind and did not feel very safe. A sergeant aimed at the flag on the next platform using a transit which was set rigidly, independently of the platform. Then he instructed the soldiers on the ground about the position of the centre line through flag signals given by a soldier beside him. Then the trees and bushes on the centre line were cut down accordingly.

I noticed the line on the ground was deviating to the right. Even though the signaller requested them to move it back to the left, it was not corrected. I observed to Mouri, 'They are not correcting the line.' He answered with a forced smile, 'They are keen to cut down a ripe banana tree. They are innocently keen to eat fresh bananas which were rarely available back home.'

When sunset approached, the team finished work for the day and came back to our camp at Ban Pong in lorries. Then I heard Mouri's enthusiastic report coming from the room of the battalion commander, 'Today we finished marking the centre line as far as 5,400 metres; cleared the ground for the length of 500 metres; decided the centre of Rukke station. All the men are in good condition.' And then he came to my room and after we had finished discussing the technical details for the next day, he saluted me formally and left. As my work for the day was over I relaxed in my room under a kerosene lamp, with a cool breeze coming into the room.

More houses with roofs and walls made of palm leaves supported on bamboo poles were built to accommodate the 2nd and 3rd battalions of the regiment who had arrived from Burma. Our work became busier, as we had to guide the design and execution of the construction work. When the survey team advanced to Kanchanaburi, 50 kilometres from the zero post, in early August, Colonel Itaru Imai arrived and took command of the 9th Railway Regiment. He had specialized in civil engineering at Tokyo University and was a military commander who understood technical matters. I and my colleagues were called to his room almost every day, and we discussed the selection of the route and the design of the basic work, looking at maps which indicated that the whole route would be through the jungle.

In early July I was asked to see the operations of the 7th Well-drilling Company who were to carry out the geological survey at the proposed site of the big bridge near Kanchanaburi. There I was shown a long wooden box which contained a neatly laid columnar section up to 20 metres deep. I was surprised that the sample had been prepared so quickly, in a day, as I had gone there assuming that they wanted to discuss with me the location of the boring. I was told that an artesian well of ten metres deep could be completed in half a day by one platoon of the company, and the water supply for a camp and water for steam locomotives would be made available.

On 17 August I left Kanchanaburi with commander Imai, our technical staff, a medical doctor, officers of the water-supply and disease-prevention units and the well-drilling company in a lighter drawn by two motor boats. The River Kwai was flowing slowly at this point with a clayey colour due to the rain of the past few days. The river then became narrower.

'Colonel, that mountain on the right is Mount Chungkai. The track will go where the mountain comes right down to the river. The mountain is all made of hard rock, and about ten thousand cubic metres have to be cut away, which is hard, time-consuming work,' I explained, using the map. I gave the mountain a name; as the track went through rugged uninhabited areas many places were given names by us.

We kept going until sunset and decided to sleep in the lighter by an isolated sand bar, as the doctor advised us that there could be some danger of malaria mosquitoes where the local people lived. I was woken up by a cool breeze. Because of the mist on the river I could not see the dense forest on both sides. I enjoyed the refreshing morning air. When the sun came above the trees, the mist cleared and the boatman started the engines to continue our journey. The river narrowed to about 50 metres, and boats followed along the winding course of the main stream, avoiding the sand bars and big rocks.

Around noon I saw a survey flag on the beach. It was the advance post of the Mouri survey team. As we came closer, 2nd Lieutenant Mouri was waving his hand and a few soldiers came running out of a tent. Mouri explained to us that we were the first visitors in the past two weeks. Nobody came there except for food supply boats every other day. Colonel Imai went into the tent and asked the soldiers, 'How are the meals? Anybody infected with malaria?' He then gave a present to Mouri as a token of appreciation.

Mouri said, 'It is terribly hot in the jungle, and we sometimes get headaches. It's especially bad after it rains and we cannot stay there for a long time. The ground is soft with piles of fallen leaves, and our feet and caps often get caught in vines or grasses. There are no big animals except snakes. We are bothered by scorpions and red ants. When we go into the forest we lose our sense of direction and it is very hard to make the track follow the line shown on the maps.'

On the third day we came close to a cliff of hard agglomerate which hung above the river. We were forced to admit that a lot of work was needed for the track to pass along there (points 103 km and 109 km).

On the fourth day we went through rapids which are difficult for boats to go up. The motor boat went up on its own and then pulled up the lighter by a rope. That night we stayed at Kinsaiyok. Next morning when we woke up we noticed that the landscape around the boat had changed. The house which had been about seven metres above us on a slope was just in front of our eyes. The cable for the anchor went straight down in the river. The anchor had been on a sandy beach but the boatman had extended the rope in anticipation of the high water level caused by the rain following upstream. It was a surprise to us that the river had risen seven metres just in one night.

In the evening we came to Takunun, which is close to a tungsten mine. A few officials and mine workers lived there. The doctor was surprised to find that almost everybody in the village was badly infected with malaria. He could see the swollen spleens even on the children. He gave quinine to an old man groaning with pain by the roadside.

We left the dangerous village and turned round. Going downstream was quick and we came back to Kanchanaburi in two days. From the exploratory trip I realised that there would be a lot of difficulties to be faced in the construction work and that we would have to work with courage and make careful preparations in order to complete the railway.

3.2   The Volga boat-song and the bridge

Masaru Tsuruta, Probationary Officer, 6th Company, 3rd Battalion,
9th Railway Regiment, 2nd Railway Command Group, Southern Army

In early October 1942, I was at the Tamarkan camp located near Kanchanaburi. The rainy season seemed to have finished early, as it had rained for a shorter time than usual. But the River Mac Khlong was still flowing vigorously. I went out to see the water-level gauge on the river, as we were anxious for it to go down so that we would be able to start building bridges over it. Then I heard the faint whistling of a march tune far away, at the other side of the palm forest. The whistling gradually came closer to us with the sound of the army boots of a big group. The tune they were whistling was the 'Colonel Bogey March' (which was later to become the theme song of the movie *The Bridge Over the River Kwai*) This was our first encounter with the prisoners of war (PoWs). They were going to the bamboo-palm houses of the PoW camp.

All that day we all talked about the prisoners.

'They've just come. They seem to be in a good mood.'

'They are unique soldiers: soldiers wearing skirts!'

'The colours of their berets in the first group and the last group are different. Are they from different regiments or is their rank different?'

'They are tall and well-built, and full of vitality. How did they come to be prisoners?'

We were told that two bridges were to be constructed across the River Mac Khlong – one steel bridge and one wooden bridge. As it takes a long time to construct a steel bridge with concrete piers, a wooden one was needed urgently to transport materials to upstream sites. Our 6th Company was ordered to work on the wooden bridge while the 5th Company was to build the steel bridge. The position of the wooden bridge was about 200 metres downstream from the steel bridge (which has remained until this day).

When the water level had gone down and the materials had been collected, we started the construction work. Second Lieutenant Hirokawa, deputy company commander, addressed us all:

> We have been ordered to work with the PoWs. The railway regiment can set them to work on our construction only. The provision to them of food, clothing, bedding, and sanitary and daily necessities is all under the charge of the PoW camp, guarded by the Kosakayama branch of the Thai PoW unit. The Red Cross Geneva Convention defines how PoWs should be treated, but our country did not ratify the treaty. However, due to humanitarian reasons, we should pay regard to the principles of the treaty. Note that General Headquarters has ordered us to employ the PoWs on the construction of the railway. We should not make PoW officers work as a general rule. Holidays must be allowed to the PoWs and their working hours must be adhered to punctiliously. The regulation wages will be paid to them. Don't inflict physical or any other punishment on them. All of you, keep in mind what I have said.
>
> 'As regards the administration, a soldier in charge of the workers will be named in each platoon. He is to go to the PoW camp at the defined time every day and receive the PoWs, and when their work is finished take them back to the camp at the set time. Keep a precise count of their numbers.'
>
> 'Avoid any trouble with the PoWs, and if any trouble should occur report it to your senior officer. Regard the PoW as part of our war potential, and make sure their strength is maintained, avoiding useless loss.'

He mentioned many other matters to be attended to by us. After the speech the men started talking to each other:

'These PoWs are a nuisance, what with so many restrictions.'

'Don't say that. They could be a big help to us; they are well-built and seem to be stronger than we are.'

'What did you say? Do you think that they will work seriously? What can we do if they rebel against us! They are probably more than one thousand strong.'

'By the way, can you speak English?'

'Don't be so silly. They are prisoners – why can't they learn Japanese? Don't you think so?'

'Who will teach them Japanese?'

'Well, if it comes to that I will be the teacher.'

'It's fun, anyway.'

'Are there railway soldiers among them? If there are, we can challenge them to a performance test.'

'England is where the steam engine was invented. So there should be some railway soldiers similar to us.'

'Even if this bridge is completed, there is a lot of work to be done deep in the mountains. We shall have to be working with them for a long time. If they are experienced in the work, it will be a big help for us. If they are exhausted it will be a loss for us.'

Talking in this way we seem to have formed our mental attitude towards accepting the PoWs. But even so we were not sure whether they would join forces with us, the Japanese army.

The bridge we were going to build was the standard one for our railway unit. We were to drive about 390 teak piles into the river bed. And our platoon was ordered to drive the piles from the right bank while the Yusaka (3rd) platoon drove them from the left bank. So the two platoons competed to get to the centre of the river first. Our senior section leader, Sergeant Nishimori, was an expert in bridge building while I was a green officer who had just arrived in the field.

As the company had only one kerosene engine, it was to be used by the Yusaka platoon, and we had to drive our piles, using a scaffolding tower on combined boats, by the human strength of the PoWs. About 30 men on the boats pulled up a weight and when it reached the top of the tower, the ropes were released, and the weight dropped to hit the top of a pile. The tower boats were assembled on the other side and moved to our side. We were ready to start.

On the day that the PoWs started to work, Corporal Yanagi and I went to their camp and were met with readiness by Lieutenant Kosakayama, the NCOs and guards. The branch camp manager alerted me, saying, 'I trust you to use your discretion with them.' To which I answered, 'I will indeed.' The PoWs were all Scots. An officer came forward, saluted me and gave orders to the men.

'Fall in!' 'From the right, number!' 'Left turn! Forward march!' They went to the gate marching in line. I thought instantly: 'Splendid! They act exactly like Japanese soldiers. It will be easier than I feared. Things should go smoothly.'

After they had gone out of the gate, they marched at ease and started to smile. It was a joy to them to be freed from restriction. (I experienced the same feeling when we were captured and went out of the gaol for outdoor work. It is delightful to go out of a restricted place.) Their smiles then changed to the whistling of the Colonel Bogey River Kwai march, as they headed for the boat pier. As our workplace was on the other side of the river, we crossed the river by a small local boat with a kerosene engine. The boatman was Corporal Azuma, leader of the maintenance section, who was very punctilious, especially about the capacity of the boat. 'Sir, please keep the number of passengers within the capacity, as the PoWs are heavier in weight. It is my responsibility if any accident happens.'

When the PoWs got on the boat they were in high spirits just like children. But the Japanese soldiers looked tense. It was just like the Japanese proverb about enemies being placed by fate in the same boat.

We heard a loud noise and saw ripples spreading in rings in the water, which put us on our guard. Was it a trick being played on us? Or a prisoner escaping? As every man kept his eyes on the ripples, a big lizard showed up from behind a bush and then disappeared into the water. Everybody laughed and that was the end of it. As indicated by this event, on the first day both sides were suspicious of each other, and only a little work was done.

It was the general opinion of our men that it was expecting too much of the prisoners to get them to do highly technical work. They were not suitable for work done in high places, but as their arms were strong they should be suitable for moving materials or pulling the ropes with the weight in them. It was agreed with the camp that the same Scotsmen should be sent to us every day, as some degree of experience was needed for any work.

The officer for the Scotsmen was Lieutenant P. He did not work but came to the workplace with the soldiers. He interpreted my instructions to the soldiers and relayed their messages to me. I told them to start the pile-driving work. We had to teach them the procedures for the work. We ourselves showed them how to do it and Lieutenant P. explained it. 'OK, OK.' They seemed to have understood what to do, and the pile-driving began. The first line of piles was on land, so it was suitable for training.

'Itch, knee, sun, yoh.' A Japanese soldier on the tower shouted the numbers 'one, two, three' loudly in Japanese, but their movements were sporadic and the weight did not go up. So again calls came from the tower, but the result was same. It looked simple but I remembered that when we were newly enlisted as privates it had taken some time before we could carry out this process smoothly. So it was too much to expect them to get used to the work so soon. Anyway they gradually got used to the work and two piles were driven in the day.

On the other bank, the Yusaka platoon had not started pile-driving as they needed time to install and adjust the kerosene engine. So we had a lead over them of two piles. But we had to drive five piles a day on average in order to finish the pile-driving in a month. Some soldiers said, 'I cannot stand this. Wouldn't it be quicker if we did it all by ourselves?'

So it was necessary to improve our efficiency in using the PoWs. Accordingly the call was changed to English, 'one, two, three' though the Japanese complained that the English calls did not co-ordinate their efforts.

While we were still struggling, we heard the kerosene engine of the Yusaka platoon start up. So a loud cry came from the tower: 'Stick to it! Don't let yourselves be beaten by the kerosene engine' However, when the pile-driving position moved from the land to the boat tower on the water, the work slowed down. On the other hand the Yusaka platoon improved their speed and were closing on us. At that point, for some reason the noise of the engine stopped. Seeing this, Senior Private Kanemoto on the tower started singing in an unconcerned attitude: 'Ei Koh la, Ei Koh la, mo-hitotsu Eikoh la.' That was his favourite song – the Volga boat-song. On hearing him sing, the PoWs applauded and sang with him. They sang in a co-ordinated rhythm. Hearing them sing, Corporal Ichiyanagi said, 'This is it. Let's drive the piles this way!'

I felt some resistance to his proposal as we were in a battlefield and the song was a Russian folksong of a Western nature. Though Japan was not fighting against Russia, we might be criticized for currying too much favour with the PoWs. But it would be more shameful if we were beaten by the kerosene engine. So I allowed them to use the Volga boat-song in the pile-driving work. When Lieutenant P. explained this to his men, they clapped their hands with joy and gave some whistles. Senior Private Kanemoto on the tower was in high spirits and sang 'Ei Koh laa', and then they pulled up the rope with all their might and the weight went up high, and when it was dropped the pile went down deep in the river bed. Senior Private Oka who was measuring the penetration of the pile cried loudly; 'It went in twice as deep!' The pile-driving in time with the song was a great success.

Every day the singing of the Volga boat-song sounded over the river, and we drove more and more piles. Sometimes a Scottish folk song was sung instead of the Volga boat song. They also liked rhythmical American folksongs such as cowboy songs or the 'Isle of Capri'.

Though the team with the kerosene engine also improved the speed of their work, we did keep a lead of a few piles over them. Both teams drove seven or eight piles a day, and the rows of piles extended from both banks toward the centre of the river.

When our pile-driving got close to the middle of the river, waves rocked our boat tower and the water got deeper. Still our pile-driving kept in the lead. Wooden beams were laid on the piles by the 4th Platoon and the construction by the 1st Platoon of the railbed for the detour line was almost complete. The deputy company commander mentioned with a smile, 'Oh, it looks like a real bridge construction site.' He did not criticise the use of the Volga boat-song at all.

Sometimes a bugle was sounded at the site. This meant that a high-ranking officer had come to inspect the construction site, but we did not stop working or singing the boat song. Once a high-ranking Thai official came to see the site.

When the work was progressing smoothly, I relaxed and talked with Lieutenant P. sitting by the river. He said he had studied at the University of Edinburgh. He seemed to have taken a literary course and was not good at technical matters. He was a cheerful sportsman-type person. He was in good command of his men and was trusted by them. He asked me, 'Are you a Captain? I am a Lieutenant.'

He saw my badge of rank which had three stars on a stripe, and thought that I must be a Captain. I did not know how to explain 'Officer Cadet' so I said; 'I am not a Captain. I am an egg of an officer (by which I meant a budding officer).'

'Oh! You are a Tojo boy.' He was thinking of the German Hitler Jugend. From then on he called me the Tojo boy. Once he said to me, 'Why did Japan start this war?'

I wanted to tell him about our guiding motto 'Hakkou-ichi-u' (The Whole World under One Roof – universal brotherhood) but it was too difficult for me to explain.

'With my English it is very difficult to answer your question. In brief it is 'Asia for the Asians'. Japan will form an Asian bloc where she will be the leader.'

'Japan is fighting to be the leader of Asia?'

'That's right. Britain formed a British bloc throughout the world and Britain is the leader. Isn't that so?'

'Really? I see.'

I wanted to speak about the liberation of the Asian races from colonization if I could, but to explain this was beyond my English capability.

'How is it you are working here in co-operation with the Japanese?'

Illustration 3.2.1　The bridge being built over the River Mac Khlong

Illustration 3.2.2   The central part of the completed steel bridge over the Mac Khlong

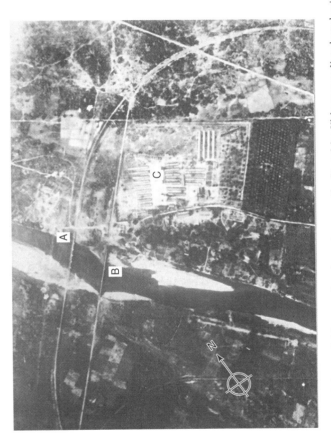

Illustration 3.2.3 Aerial view of the two bridges, steel and wooden, over the River Mac Khlong near Kanchanaburi. Three spans of the steel bridge were demolished by American B-24s on 13 February 1945, temporarily repaired but demolished again on 22 April. The wooden bridge was destroyed on 4 February and despite repeated air raids, it was repaired again and again and was being used on the day the war ended. (A) Wooden bridge   (B) Steel bridge   (C) Prisoner of War camp

'We maintain our military discipline even as PoWs. We want to complete this railway and go home on this line. We will be welcomed as heroes back home.'

According to him to be a prisoner was proof that he had fought until the last moment, unlike the Japanese who feel it a great disgrace to be captured. He took out a photograph from his pocket and showed it to me.

'A very pretty girl! Is she your sweetheart?'

'No, she is my sister. My home is in Wales and she takes care of it by herself.' He wanted to see a picture of mine, but I did not have any picture of a girl.

'When the war ends, I would like to meet you in Scotland.' As he said this he looked at the flowing river. His men came up closer from behind us and started singing 'Home on the range'. It was a time to be sentimental.

When the pile-driving was 80 per cent done, the level of the river went up, even though there was no rain on our site. The water increased rapidly, passed the critical level and came very close to the bridge beam. Through the night all the men in the company worked to protect the bridge, using all the available lights. The bridge had to be protected from big trees and bamboo roots floating on the swollen river. If they stuck to the piles, they would form a kind of dam and the bridge would be washed away because of the enormous pressure of the big river. Luckily the water went down from the next day and we suffered no damage. After a few days the work was resumed. Soon afterwards a Scot fell from the scaffolding stage into the river. Senior Private Fukuhara who was near him jumped into the fast-flowing water and rescued him.

As both sides advanced and it was dangerous to come too close, we were ordered to move to Tamoan. That was the end of the competition. It was early November 1942, one month after the start of the pile-driving work.

We next built three bridges of 20 metres in length on the line to Kanchanaburi for the Thai government. When we came back to Tamarkan in the middle of December the big wooden bridge was complete. It was used very effectively for more than five months until the steel bridge was finally completed on 15 May 1943. (The steel bridge is still used by the Thai railways in its original state, except for the two spans in the middle which were destroyed by British bombing and were rebuilt after the war.)

3.3 My touchstone – the Chungkai Cutting

Second Lieutenant Juji Tarumoto, 3rd Company, 2nd Battalion,
9th Railway Regiment, 2nd Railway Command Group, Southern Army

On 10 September 1943, 60 men of the 3rd Platoon under my command landed on the beach of Chungkai (Kaopon village), where we had come on motor boats of the transport unit from Kanchanaburi. Since tall pampas grass grew on the beach, we cleared it, made some open space and set up tents to stay in. Some men moved bamboo poles and *chak* (roofing material made of palm leaves) from the boats and some made preparations for cooking. These jobs were done quickly, being routine work for soldiers in the field.

Kanchanaburi was on the edge of the developed area and once we had crossed the River Mac Khlong we were in dense jungle. The proposed railway line went roughly along the River Kwai in order to use the river for the transportation of men, construction materials and food. However as the line was close to the river we were faced with the hard work of cutting rock beds, starting at Chungkai.

From the next day we started to build semi-permanent buildings which were similar to the ones we had at Ban Pong. We did the building work carefully as this was the first time we had built anything for ourselves. A barracks with enough space for 60 men was completed together with a kitchen, bathroom and tool store. The trees and pampas grass in front of the barracks were cut down over a wide area, and a passage to the work site was opened up. The children of Kaopon village watched us curiously while playing hopscotch. We noticed that a simple stall had started selling fried bananas in front of our barracks. I remember that we each ate a chicken leg prepared by the cooking team as a token celebration of finishing our barracks.

We had to start working as soon as we had settled in. On 14 September I went to the Chungkai mountain with the 2nd section which was specially organized for the blasting work. The company commander transferred those soldiers in the company who had some experience in blasting to the 2nd section of my platoon. I had done a little blasting drill after I came to the railway regiment, but as I had no civil engineering experience I had no confidence in blasting. So I studied the blasting manual that the battalion commander lent me and gave makeshift lectures to the men. The soldiers perhaps noticed that I was worried, as some encouraged me by saying, 'Everything will go well. Please do not worry.'

As a trial we dug a hole about 30 cm deep, put in dynamite and blasted. As a result, about one cubic metre of rock came out. As ten thousand cubic metres of rock had to be blasted away, only one-ten-thousandth of the work was done in this trial. We had been ordered to complete the work by early February; this meant that an average of 67 cubic metres of rock had to be blasted per day. However we still did not have enough chisels, hammers and men for that workload. Even if we had them, I was not sure whether it would be possible to dig such a number of holes in the narrow rock bed or not, and I had other doubts. I feared that my duties might not be completed by the set time, and I felt lonely and desolate.

Next day 60 PoWs from the 2nd PoW camp came to Chungkai escorted only by Sergeant Joutani. Each of them carried a big kitbag and they set up temporary tents in front of our barracks. In the evening they started a simple entertainment of comic dialogue and harmonica music. One man stood on an earth mound, and the PoWs around him laughed and sang together. It gave an unexpected touch of liveliness to the evening in this lonely place. They were also perhaps affected by their first step into the jungle. Maybe they wanted to make up for their loneliness and wish themselves happiness in the future. I stood behind them with many Japanese soldiers, and watched them. It was not a long performance, and when it ended the Major who was leading them came to me and asked for permission to sing the British national anthem. I was not the administrator of the PoWs and did not object to it. They all stood up and sang the song earnestly in the dark evening. There was no accompaniment on the harmonica. They sang 'God save our gracious king' loudly in good harmony, fanned by a breeze coming from the River Kwai. It was a scene that would have made any human being sentimental and sympathetic. However these human sentiments had to be actively discarded as we were on a battlefield. One could not distinguish between humane and inhuman beings. Man fluctuates between a god and a devil. What causes that fluctuation must be war. Sergeant Joutani had planned to use the 60 PoWs who had come with him to build barracks for the 2nd PoW camp which was to move to Chungkai. He had received such orders. But I wanted to use this labour force immediately on our work, as I had been instructed. So I negotiated with the sergeant and we agreed that they would be divided in half and 30 men were to work on building the barracks and 30 men with us. We in the railway construction group wanted to start working as soon as possible, but our 60 men were too few for the job and we needed a much bigger labour force. It was essential that the camp should be completed very soon. So as compensation for borrowing thirty men for drilling holes in the rock bed, I lent them ten of our men of the 1st section led by an experienced carpenter for building the barracks.

However the building of their barracks was not as simple as that for our own platoon. The plans for building houses that Sergeant Joutani had received from the camp headquarters were too ambitious, with a vast open area, officers' houses, barracks for NCOs and soldiers, an office, a kitchen, toilets and bathhouse, which needed a long time to complete. The opinion of the camp director that the PoWs could not be sent without having a place to stay was correct, and I could not refute it, but I was really uneasy as my job had to be completed within a limited time.

The staff of the PoW camp at Chungkai consisted of Sergeant Joutani and four Korean guards, and the sergeant had to arrange the preparing of the meals as well as the building of the large-scale camp himself, so he was really too busy. I felt that the camp administration was not adequately staffed, even supposing it stayed in one place. Once the PoWs had to be moved its deficiencies would be revealed immediately. In the construction of the railway they were moved very often, and as soon as they were moved urgent construction work was waiting for them. As the railway could not be completed without the PoWs, it was surely better for the railway regiment to co-operate fully with the camp so that their labour could be used as early as possible.

The PoW camps and the railway regiments were quite separate organizations. The railway regiment borrowed PoWs from their camps under the conditions set by the camps. The director of the 2nd PoW camp (Accommodation), Lieutenant-Colonel Yanagida, issued a strong notice to all units employing PoWs that included 'Never beat the PoWs. Do not make them work beyond the set working hours.' He even stopped lending the PoWs to a unit where a man slapped them in disregard of the notice. This action was the kind of humane treatment that the camp should rightly and properly adopt, to which we, the employing unit using them, could not openly object. However there were voices in the unit saying, 'When a Japanese soldier neglects his work, he is slapped. Why can we not slap a PoW?' Or 'Did we come here to build the railway or to learn how to treat PoWs?' Even so the norms Yanagida set for treating PoWs were generally followed. The camp itself supplied food, housing and other necessities, independent of the railway construction units. As a matter of fact there was partial co-operation between the local railway units and camps in such matters as loan of tools, transfer of building materials and transportation. But this happened sporadically on the spot, and not as a general rule. The army organization was set up so that its units should concentrate all their efforts on the completion of the orders issued from above, but not take any interest in other matters, just like a horse pulling a wagon straight ahead without looking sideways. While the chain of command was established by strict regulations, lateral liaison and co-operation were very much neglected. This contradiction was at its worst at the lower levels. Co-operation could not be practised unless an arrangement had been made at the upper levels. However this tendency towards jealously defending sectional authority was strong even at the highest level. So this contradiction was bound to appear everywhere at the lower levels. And it was at its worst in the relations between the railway units and the camps in the Burma–Thailand Railway.

One day regimental commander Colonel Imai came to the rock bed in person. When I hurried there, he was standing on the slope of the rock. I explained the work situation and stressed the need for hammers, good quality chisels and a labour force. He listened to me, nodding, and then said, 'The laying of the rails will reach this point by early February. Can you be ready?'

Though the answer depended on the availability of labour and tools, I answered in the army style, stressing my will to perform. 'Yes, we can.' And I continued, 'It will be difficult to give a slope of 3 in 4 to this cutting. I would like to cut straight down to a width of four metres. What do you think?'

He smiled and answered. 'That is all right. The sloping can be done later. It is essential that the railway should be complete and trains run on it.' He encouraged me and briskly left in a boat. I felt relieved that the commander had not scolded me about the progress, and thought I should have some visible results ready by the time he came next. The progress of the work did not change, even though I was in a hurry, as we had just one platoon and 30 PoWs. About the end of September, an engineer came from the Railway Command Group and had the design changed and reduced the amount of rock blasting to 8,000 cubic metres by increasing the amount of the easier earth-moving work. This was a great help. In early October the 2nd Thai PoW camp moved to Chungkai with many PoWs whom we were anxiously awaiting. We were able to borrow 500 men each morning.

I assigned the experienced 2nd section to blasting the bigger first rock bed (6,000 cubic metres), the 3rd section to blasting the second rock bed (2,000 cubic metres), the 1st section to building an earth embankment in my area (61 km to 63 km) and the 4th section to crushing the broken rocks and moving the rock chips. Also I assigned more than half of the PoWs to earth moving where there was enough space to work, and

150 PoWs to the blasting work. These 150 men lived close to our barracks so that we could keep the experienced men on the job without rotation. Their meals and sanitary arrangements were looked after by the camp, and two officers lived with them as leaders.

All the drilling of holes for the blasting was done by hand. A PoW officer said to me, 'Why do you use such a primitive method. Isn't it more efficient to use drilling machines?' This I knew quite well, but the regiment had not been equipped with such machines. Not only did we have no machines, we even did not have enough chisels for hand drilling.

Though I had requested the battalion to send what I needed: workers, compressors with drilling machines, hard chisels and hammers, ignition fuses, coke and forges (for re-hardening the chisels), strong shovels, and so on, they were seldom sent to us. Every time I saw boats at our pier I ran to them, but most of the cargoes were explosives. 'Explosives again!' Our men seemed disappointed and carried the cargo to our store-room. One day the battalion commander and the company commander came together and ordered me to store the explosives in a separate building. I had been more focused on the daily work and had forgotten about the storage of explosives, though I was aware of the damage that might be done to the local inhabitants and passing boats by an explosion. As the storage place had to be big and strongly built, it took a lot of our valuable manpower.

The Chungkai cutting was the first bottleneck in the regiment. I had to do my best to break through the rock. However my assignment was not only to make the cutting but also to build the railbed over three kilometres and construct two bridges of a total length of 50 metres. Of these, I did not start on the bridges because of the manpower shortage.

In order to build the rail bed embankment we had to clear dense jungle which was also very hard work. We felt the shortage of tools such as axes, hatchets and saws. After we moved to the railbed construction we suffered from the poor quality of the shovels bought in Thailand, which buckled if too much pressure was put on them.

It was human strength that decided the progress of the earth moving. As about ten men of the 1st section were in charge of the railbed, sometimes a private had to watch 60–100 PoWs. When I went to the earth-moving section every soldier complained to me, 'The PoWs do not work hard. They seem very idle. Please say something to them.' As I watched, they piled a small amount of earth on a shovel and after one scoop they took a rest. So I said to the officer who came with them as an escort and liaison man, 'Can't they move more quickly?'

Illustration 3.3.1 Preparing the cutting for rail-laying. *A* A hole of 1.2 metres (4 feet) deep was dug in the hard rock using chisels and hammers. Digging one hole was a day's quota. Pneumatic drills were used at the overhang (109 km) where hand-drilling was not possible, but most of the cutting was done by hand

Illustration 3.3.1B Blasting rock using dynamite. Dynamite was pressed into the hole and the fuses were ignited by Japanese soldiers using lighted cigarettes, not by PoWs as this was a dangerous job

Illustration 3.3.1C All the charges were detonated simultaneously causing a huge mass of rock to collapse

Illustration 3.3.1D The fallen rock was removed by hand. Some of the peices were big and heavy

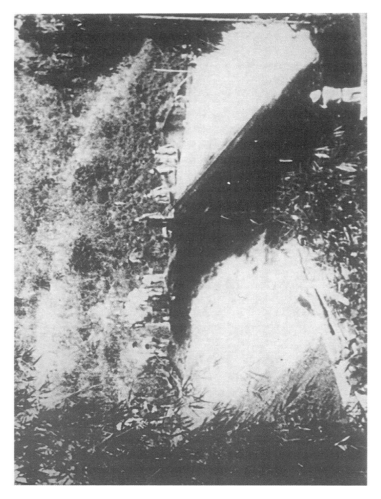

Illustration 3.3.1E An embankment was built to the side of the cutting

Illustration 3.3.1F The cutting was then nearly ready for laying the rails

Illustration 3.3.2   Prisoners of war laying rails

Illustration 3.3.3 A train laying ballast. Track beds needed constant maintenance to keep the trains running

'They were completely worn out by the work on the first day', he replied, 'Our meals are not satisfactory; there is a lot of rice, but we are fed up with rice which does not slip down our throats. When I go back to England I will beat my wife if she serves me rice. There is a critical shortage of meat and raw vegetables. So if they work for a while, they get too tired to move any more.'

I felt that what the officer was saying was correct. However what my soldiers said was also correct in terms of our objective. Would there be any way to bridge the gap? The PoWs must surely be aware that the railway was for transporting military supplies even though we tried to hide it. It was quite natural for the PoWs not to co-operate with the work of the Japanese army and to try to disrupt the work. I had been told that PoWs had been instructed to escape or to obstruct the enemy's operations. It was possible to stop them escaping by vigilant guarding, but it was very difficult to get the PoWs to offer their labour activity. Persuasion could only be effective when there was an advantage offered to those persuaded or when the amount of labour expected was small. The work on the Thai–Burma railway was very hard, so how could I expect any effect from persuasion? I made a speech in English with the help of a PoW officer and read it out twice in front of PoWs. It was an abstract speech asking them to participate in the railway construction work as a combined team of the PoWs and the railway unit. My speech did not achieve anything and was once laughed down by them, so I gave up doing this.

As the PoWs were newcomers whose working ability we did not know, they were working from 8 a.m. to 5 p.m. with one hour for lunch and other short breaks. But as the level of achievement was so low, I discussed with them and adopted the piece system of 1.1 cubic metres per man per day. That meant allocating the workload according to the number of men in the group every morning. 1.1 cubic metres was a figure given by the company commander which was based on the experience gained at Tamarkan.

The next problem which arose was Sunday. All the Japanese soldiers were working without any holiday through Saturday and Sunday, so I asked the camp to let the PoWs work on Sunday. But as there were various strong complaints, I proposed a compromise. That was to change from the daily allocation of the work to a weekly allocation. If the allocated work was finished in six days they could rest on the seventh day. This plan was discussed at the regular meeting on Friday attended by Lieutenant-Colonel Yanagida with the camp staff and representatives of the PoWs and was agreed on. I sometimes attended the meeting as an observer.

At the meeting the PoWs raised many points. The first was that 1.1 cubic metres was too much. With this figure it might not be possible to get any holidays. This was certainly true, judging from the rate of performance so far, but I could not lower the figure. I said, 'Please encourage all the soldiers to improve the performance to get the rest day. For that purpose you can rest any day in the week if you are sure to complete the allocation within the week. As the standard rate of earth-moving work in the Japanese engineering corps is 5 cubic metres, 1.1 cubic metres cannot be so severe.' Hearing my explanation the representatives were convinced, but asked me to reduce the quota when the earth was hard and difficult to dig, which I agreed to. Then they wanted the tools, especially the shovels, to be in good condition, and I agreed to improve them. They brought up many detailed matters and it was decided to adopt the new weekly quota system from the coming Monday.

On Sunday I allocated the earth-moving works accompanied by the PoW officers who led the groups. The officers had prepared a measuring rod and checked the allocation and complained when there was some disagreement. After the weekly quota was allocated the PoWs set to work without resistance. Some groups finished the quota in six days and rested on the seventh day. However most of them had to work till Sunday morning. Sometimes a group found it difficult to finish the work in the full seven days, and then they became discouraged and their work-efficiency dropped. It was a rule that they had to work into the night if the work was not completed in seven days, but as the men were driven to despair, resulting in a low performance, I had to say, 'At this point you can finish working on this week's quota, but next week's quota will be slightly increased.'

The PoWs came from different units – infantry, signals or artillery. As the group composed of those who had done clerical work was apt to lag behind, I once proposed redistributing the allocation among the groups. But this was rejected by the PoWs as being unfair to the group for which the quota was to be increased. Generally speaking, this weekly quota system was a success, as the Japanese soldiers did not have to interfere with the details of their work. One Japanese soldier in the 1st section, who was assigned to one PoW group, acted like a platoon leader of a hundred men, and was eager to complete the week's quota of the group in six days, working together with the PoWs. He was also busy on Sunday when the PoWs were resting, as he had to mark out the next week's allocated area and provide all the necessary equipment.

He tried to communicate with the PoWs by sign language and the famous 'speedo', but things did not always go well. One day I went to the earth-moving workplace and saw a PoW standing with a shovel, his hands above his head. I asked the soldier in charge for the reason. He explained to me that the PoW had not followed his instructions, but taken a hostile attitude, stamped on the shovel and broken the neck of its handle.

I knew from the note issued by the PoW camp commander that we, the railway unit supervising the work, should not physically discipline a PoW. But the hostile action on the part of the PoW was of a serious nature by our standards. According to the code of the railway regiments or any part of the Japanese army, anyone who intentionally broke a tool (owned by the army) was to be held in a confinement cell (a simple room in a barracks area) for several days. As our men had been trained under such rules, I understood the agony of the soldier who could not communicate well with the offender. I felt that as there was no effective alternative I could not blame him for his instant punishment, which was more generous and practical than sending him to a confinement cell via a higher commander. So I connived at it and did not tell my soldier to stop the punishment. When I went round the site about an hour later, the PoW was working together with the others, so I felt relieved that the punishment had not been too heavy.

There might be a disorderly man among the PoWs and some action to get him back to orderly work was certainly needed. There may have been many incidents between Japanese and the PoWs but most of them seem to have been forgotten soon. Such a poor reaction by a Japanese soldier to provocation by a PoW came not from the personal character of the individual soldier but from the Japanese military training and the social characteristics of the Japanese. The railway soldiers were happy, good-natured men as long as the work went well. The case of the PoW holding up the shovel was the only one I remember, and no other punishment was reported to me.

At that time most of the company I belonged to were moved to Wang Lan, 8 kilometres upstream along the river. This affected my job. As the headquarters of the PoW camp was only 100 metres away from my barracks, I often attended the Friday meeting with the PoWs. As the head of the camp was a Lieutenant-Colonel and I was a 2nd Lieutenant, I asked the senior commanders when they came to Chungkai to negotiate the difficult problems, but I did the routine negotiating with the camp myself rather than going through the company commander who was located elsewhere.

One day a young officer came to my office to pay his respects. He was officer cadet Toyama. Soon he was moved to my barracks with his 4th

Platoon. So far I had been sleeping in a corner of the soldiers' barracks. Now that Toyama had come, a small hut was built for the two of us. It was a relaxation for me to play the harmonica with Toyama. Almost every day the sound of a harmonica could be heard from this small officers' room for about an hour after supper. I sometimes thought it was foolish, but it enabled me to escape from the harsh reality of the work responsibility. Talking with him was valuable. His pure and young mind was a fresh environment for me. He told me about our homeland and I talked about Burma and Malaysia. He listened to my poor talk without tiring of it. He frankly said, 'I was disappointed to have come straight from Japan to this railway construction work. When it is finished I want to be engaged in an operation.' He had come here and found himself faced with the plainest but most painful jobs. Whenever he confronted a difficulty, he thought about it and then asked my opinion. As I myself was under great pressure, I could not help him. It seems as if the pure young man gradually became overpowered by the militaristic objective or the idea of the absolute authority of the orders, which was implanted in him.

In late October the compressor and drilling machines which we were eagerly waiting for were delivered to us. Now the first rock bed was drilled by machine, but hand drilling was still used on the second rock bed. Through the use of machine drilling the amount of the broken rock increased and hence the moving of rock chips by our 4th section was moved into the night. I had to negotiate with the camp to increase the number of PoWs employed in blasting. They were divided into three groups; each worked on one of three shifts. As the average working hours of every shift were about seven hours, no complaints came from the PoWs.

Late in the evening of 30 December I got a message saying that the 3rd Battalion headquarters at Tamarkan had been shot at by a rifle, but I just told our men the situation and let them sleep so as to continue the next day's work smoothly. I should have paid more attention to guarding ourselves, and also to the dangers of blasting as well as giving more consideration to the PoWs. But I admit that I did not have the capacity to pay full attention to these matters. I had been fully occupied in the completion of the work assigned to us and had neglected most of the other duties. But I was protected by the Japanese military organization and its orders to complete the railbed in the Chungkai area by early February. Besides this, there was a line of reasoning in my mind that strengthened my resolve. This Chungkai cutting was the first touchstone testing my ability as a member of society, not just a student.

While it has been said that war is always destructive, my work was constructive, and had the fascination of giving a pale-faced young intellectual a chance to test his ambition of leaving something concrete behind on the earth.

By the use of drilling machines and the three-shift system of working, I could expect that the blasting of the two rock beds would be completed by the assigned date, 4 February. However the number of the PoWs did not increase as we had hoped, and I had to worry about the earth-moving work, and the building of the railbed. The absolute workforce available to us was not sufficient. There were two possible ways to achieve a breakthrough: one was to increase the amount of earth-moving work per person, and the other was to request an increase in the workforce. It was difficult to increase the daily allocation of 1.1 cubic metres, as the piece-work system had been going well and the work was getting heavier as the railbed became higher, but this was compensated for by the increased proficiency of the PoWs. It was observable that from that time the number of the sick increased and the number of PoWs actually working gradually decreased. Whenever my superiors came to Chungkai, I asked them to go to the camp to negotiate an increase in the workforce. However, though the supply of medicines and nourishing foods such as green peas for the prevention of beriberi was earnestly requested by the medical doctors at the Friday meetings, the camp staff were able to answer that they would do their best and few supplies appeared. Under such conditions the camp inevitably tended to take the conservative attitude of trying to reduce the workload in order to maintain the health of the PoWs. This was against the wishes of the railway units who had to build the railway by the set time.

In the latter part of January, I moved the 3rd section, which had completed the blasting of the second rock bed, to Wan Tao Kien for our next assignment. The last work on the second bridge was completed by the 1st section on 4 February, and three days later rails were laid on the cutting, railbed and bridges that the platoon had completed. I left Chungkai hurriedly by boat with the 2nd and 4th sections, bound for my new area, Ban Kao, without seeing a train running on the railbed we had built with so much effort.

3.4   The Painter

Second Lieutenant Yuuji Wakatsuki, 8th Company, 4th Battalion, 9th Railway Regiment, 2nd Railway Command Group, Southern Army

In late September 1942, I left Kanchanaburi in a motor boat which was pulling a lighter fully loaded with food and construction materials. The boat went up the River Kwai where the water was dark after the continuous rain. We slept in a deserted temple and arrived at Wang Yai on the third day. There were no inhabitants' houses, and our tents had been set up by the advance party of the platoon in a tall bamboo forest. On the first night I offered local liquor to my men, though it was only one bottle per section.

As I was their platoon leader, I thought it would be courteous to send greetings to the families of my men and the best thing would be to send their portraits to their homes. However no photographs could be taken in a short time as we were in a remote place and also we were only allowed to mail postcards to Japan. While I was wondering what to do, Corporal Kaneko brought to me a PoW who was called the Painter.

From the next day my men were sketched from life one by one. As it was the natural wish of every one to send home a better-looking healthy image, they not only shaved but borrowed a new cap from a comrade and so on, though I thought this would not make any difference to the sketch. In fact I strictly ordered the Painter not to make any adjustments. When the sketching was finished the soldier who had posed stood up and looked at the drawing on the postcard with a smile, and the next man sat in front of the Painter. However the happiest man was the Painter himself, as not only he did not have to work in the field but he could practise his skill and earn cigarettes which were hard to get.

It took about two weeks to sketch all the men. I wrote my greetings and a short sentence in a space by the portrait saying that the man was in good health, and sent the cards to the families.

Some twenty years later I had an opportunity to visit Mr Yuukichi Ishii, who was a member of my platoon, in Ashikaga city. His wife said to me, 'You, commander, are good at drawing pictures. Do you still paint as a hobby?'

I was puzzled to hear this and did not know how to answer her, as I had never practised painting, and my art grade at school was the lowest one. Then she showed me a military postcard. I recollected that it was the one that I had sent from the Thai front. I was just going to tell her the truth, when she added, 'The card made me very happy and the children were delighted, pointing to his moustache in the portrait.' I looked at the picture and imagined how the family had gathered round happily when they received the card, and lost my opportunity to confess the truth. While Mr Ishii was smiling, a comrade who had come with me stepped in immediately trying not to put the former platoon leader to shame.

'Well, Mr. Ishii's moustache was nicer at that time than it is now.'

I wonder if she felt that the picture had been painted by someone else.

3.5   A new company commander at Konyu and Hintok

Lieutenant Shuji Otuki, 7th Company, 4th Battalion, 9th Railway Regiment, 2nd Railway Command Group, Southern Army

On 6 March 1943, I reported to the regimental headquarters located at Kinsaiyok and was appointed commander of the 7th Company. I was very much moved at being given the responsibility for this important job.

As I went round my area, I found there were a lot of rocks, especially at Konyu and Hintok where nearly 20 metres' depth of rocks had to be blasted away. Also many bridges had to be built, with a total length of one kilometre. As the target date for the completion of the Burma–Thailand Railway was October 1943, we had to have the line in my 7th Company's area ready for laying the track by July at the latest, which would require a lot of hard work. At that time the 1st Platoon was located at Malayan Hamlet (Konyu), the 3rd Platoon at Hintok and the 4th Platoon at Tampi, spread out over a length of 10 kilometres. To my disappointment the 2nd Platoon was not with us as they were installing telephone lines. There were nearly 5,000 PoWs there, located in several camps.

Every day PoWs and our men worked together to blast the rock beds by repeatedly drilling holes, blasting, and moving away the broken rocks under the strong sunshine. There were only five drilling machines, and the rest of the drilling was done manually by PoWs who worked very hard to drill holes one metre deep. However the steel rod chisels provided to us were made by the regimental supply depot and their cutting quality soon deteriorated. So our tool section had to make strenuous efforts to harden the dull ones again using a furnace and poor quality local charcoal.

On 14 May the leader of the 1st Platoon was changed to Warrant Officer Kamuro (who was soon promoted to 2nd Lieutenant), a young and energetic officer. Late in May, the 2nd Platoon returned to the company and was assigned to building bridges and the railbed. Also 40 elephants and about five thousand local workers along with some of their families, came to the company. The troublesome business of handling the local workers was undertaken by the organised effort of our command unit.

As we had to use many PoWs I often contacted the PoW camp office and kept an eye on the situation at the work places, hoping that there would be no serious problems. Obviously it was not possible for three hundred Japanese soldiers to watch ten thousand PoWs and local workers. As a temporary measure I increased the numbers of soldiers carrying rifles and paid special attention to the storage of the dynamite.

I went round my area at least once a day, and tried to talk with all the platoon and section leaders. One day when I sat down on a rock just to rest for a while, I went to sleep, I regret to say. The 3rd Platoon headed by Second Lieutenant Hirota worked at the Hintok cutting (called Hellfire Pass by the PoWs). When I went there with the battalion commander, Hirota was drilling a hole, working like one of the PoWs. The commander asked him, 'Why are you doing this?' He straightened up and answered, 'As I have very little experience in blasting rocks, I wanted to know by trying it myself how many hours it takes to drill a hole and how long one can continue to work under the strong sunshine.' He drilled one hole a day, the same quota as the PoWs, for one week, and was convinced that he was not demanding too much work of them.

In June the blasting of the rocks made good progress and the difficult bridges began to be constructed, though there were not enough bolts, and they had to be temporarily replaced by clamps. It started to rain from the latter part of June and the transportation of food and supplies became inefficient, both by lorry and by ship. As the water increased, the river flowed faster and drifting trees disturbed the movement of boats. We caught fish in the river and collected bamboo shoots, a kind of butterbur or anything else edible for our meals.

In mid-July when, with the assistance of the 8th Company, the rock blasting was finished and the big bridges were near completion, two disasters happened. One was a landship affecting the earth embankment and the cutting at point 155 km, which formed a canal in just one night. The other was the collapse of a temporary bridge in the 4th Platoon's area. Though these were put right using the full strength of the company, I regretted the delay in the overall construction schedule of the regiment.

Despite these drawbacks the rail laying progressed through my area, and I was excited to see a light train running on the track. I was really grateful to our men as well as the PoWs and local workers for their efforts and co-operation.

3.6 The Konyu Cutting

Second Lieutenant Takumi Kamuro, 7th Company, 4th Battalion,
9th Railway Regiment, 2nd Railway Command Group, Southern Army

I graduated from the Military Academy late in 1942, underwent training at Tsudanuma railway centre, and was sent to Thailand. When I visited the command group headquarters to report my arrival on 13 May 1943, the chief of staff shouted at me 'Why are you so late?!' Next day when

I arrived at the regimental headquarters in a light train, the adjutant Sudo told me to stay overnight there, but regimental commander Imai didn't agree and ordered me to go to my battalion immediately. I arrived at Tampi after dark and was met by the battalion commander Yabe who was unshaven and looked very exhausted. Then I went to the office of the 7th Company at Kanyu Hill and was appointed leader of its 1st platoon. I slept at the office but could not go to sleep as my heart was too full to adjust myself to a new situation with heavy responsibilities.

On the 15th I went to point 150 km (which was called Malayan Hamlet) where the platoon was located and took command of about sixty men of 1st Platoon and 27 men of the 4th JNR Tunnel Unit. The latter group was composed of men who were experienced in constructing tunnels for the Japan National Railways. Their special skills such as the selection of points for drilling holes by looking at the rock strata were very valuable for the efficient blasting of a large amount of rock bed. Also about 1,300 PoWs, who were in the branch camp, administered by a sergeant and four men, were to help us. About two thousand local labourers (*romusha* as they were called) were to be assigned to us. As I went along the two kilometres of line for which I was responsible, great masses of hard rock loomed up precipitously as if they would resist any kind of work, and the centre of the proposed rail line marked on the rocks with white paint caught my eye. I assigned single-bank excavation cutting at 150 km to the 3rd section, both-banks cutting at 151 km to the 2nd and 4th sections and single-bank cutting at 152 km to the 1st section. Each section had about ten men, but half of them worked on a shift which started at either 7 a.m. or 7 p.m., as drilling and other kind of work had to be done continuously for 24 hours. I decided that the blasting work should be started on 25 May as we had to wait for the arrival of tools and the completion of the barracks for the PoWs and local workers (25 May is the memorial day for the Japanese patriotic warrior Kusunoki Masashige, whom I respect).

The PoWs and workers had to clear the jungle and build a simple, very basic barracks, and were then ordered to work at the construction site. All the supplies came by boat on the River Kwai as the rain-soaked roads were muddy and barely usable. Food and supplies were all carried by men who walked up the muddy slope for two kilometres from the river to the barracks, as we had no other means of moving them. The mud was so sticky, sometimes the soles of shoes were ripped off, so the soldiers tied ropes around their shoes. Unfortunately we were in the worst period of the monsoon.

Every morning our soldiers went down to the construction site carrying bamboo to provide lighting, and on their return to the barracks brought up stone to pave the passages. As there were not enough floodlights, we burned bamboo to provide light for the drilling work at night. Where the both-sides cutting was in progress, the mixed sounds of hammers and steel tap drills echoed in the pass. The number of our soldiers who worked at the site was a little over 20, working in two shifts of 12 hours each. There were about 400 PoWs, working in three shifts of 8 hours each, and a maximum of about one thousand local workers on the site. This meant that an average of 70 of these men worked with one Japanese soldier.

The local workers were badly needed for the completion of the hard work, so poor-quality cigarettes and other luxuries were given as an incentive to those who worked regularly. We were not able to force workers from friendly nations to work. But I thought a good wage of 80 yen a month would surely be a good incentive for them, as it was better than my salary. However one major problem was that many of the workers left for home after they had received a certain amount of money. In this respect the PoWs were a more dependable workforce.

A special team of ten men headed by Sergeant Kawasaki dealt with all the ancillary services such as handling food supplies, feeding the Japanese soldiers and local workers, paying wages to the workers, providing sanitation and many miscellaneous jobs. This was very hard work for them. However it was a pity that these 11 capable men could not have been involved in the construction work. As a matter of principle, these other works should have been done by the battalion headquarters, which had an adjutant, extra officers, a medical doctor, intendand (a quartermaster) and assistants. But as the battalion was spread out over 50 kilometres and the supply system was weak, we inevitably had to spare these men for the work.

At Malayan Hamlet a detachment from the regimental headquarters was installed and 2nd Lieutenant Someya was posted there. Though I was told that the commander, who was a civil engineer, wanted to assist me as I was a green officer just out of school, I felt that my platoon must have been regarded as the bottleneck in the regiment's efforts. I made up my mind that I would make a desperate drive to complete the task.

At the end of May two air-compressor units, each with two pneumatic drills, were delivered to us. These were what we had been waiting for. The sound of the pneumatic drills improved the morale of the whole platoon. Our soldiers often did not ask for a rest, even if they had a

Illustration 3.6.1   Barracks for PoWs and Japanese soldiers were made of bamboo pole with palm-leaf roofs and walls

Illustration 3.6.2 Barracks at Takunun (218 km) for a Japanese platoon with storage

fever, and kept on working with flushed faces. When the night was coming to an end and the men on the night shift got 30 minutes' rest, everybody fell asleep like dead men. Then a morning mist came up from the River Kwai which somehow made me homesick. While the crucial 10,000 cubic metres of rock were being blasted, I never took off my clothes. I slept in the shade of the rocks with my clothes and boots on.

On 25 June we were told that the laying of the track had been started from Wang Yai. Judging from the speed of our work, I estimated that our blasting should be completed at the latest by 10 July. The urgings of the company commander and battalion commander became more intense day by day, and one evening the regimental commander went round the work site with a stick in his hand. Even though the commander repeatedly emphasised that the construction workers should be respected in the same way as our soldiers, the paramount order was to cut through the rocky mountain as soon as possible. So I was under great pressure. I stood on top of a rock day and night and shouted and threw small stones at those who seemed to be idle.

In the blasting I ordered one person to ignite 30 blasts though I knew this could be reckless. I gave the orders 'Get ready to ignite' and then 'Ignite!' By the time the 30th fuse was being ignited by a soldier, the first and second ones were starting to detonate. Fuses were not available to us in sufficient quantity, so we could use only 40 to 50 centimetres of fuse for a blast. The combustion speed of a slow-burning fuse is one centimetre per second. So if one igniter can be allocated to one hole, he has enough time to escape. But we did not have enough igniters, as we did not let the PoWs or local workers do the dangerous job of igniting the fuses with mosquito coils in the rain. That was why each of our soldiers had to ignite thirty fuses. They could not do the job wearing heavy steel helmets, so they wore caps made of woven tree stems. If the sharp edge of a blasted rock hit a man's head, he would be killed instantly. Every day they faced death.

On 3 July, it seemed as if the greatest task, the both-banks cutting, would be completed in a week, so I moved some soldiers to 152 km which was behind schedule. The Mizutani platoon from the 8th Company came to help with the cutting at 150 km.

At 11 o'clock p.m. on 9 July, the both-banks cutting finished with the 'big bang' of 150 holes. In the drenching rain, our soldiers, PoWs and local workers gathered in one place and all grabbed at big balls of rice, tiny presents to celebrate the completion. There was joy at having done the tremendous task and a feeling of relief.

Illustration 3.6.3 The cutting at Konyu (152 km), where PoWs were forced to work around the clock in shifts, while oil pot lamps and bamboo and wood fires were kept burning all night. The PoWs called this cutting 'Hellfire Pass' as these fires viewed from above gave the impression of working in the jaws of hell

Illustration 3.6.4   Wooden viaduct near Konyu, which was later filled with earth

3.7 Cholera

Corporal Tatsuo Morohoshi, 7th Company, 4th Battalion, 9th Railway Regiment, 2nd Railway Command Group, Southern Army

In May 1943 I was despatched from the command unit of the 7th Company to the 1st platoon as a staff worker in charge of its sanitary arrangements (disease prevention). The 1st Platoon led by 2nd Lieutenant Kamuro was at Malayan Hamlet (point 150 km) and was struggling to cut through the big rock bed at Hintok.

My biggest concern with the Kamuro platoon was the danger of cholera, as I had been notified by the disease-prevention unit of the Southern Army that cholera had broken out on the Burmese side of the River Kwai further upstream about two months ago, and had been gradually spreading in our direction. My concern became a practical problem when we were informed that cholera patients had been found at Nikhe on the Burma–Thai border. Though it was 130 kilometres away from Malayan Village where we were located, the spread of cholera to our area seemed inevitable, just a matter of time.

The first measure to be taken by us in the field was inoculation. Cholera vaccine was hurriedly sent to us from the army. This vaccine must have been of a high potency, as the hypodermic injections were very painful, and were accompanied by a feeling of numbness which went up to the top of the brain. Careful washing of the hands and fingers was strictly ordered as cholera was passed on through contact, not through the air. Antiseptic solutions, such as formaldehyde or cresol were distributed to each section, and shoe-cleaning mats dipped in an antiseptic solution were placed at the entrances of all buildings, and men were ordered to clean the soles of their shoes. Soldiers on cooking duty placed all used and washed tableware in metal baskets, which were dipped in boiling hot water for sterilisation. As our men had been in a tropical area for nearly two years, no man dared to drink unboiled water. These preventive measures were not perfect, but our men understood the seriousness of the situation and voluntarily co-operated in the prevention of cholera. While we were working hard on preventive measures, the cholera came closer to us, as far as the neighbouring village Kinsaiyok, 10 kilometres away. On the following day one Australian PoW who worked at the river pier unloading supplies was taken with cholera. I did not hear how he had been infected; maybe he had drunk water from the river as the work had made him so thirsty, or had eaten raw fish or contacted local people who had been infected.

The patient was immediately transferred to the isolation hut. However four patients were found two days later, infected by some unknown route, and the number of the patients increased rapidly to about one hundred one week later; there was nothing we could do about it!

In order to treat the patients a large amount of injectable saline solution was needed but it was not possible to get enough of this due to the poor transportation conditions in the rainy season. What was called the isolation area in the PoW camp was just a small hut in the jungle of about one thousand square feet, to which even men who suffered some diarrhoea were sent as suspected patients. One day when the cholera was at its peak I visited the place, led by an Australian medical officer, though going there was quite outside my responsibility. Being a young man, I wanted see the patients with my own eyes. It was about 2 p.m., when there was a short lull in the rain. Here and there patients were shrieking in agony, in postures of evacuation, which was just like the pictures of hell in Buddhism, and I could not go on looking at them. There were about 130 real and suspected patients, out of 1,300 PoWs who were working together with us.

Fortunately none of us Japanese soldiers were infected. And though we were very worried about the sanitary conditions among the local workers who were under our command none of them fell sick. Though we were seriously concerned by the prevalence of the cholera, not knowing what the end would be, it happened that no more new cases appeared after a fortnight. I wondered if our people had become immune, but then a cholera outbreak was reported downstream.

I worked hard, and was enthusiastically involved in the prevention of cholera. One unforgettable memory from that time is the noble figure of the Australian medical officer Major Fagan running around caring for the patients and encouraging the dying.

3.8   The Hirota platoon at Hintok

Sergeant Jiro Sakai, 7th Company, 4th Battalion, 9th Railway Regiment, 2nd Railway Command Group, Southern Army

We moved to Hintok in April 1943. I was told that Hintok meant 'below the cliff' in the Thai language. We were on a rocky plateau and could look down at the River Kwai far away in a sharp valley. A small river flowed by our barracks which was roofed with *chark* (woven palm leaves) and bamboo poles. About 200 metres from our barracks was a PoW camp.

Before the platoon moved in, our leader Hirota and I had gone to reconnoitre the situation in the area assigned to us. The time allowed us was only three months from April to June, part of which would fall in the notorious monsoon when all the roads would be like rivers and supply by land would not be possible. After we had looked around the leader asked me, 'Do you think the work can be completed in the period assigned to us in our orders?' I immediately answered, 'If civilians undertook this work it would take more than a year. However as we are in the army, we should be able to do it.'

I made up my mind that I would strive to perform any work however hard at Hintok. I had been in the China War for two years and seven months, and had been enlisted in this war leaving behind two children and another one on the way. I was always encouraged by the letters from my wife in which she said 'I will guard the home front, so you do your best for the country.'

My section undertook to blast one side of the first rock bed in April. At that time a team of cameramen came from Tokyo to make a film of the construction work which was to be shown to the Emperor. The ignition was done by two men and myself using cigarettes. While we were being filmed, a big rock fell very close to the battalion commander who had happened to come and was watching the work. If he had been hit it would have been a great shock to us.

At that time every company was hurriedly working to extend the track as far as possible, as it was needed to supply materials for the work. Where large amounts of earth had to be piled up for the railbed, a temporary wooden bridge was built to enable light trains to go through, and then the bridge was gradually buried with earth while being used by passing trains. In our platoon, the Ikeda section was working on filling in the temporary bridge for a length of 300 metres.

We moved to the second rock bed in May. Our leader Hirota asked me, 'Sakai, when can you finish this?'

'This should be just about completed by around 25 May'

'Sakai, you don't let your work get you down, do you?'

At that time the number of men available for work was reduced to almost one-third due to missions to headquarters and disease – malaria and dengue fever. So we had to use all the available men efficiently. Lance Corporal Arii worked hard and helped me very much. The numbers of PoWs despatched to my section was not much at first but was increased to 160 men. Their commander was a warrant officer who led the men well. We made up 40 drilling teams of two men each and the remaining 80 men worked on moving the rock chips after the blasting.

We needed a minimum of three chisels for each team; a long, a medium and a short one. But we did not have enough, which decreased our working efficiency. We were impatient to get them by every possible means. I once had a lengthy discussion with the platoon leader. He argued with the battalion headquarters, asking for more chisels, but was told it would take one week to get them as they needed chisels everywhere in the regiment. But one day he brought us chisels which had been allocated to somewhere else, to our great delight.

The PoWs worked during the daytime only, but we could not be so leisurely. We continued to work day and night. The drillings by the PoWs were done on the piece-work system, so they could go back when the day's work was finished. Sometimes they went back to the barracks at 11 a.m. Those working on moving the rock chips had to work throughout the set working time.

The assigned depth of drilling was 1.2 metres, but when we tried to increase it by 10 centimetres, a hot discussion arose between the platoon leader and the PoWs. The PoWs insisted, 'The Japanese soldiers get three meals, but we are given only two meals a day. With this we cannot dig one metre and thirty centimetres.' I did not know exactly whether they were given two meals or not, as their feeding was done by the PoW camp. However, when he heard that, the leader himself set an example of drilling, and eating two meals like the PoWs. As he went around his area till dark after finishing the day's quota of hard drilling work, I worried about his health and advised him to stop drilling and eat three meals but he did not accept this. He was a man of great endurance, to live on two meals a day. And he continued eating two meals a day while we were working with the PoWs.

One day the leader did not come back to the barracks even at 8 p.m. after the sun had completely set. We were worried that he might have met with an accident and were contemplating whether to send out a search team. Then he came back with his whole body covered in mud and sweat. He told us:

I was nearly eaten by a tiger. After I finished the drilling work, I went round to see the day's progress and the preparations for tomorrow. As the workplaces are all reached by winding bridges, shaped valleys and dense forest, I mistook my regular route and got lost in a maze. The sun had already set and I couldn't find my way in the darkness. I lit my lighter, took a look ahead and ran five or six steps, and then lit my lighter again and ran several steps. But after a while my lighter began to run out of fuel, I lit some tissue paper and ran as far as

I could see in front of me. At that point I was not so worried, but when I lit the last sheet of tissue I felt hopeless. I took out from my leather bag the folder of a paperfile and burnt it as a last resort, then with God's help I found the regular path. I'm safe, but I am sorry to have given you trouble.

The Ebina section of the platoon worked on the night shift. When they went to the workplace our platoon leader went with them in the jungle, where tigers were living, personally taking command. Once he saw a light in the darkness. When he moved close to it with his sword in his hand, it proved to be just the root of a tree.

On 25 May we moved to the third rock bed, as the second one was almost completed. The rest of the second rock was to be dealt with by 30 men.

On 22 June our platoon leader came back to our barracks in the morning very exhausted. He had been to attend the battalion officers' meeting to receive important orders. He ordered all the men to assemble and said in a serious tone, 'You are to complete the work at Hintok even if everybody dies of exhaustion.' Some of the men trembled with excitement. The completion of the railway by October was essential though the work was being hindered by rain and big rocks.

As every man was so concerned I surveyed the remaining rock bed. My conclusion was that we should cut to a depth of 4.5 metres for a length of 70 metres. So I judged that if we dug down half a metre a day, we would be able to complete the work by the date assigned in our orders. The regimental commander moved his command post to Hintok after asking everybody to put forth his utmost effort. One day he came to my work area and said, 'Sakai, I see you are doing a good job!' I jumped up straight, fearing that I had failed to salute him. But he said gently, 'Stay where you are. Keep doing your present job.' This is an unforgettable memory.

On 2 July the battalion commander came to my area. At 4 p.m. the last bit of rock was blasted away. Our leader Hirota grasped my hands. He just said, 'Sakai, well done!' but could not continue, and turned his face away so that it would not be seen by others. Big tears glittered in his eyes, and I could not hold back my flowing tears. It was a time of strong emotion.

Our platoon leader, 2nd Lieutenant Hirota, had a strong sense of responsibility, and put his whole heart and soul into the completion of the construction work. He was a leader who himself proved that he was not forcing an unreasonable workload on the PoWs. Under such strong pressure to complete the work by the given date, the quota he forced them to finish could be a reasonable one. Why did he have to be sentenced to death by the victors? Was it considered vindictiveness or the venting of someone's anger? Whenever I think of our leader Hirota, I feel a strong resentment. However, what is done cannot be undone. All I can do now is to tell our children that war is an evil when such a fine young man had to be killed, and hope that our children who understand such evil will lead Japan to be a peaceful country. This is the only way that his death can become meaningful and form the basis for the creation of a peace. I pray for the repose of his soul.

3.9   Lt-Colonel Banno and the PoWs

Captain Saburo Hasegawa, Adjutant, 5th Railway Regiment, 2nd Railway Command Group, Southern Army

On 16 April 1943, the 4th Battalion of the 5th Railway Regiment, whom we were eagerly awaiting, arrived at Nikhe near the Thailand–Burma border via Bangkok. The battalion had been in south China, had taken part in the attack on Hong Kong, operated the South China railway and finally managed to return to its original regiment for the construction of the railway.

I was ordered to visit the 4th Battalion to deal with personnel matters and to help set up the Banno (4th) branch camp for the Malay PoWs who were arriving from Singapore by train and then on foot. On 7 April I left the headquarters at Thanbyuzayat with my messenger, Senior Private Nagayama, in a Ford commercial car driven by Lance Corporal Nishida. Around noon we came to Ronsi (60 kilometres from Thanbyuzayat). I dropped in at the work site of the 3rd Company and had lunch with their commander Asakura, a good friend of mine.

Five kilometres from Ronsi, in a round valley, I located pile-driving work being done at a branch of the River Unyou. I got out of the car, walked 300 metres in the field and met the battalion commander Masaji Saito who was standing in the sun. He wanted me to stay overnight for a drink, but I declined his offer as I had a tight schedule. I stayed there about an hour to watch the pile-driving.

It was very hot without any wind in that desert-like basin, so the work had just been started at 2 p.m. after a long lunch rest to avoid the heat. A Senior Sergeant with a moustache gave the order 'Start!', and some thirty PoWs standing on both sides of the river pulled on the ropes; the weight went up and dropped on the pile in time with the whistle of a PoW officer. I said to the commander, 'These men are doing very well, all pulling together. Are they engineers?'

'No, they are mixture of infantry and gunners. The sergeant had a hard time training them. First he tried the Japanese style and called 'one, two, three' in English and they released the rope on three! But the English pronunciation of 'three' begins softly and they did not release the rope in unison. After many failures the PoW officer thought of the whistle we use when a train is leaving and asked us to borrow one. The whistle worked well, as they had been trained to move in combat in time with a whistle. Using the whistle it became possible to lift the weight higher with greater efficiency.'

I said goodbye to him and moved on. After we passed Mezali (70 km) we were deep in the mountains and went through many valleys. We saw no local inhabitants' houses after Apanon (85 km). All we saw were the temporary huts of working crews here and there. I felt as if the sun had set as it had got darker and animals with shining eyes came running out. But when we came to the open country of Kyando (95 km) it was still bright with sunshine. We had been in the shade of high mountains and trees. We turned into a side road and found rather neatly built palm-leaf houses. When I got out, the battalion adjutant Sato came running out and greeted me.

'Iyoo, welcome, regimental adjutant. Please come in'. (This 'Iyoo' was his own friendly expression.) 'Your face is covered with dust. Go to the river behind the building and have a wash.'

The faces of the three of us were really dirty; only our eyes and mouths could be seen. A sergeant led us to the river. After driving along a dusty road in the dry season, it was a real treat to have a bath in clean, cool water. It was the River Zami, which was 20 metres wide and 50 centimetres deep. Zami meant 'angry turbulent river' in the local language, and it was not uncommon for the water level to go up 10 metres in a night after a heavy rainfall. We had to build the railway in this difficult area, and we hoped that the river would not be angry.

While we were resting by the river after bathing, battalion commander Kawano came back in an ox-cart. He had been to see the work of the 5th Company. That evening Adjutant Sato and Lieutenant Tanaka drank the local brandy made in Moulmein that I had brought with me, and I retreated to the commander's room to rest. But as I and commander Kawano had been in the same units several times after 1934, we had a lot to talk about and went to bed just before sunrise.

Though I was sleepy, we had to leave early to avoid the heat, so I got up and went to the river to wash my face. Commander Kawano was already there and told me that big fish could be caught in the evening and the night but not in the daytime. The sergeant showed me a fishing cage made of wood branches in which he had just caught a carp 40 centimetres long.

After a quick breakfast we left the battalion headquarters.We drove in the morning mist among the tall trees along the River Zami. After an hour the road changed to steep hairpin curves. We crossed over wooden road bridges formed with two layers of big tree stems, built by the 5th Company. We left the river and entered a plateau, and there we saw the temporary tents of working crews. Suddenly we came to a plain scattered with thickets of thorny bamboo. I heard men talking, so I got out of the car and went over. They were the Abe platoon of the 6th Company, who were pulling out the bamboos. Platoon leader Abe was giving the orders, speaking fast. An elephant was trying to pull out a large clump of bamboo one metre in diameter, and exerting all its powers, with a glint in its little eyes, on the commands of the mahout. The soldiers nearby were also straining at the task. It might be thought that the men's straining bore no relation to that of the elephant, but the elephant is a clever animal and is stimulated by judging the feeling of the men. With the sound of tearing, the shrub of thorny bamboo came down. A cheer went up from our soldiers and the men of the Burmese labour-service group. As the leader raised his hands with a cheer, the elephant seemed to answer it by raising its trunk high and trumpeting. The elephant seemed happy too. The proposed railway line was full of big holes from pulling out the bamboo, and these would have to be filled and tamped down, a hard construction job.

After driving for ten minutes we came to a barren field of red earth and red stones which might have been baked by a forest fire. There were a few tiny plants in the ground, which reminded me of the Children's Limbo of Buddhism.

Soon we met a party building an embankment. Several men came running out crying 'Ow!' It seems they had hit a beehive in the ground. Numerous bees came and attacked them. The leader promptly lit several pine-torches and handed them to the men saying 'Kill them with these', and the torches were pushed into the hive.

We drove through a mountainous area, up and down hills and valleys, and arrived at the Burma–Thailand border, as I judged from my map, though there were no signs of border guards. The railway was to go east of three pagodas which were standing away from the road. I took out my binoculars and just managed to see the upper part of the three pagodas, which I could not approach as there was no path. I looked to the west and saw the thin line of the planned railbed cut in the woods winding its way up. This was a scene that I would never forget. I saw smoke coming up from far below – probably a unit was cooking lunch. I felt grateful for the hard work of our men in the regiment. We crossed the River Kwai further upstream several times, and at about 2 o'clock arrived at the village of Nikhe, where soldiers of our 4th Battalion who had just arrived from south China were moving around busily. I met the commander and the officers and congratulated them on their safe arrival after the long journey and spent the night there talking on personnel matters.

Though Nikhe was close to the border and deep in the mountains, it was not affected directly by the war, and many more goods were sold in the village than in Burma. This was very different from the Burmese side of the forest where inhabitants' houses were rare, and I envied the unit which was assigned to Thailand.

The morning of 9 April was cool as it had rained in the night. As we drove along we saw the River Kwai on the right at Konkoita. The road had been built hurriedly by the 3rd Company in late March and had many curves and slopes in order to reduce the amount of earthmoving work. We arrived at the lodgings for military travellers at Tamuron Part (244 km from Nong Pladuk) around noon. The lodgings seemed to be very new, as construction materials were scattered here and there.

I met an elderly officer, the chief of the lodgings, and asked to be given two or three days' stay. He said, 'Ha, you are the adjutant of the 5th Rail. I will put you in the hut over there. Please do your own cooking.' He gave us dried fish, onions and raw *miso* (fermented bean paste). The raw *miso* was a luxury for us, which we had not eaten since we arrived in Burma a year ago. It must have been made in Bangkok by Japanese. We had been eating soup made of dried powdered *miso*. There I met the quartermaster of the Banno PoW camp, who had come in an advance party. He told me the materials for building the barracks had already arrived; and tents to accommodate the PoWs during the building period had been sent by courtesy of the 9th Railway Regiment, so he had the necessary facilities for them to camp. I decided to wait there for the arrival of the main body of PoWs. In the evening I went to the liaison office of the 4th Battalion and sent a report by telephone to 4th Battalion headquarters, and then by radio to the regimental commander.

On 10 April, hearing that the first group of PoWs would arrive by the evening, I set out in the afternoon to meet them. The sun shone for a while, then dark clouds covered the sky and it started to rain, and then the sun came out again. This squall was an indication that the monsoon was nearing. I was worried about the hardship the PoWs would suffer walking in the rain. The road was new and slippery, and I was concerned that this soft road might not be usable during the coming monsoon.

I passed a long line of PoWs. They seemed very tired and would need several days' rest after arrival. At Tamajo (237 km) it started to rain heavily. At the entrance to the village I saw about 15 PoWs sitting in a storehouse. The guard with them told me that they were sick and had difficulty in walking. So I offered to take them in my car, but as the car was small not all the men could be carried in one trip. Since there was only one guard I offered to take the first party of PoWs myself. I loaded my pistol and got in the rear, watching them, and handed them over to the advance party at Tamuron Part. By the time the car had gone back and brought the rest of them, the sun was setting.

As requested in a message, I telephoned Nikhe and was told that my commander wanted me to come back to the headquarters in time to attend the adjutants' meeting at Kanchanaburi on the 18th. So I decided to stay at Tamuron Part until the next day.

It was fine on 11 April. Because of the squall in the night it was humid from the morning on. We left our luggage at the lodgings and carried rice balls with the delicious *miso* for lunch. Our car went slowly along the rutted road which had no gravel. After driving for 12 kilometres I met the leading men in the party of PoWs who told us that Lieutenant-Colonel Banno was about four kilometres behind. A large group was climbing up the steep slope from Namchong. It was humid and the sun shone down ruthlessly on the moving line of PoWs, who were panting in the heat. After the main group had passed, a small group came and sat down in the shade of the roadside, staggering unsteadily. A tall officer was attending to a PoW who was lying down. I went up to the officer.

'You are Colonel Banno? I am Captain Hasegawa, adjutant of the 5th Railway Regiment. I came to liaise with you on the orders of my commander. Thank you for coming here all this long hard way.'

'You are the adjutant. It was very thoughtful of regimental commander Sasaki to send you all this way to welcome us.'

'How are these PoWs?'

'They have been in a bad condition since yesterday and are worn out. I left five men to rest in the rear.'

Illustration 3.9.1 PoWs being transported using type C56 engines to Ban Pong or to Wang Yai (124 km). It took four whole days from Singapore in overcrowded box cars

Illustration 3.9.2 PoWs walking through jungle. The PoWs had to walk 22 km per day on average to Banno PoW camp at Nikhe or Tamuron Part, often troubled by showers. When they arrived at the camps, 35 per cent were regarded as patients

I went further on to pick up the worn-out men and found them resting in the shade of a pagoda at Namchong with a Korean guard. I told them my purpose and put them in my car. They seemed to have recovered somewhat after bathing in well water in the village but were still staggering. The sun in the west was heating up the road, and I was sweating just sitting in the car, so it must have been terribly hot for the walking PoWs. As I wiped away my sweat, I saw several men resting where the tall Colonel was holding a PoW and giving him water with words of encouragement.

'Don't go to sleep! Don't go to sleep. Just a little further to go.'

The man seemed to be suffering slight sunstroke.

'Mr. Hasegawa, may I oblige you to take this man in your car to Tamuron Part? He is not able to walk.'

I was impressed to see him taking as good care of the PoWs as if they were his own men. He was tall, always stood up straight and had something of the samurai (feudal warrior) about him. He could have been an excellent infantry commander, who loved his men and trained them to build up a strong fighting regiment. I was sorry to see him as the commander of a PoW camp.

I delivered the sick men to the advance party at Tamuron Part, and left for Nikhe where we stayed overnight. Next day we left there early and were able to arrive back in Thanbyuzayat soon after sunset, thanks to the downward slope, and reported the details to the commander.

Note

After the war most of the commanders of PoW camps were sentenced to death by hanging in the war-crimes court. Though more PoWs died in his camp than in the other camps, Colonel Banno was only sentenced to three years' imprisonment, the lowest penalty at that time. This was because of the favourable affidavits that the PoW officers presented to the court.

3.10 A hard struggle in the remote jungle

Sergeant Kazufumi Kamiya, 7th Company, 4th Battalion,
5th Railway Regiment

On the evening of 15 March 1943, we disembarked at Bangkok after 15 days' voyage from south China. Several days later we sat on top of the supplies loaded on railway goods wagons and headed for Kanchanaburi, taking the utmost care not to be shaken off the wagons, while at the same time brushing away the sparks falling from the wood-burning boilers. The train stopped at a place where there was no station, to load firewood on the locomotive.

From Kanchanaburi we trans-shipped the materials to light trains (four flat wagons pulled by a rail-tractor) and went to Wang Po (114 km), then went up the River Kwai in small boats to Kinsaiyok (172 km), where our platoon was building an embankment together with about two hundred Australian PoWs. I was half-impressed and half-amazed to see the PoWs marching back to their camp in a lively column to the calls 'left, right, left, right'. Though they were wearing torn clothes and shoes with big holes in the soles, some of them called out to me, 'In the long run this railway will be ours.' The guards were Koreans who wore the same badges of rank as us Japanese.

In August we embarked on boats and advanced to Konkoita (262 km). My section was to survey the route. As my speciality (obtained by private training) was telecommunications, Corporal Kikuchi of the section led the survey and I cleared the line of vision for the transit theodolite, riding on an elephant, which was not as comfortable as it looked from the ground. It had a peculiar smell after getting wet in the rain, and swayed badly when pushing down trees of up to 20 centimetres in diameter with its trunk.

Around the end of September 1943, all of our battalion were in the Nikhe area (282 km) and Captain Goto became the commander. Nikhe was about 300 metres above sea level and we did not feel so hot during the daytime as we had got used to the tropical climate and also it was monsoon season. Heavy rain continued for several weeks and we were often drenched to the skin. We dried our wet clothes over a wood fire during the night and wore the nasty-smelling ones next day. Because of this, we railway engineers as well as the PoWs, the volunteer workers from Burma and the coolies from Thailand, all worked with no upper clothes when it was not raining. At that time a large number of volunteer workers, ox-carts and elephants were sent from Burma. There were local doctors among the group of Burmese workers, who were treating tropical ulcers and other ailments with herbal medicines.

Because of the heavy rain many wooden road bridges were washed away and our meals were reduced, though we were supplied with a small amount of food by elephant transport. The river was in spate and boats could not be used.

The number of sick increased among the volunteer workers and PoWs. Not only malaria, but also dysentery, cholera and even smallpox. At that time I was in charge of the volunteer workers and once I had to go to their isolation ward to pay their wages – an awful experience.

Illustration 3.10.1 Transport in the rainy season. The roads became muddy and it was difficult for lorries to move, so supplies were carried by river boat as far as possible

Illustration 3.10.2 Elephant transport. Elephants proved powerful transporters in many situations. Many were brought as far as north Burma

135

Illustration 3.10.3 The base for boat transportation at Takunun. The railway was built along the river so that supplies could be transported by water

The incidence of dysentery increased among the PoWs and a man died almost every day, increasing the number of the wooden crosses in the cemetery. Therefore charges or complaints from the PoWs about the working conditions were at their highest at this stage. We heard a rumour that a PoW had a radio set hidden in his canteen. Under these conditions the number of PoWs coming to work decreased drastically. However we were not allowed to delay the work for any reason, as the completion of the railway by October was an absolute order. Corporal Kanji Yoshimi, who had the duty of liaison with the PoW camp over the workforce, was ordered to collect a certain number of PoWs for the work. However he was a good-hearted man and was not able to pull out weak and sick PoWs and force them to work against his conscience. He was in a serious dilemma between the demands of military orders and his human feelings, from which he could not escape. His strength left him, and he chose to die. I deeply sympathised with him as his comrade, and prayed in front of his coffin in tears with my head bowed down to the floor. This is the most unforgettable memory in my military service.

A few days later I returned to the Yamada platoon and we advanced to Sonkrai which was close to the Burma–Thailand border. Here the workforce was just like an exhibition of racial types. There were PoWs, Malayan and Chinese coolies from Thailand, and Burmese and various Indians from Burma. As so many workers had been sent to this remote place by the border we imagined that the laying of the track and the movement of trains had advanced closer to us. I really enjoyed the boiled turtle and bamboo-shoot dish served to us one evening. We had been short of food.

Once an Australian sergeant had some complaint about the work allocation of the day, and called us 'baby' or 'Jap'. Sergeant Takeuchi and Corporal Sakinobu who were close to the tall sergeant jumped up and hit him. Though he did not resist, I admired their fine fighting spirit. On the other hand, we sang songs together with the PoWs during the rest periods and each thought of our home countries. At such times they always took out pictures of their parents, brothers, sisters and girlfriends with affection and wanted us to look at the photos. One day they asked me for permission to collect *poros* near the eaves of a local house. The *poro* was a tropical fruit the size of a human head, and its seeds were eaten steamed or baked. I was in a fix as it was in Thai territory, where we were not allowed to take anything without the consent of the owner. Conveniently for me there was no one in the house and as our platoon leader was not about, I allowed them to collect the fruit although I felt insecure in my mind about it.

Around that time the sun came out occasionally from behind the clouds and a local bird, the tokkei, started singing his peculiar melody, and after a while we moved on to our new duties saying goodbye to the hard struggle with the jungle in the monsoon season.

3.11 Matoma, the hardest time of all

Second Lieutenant Juji Tarumoto, 3rd Company, 2nd Battalion, 9th Railway Regiment, 2nd Railway Command Group, Southern Army

In the middle of April 1943, my platoon moved from Point 103 kilometres to Matoma (175 km) by boat. As the water level was low, sometimes two boats had to pull each other up or everybody had to get off the boat and get into the water and push it up. We went up the river in deep jungle one after another, feeling as if we were going into jungle where no human being had been before. Unexpectedly I saw a small pier with two or three small boats and then soldiers and PoWs. That was the camp site of a construction team. From the big beetling rock at 109 km, the planned course of the railroad left the river and we could see nothing but huge untouched jungle.

We arrived at Matoma soon after sunset and slept in the tents that the advance party had prepared. Our accommodation in Matoma was all in tents. We had borrowed enough tents for ourselves and for the expected number of PoWs who had not yet arrived. One tent was allocated to each of our sections in which a bamboo floor had been built one foot above the ground. A small stream nearby was the only source of water. After the tents were finished we all built a tool house. From experience we knew we needed a wide open space for a large number of PoWs to receive tools, baskets, axes, saws and ropes, laid out on a platform. Then we cleared the proposed camp site for the PoWs. Almost all the members of the platoon lined up in a row and advanced cutting bushes and vegetation. This was done in less time than expected.

My area extended for six kilometres from Matoma to Rinteng, where we were to build seven wooden bridges with lengths of 30, 10, 40, 120, 20, 12 and 12 metres respectively. Though it was not easy to build a total of 250 metres of bridges, I thought it would be more efficient than to build up high earth embankments as my platoon was well experienced in building bridges. My pressing concern was whether we would be able to finish the work in the given two months, and when the monsoon season would come and how it would affect our work.

Some PoWs came from Kinsaiyok with a Japanese lance-corporal and several men. We helped them in setting up their tents and the transportation of food. As a principle, the PoW camps and the railway regiments were two independent units with different duties. However our situation was fairly different from that of Chungkai, the headquarters of Lieutenant-Colonel Yanagida, the branch commander, to whom we in the railway unit had to apply for various things. Ambiguously in our case, the barrier between the two units seemed to be lowered, especially as the lance-corporal often went to Kinsaiyok for liaison purposes, and then the remaining men did not know what to do and said to us, 'Please do as you think fit.'

The work at Matoma was the most wretched of all the construction work done on the railway for us, and probably for the PoWs as well. Compared to Matoma, conditions at Chungkai and Ban Kao must have been much better for the PoWs. The PoWs who came to Matoma were all tired as they had been working hard at their previous sites. Among them was a company led by an elderly man, Lieutenant-Colonel Baker, which I had employed in earth-moving at Chungkai. Colonel Baker himself looked worn out. Though he had had full freedom from labour at Chungkai as a company commander, he now walked around in the jungle to collect firewood for making tea and sometimes he himself carried the wood back to the camp. Also Captain Whewell* who had led the PoWs in the blasting work at Chungkai, had become thin, with a long untidy moustache, and looked a sick man. Though I did not know what had caused the two to decline in health so much, I felt sympathetic towards them. I was sorry that I could do nothing for them.

Not only these two officers but all the PoWs were in much the same condition. Those who had not dropped out from the previous work were in relatively better health, while many had been sent to hospitals behind the front line. It was hard to make them bear the heavy burden of completing the work by the set date. But what could I or the railway unit do about it?

The bridge-building was being done with the full power of the platoon and good progress was being made. However the earth-moving work could not be left off as it had to be done before the monsoon season arrived when digging would be difficult, so we had been repeatedly asking for an increase in manpower. Suddenly several hundred Thai coolies were sent to us, followed by some workers from Malaya. Naturally the

---

*The name Whewell is the closest English surname I can find to translate the Japanese version of the Captain's name given in the source.

coolies were not under the command of the PoW camps. They were supposed to live independently, led by a head coolie, and the railway unit paid wages to them for their offer of labour. As a matter of fact they could not live in the jungle on the wages paid to them, and their living conditions such as tents and their daily meals had to be taken care of by the railway unit. In this sense they were practically administered by the railway unit.

We preferred to use PoWs rather than coolies because of the working efficiency of the former and the administrative burden of the latter. I complained to the battalion headquarters about the haphazard allocation of coolies to us. Their efficiency was generally no more than could be expected. However, the coolies from Thailand were exceptionally good workers. They moved two cubic metres per day right from the start. Probably they were professional earth-movers. They performed better at cutting the earth than piling it up, which was useful as there was plenty of cutting to be done before and after constructing the bridges. This was the reverse of our soldiers and PoWs, for whom piling was easier than cutting. Anyway the large number of coolies solved the earth-moving problem, and for this I was grateful to headquarters.

At Matoma all the coolies employed by my platoon camped by the first bridge, on the Matoma side of the stream, while the PoWs were on the other side of the stream. We divided them in this way as the PoWs asked not to be put together with coolies. Still the PoWs complained that it was dangerous to use the same water from the stream, but we could not accept their request for a different arrangement because of the problem of the transportation of food and other things.

At last the monsoon season came. When we first arrived at Matoma it seldom rained. After the middle of May, squalls came every day; they came suddenly and soon ended, just enough to moisten the dried-up earth, and the shirts of the workers soon dried. Then the length of each shower gradually increased and it rained twice a day. When June came it rained all through the morning for several days and then it always started to rain soon after noon and continued till the evening for several days. We had experienced the heavy rains of October and November at Chungkai, but we did not know what it would be like in June in the jungle. We had heard that there were two peak raining periods with floods, one in June/July and the other in October/November. We could not stop working just because it was the rainy season. When it was raining lightly the soldiers went out to work as on a fine day. Even if they were delayed in leaving the barracks or had to take temporary shelter in the event of heavy rain, they started to work when it changed to a drizzle.

Our soldiers went out to work wearing caps and shirts in order not to be rained on directly, but even so they were completely drenched when they returned in the evening. It was the job of those remaining in the tents to burn firewood and hang up the wet clothes to dry for the next day. In the end the wet shirts and trousers could not be dried during the night and the number of those without shirts gradually increased and many wore only loincloths.

The PoWs were more miserable. Almost all of them wore tattered shorts or just a loincloth. Nobody had the kind of extensive baggage we had seen when they arrived at Chungkai, as most of it must have been given to the inhabitants there in exchange for food. Though there was plenty of rice, the PoWs did not like it and satisfied their appetites somewhat with fried bananas or small local puddings. There were a few stalls with local people selling such foods, but not so many stalls as in Kinsaiyok or our previous locations. This was partly because the PoWs had already sold most of their belongings. Their meagre uniforms had to be used as bedding, so they had to go to work in just a loincloth.

'A Japanese loincloth is convenient,' a PoW said to me as if it was a new discovery, but when he was trudging through the rain he could certainly not be described as enjoying the new discovery. A few PoWs wrapped a piece of a jute bag around their waist. Their way of walking to the workplace was not orderly, unlike the past, but in a loose long line, with everybody drooping his head and straggling. Some had rashes all over their bodies and some were limping with water-eczema. I felt there was something abnormal about their thin faces. They seemed to have completely lost the military pride characteristic of Great Britain or the Netherlands. Meeting their fate with resignation, they moved obediently as the Japanese instructed. Their feet were covered with mud just by walking on the muddy path. They all wore shoes with holes in the toes and were walking with lumps of mud on their toes. And when they started to work their bodies were covered with mud.

When I was at the work site a pale-faced PoW would come up to me saying 'Benjo (toilet), speedo!'; he wanted to relieve himself because of loose bowels. But in most cases he could not contain himself and went quickly into the nearby bushes before I had time to answer. We made simple toilets at the work site but we could not stop the scattering of loose faeces and the foul odour, a miserable situation. I deserved to be called inhuman for employing such men. But how many men could I get if I allowed all these men to rest and picked out only the healthy men for the work? It was not only my platoon that was affected, but the neighbouring Takizawa platoon, and all the companies and battalions were in the same situation. Japanese soldiers and PoWs alike were forced into the most miserable of situations in the construction of the Burma–Thailand Railway. One day I did not see the leader of the PoWs, and was told that he was attending the funeral of a PoW who had been suspected of having cholera. I was worried when I heard this, but when I got back to my barracks I was told that he had not died of cholera. The officer, who came to the work site the next day, was very happy that it had not been cholera. I too felt relieved.

About the same time three coolies employed by the Takizawa platoon were infected with cholera and soon died. Takizawa was deeply disappointed as he had been paying close attention to the living conditions of the coolies. The Takizawa platoon as well as mine tried hard to stop the prevalence of cholera; bamboo shelves were made so that everybody returning from work could sterilise their hands, and a disease-prevention team was despatched from Kinsaiyok. By the combined efforts of these people and ours, no more cases of cholera appeared at Matoma, to our great satisfaction.

Many Japanese troops came marching along the Burma–Thailand railway line to go to the front in Burma. Their movements greatly inspired us to complete the railway before the assigned date. Their marching continued every day in the rain and the mud. Where there was no road they walked on our embankment which was soaked with rainwater and sometimes crumbled away, so we had to repair it every day. When the river level was high the troops went over a bridge which had not been finished, and its upper surface was still round wood. So it was dangerous to walk on it as it was wet and slippery with the rain. Two infantrymen would hold hands to get a good balance for walking over the bridge, but once a man fell five metres from the bridge, and was sent to the rear and diagnosed by the military doctor at Rinteng as having a broken spine. Whenever our soldiers saw these marching troops they said to each other, 'Our work is very hard, but the infantry are also having a hard and trying time. We must complete the railway quickly so that they can go by train.' Most of these troops were going to the Indian front in Burma, but there were still four months to the date in October by which our orders were to complete it.

In June new orders were issued by the high command to complete the railway by August. This must have been because an important military operation was planned in Burma, but I wondered whether it would be possible to shorten the time for completing the whole line by two months. We could hardly even complete the work by the initial date of October. Was there an ingenious secret plan? Some infantry battalions, engineers, house-building units and work units were added to the command of the 9th Railway Regiment, and the number of coolies was increased. This was all that could be done by the Japanese army at that time, and in fact it was only an increase of manpower. I did not think the shortening by two months could be achieved by this increase, but I determined to do all I could to comply with these orders. My platoon had to complete the given task at all costs. That was all I could do. But the consequences were to be expected. One by one our soldiers collapsed from sickness. At the most 35 men out of a total of 60 in the platoon were able to work. The number of men sent to hospital in the rear increased, and those who got sick never recovered their previous state of health. Except for a few, most of the men had to rest for several days after they had worked for a week or so. Every day I had to worry about how many men could come to work, and I got a shock whenever the doctor told me that a man had had to be sent behind the lines. Most of them suffered from malaria, and many were suffering also from abdominal pains or a sickness of indeterminate character. All the parts of every man's body became weak in the last extremity of fatigue. I had a fever once every ten days. One day when I was at a work site a private suddenly started to shiver violently, so I sent him back to the barracks in the rain. Soon afterwards I myself started to shiver with cold.

It was the same for the PoWs. The ones who came to work were different every day; they could not work for three days in a row. The number of those who turned pale while working and had to rest increased. Some went back to the barracks supported by a comrade. Often a PoW was sent to the company command unit at Matoma from the barracks by the first bridge. When I met him on the way and looked into his face, he seemed to be almost dead with sunken goggling eyes. Some were very thin and seemed to have no hope of recovery. Was it my responsibility for keeping them working until that stage? I could dare deny it.

It rained heavily every day, and the River Kwai and all the rivers that we were bridging flooded, and the dip in the ground near the fourth bridge was filled with water, which made it difficult to carry food between the barracks. Some of the PoWs walked over the almost completed bridge but most of them waded or swam in the water and returned to the camp wet through. The scaffolding on the fifth and sixth bridges was washed away and had to be rebuilt in the turbulent water. Water flowed just like a river in the cutting for the rail bed, breaking down both sides which we had to dig out again. At this juncture we were ordered to complete the work by 24 June rather than the original target of completion by the end of June. This was because the target completion for the whole railway had been brought forward.

In order to speed up our work, one elephant from Malaya and ten men from a building-construction unit headed by a sergeant were added to us. The elephant was very useful in bringing out wood for the bridges. One night when the work was almost finished this useful elephant disappeared and the driver, who was about 30 years old, and his young assistant hurriedly went off to look for it. I was told that the elephant was found later.

I had accepted the men from the building-construction unit gladly as a replacement for the increasing numbers of sick men, but this was a miscalculation, as I was forced to recognise later. I assigned the newly arrived unit to cutting and moving the wood, replacing the third section, whose men were then allocated to the bridge-building sections.

On the first day of the new assignment, the soldiers from the pile-driving section suddenly complained that 'the wood that the building unit has cut is bent and hard to hit. The quality of the wood is not good, so the ends crack.' In fact the wood that the building unit had cut was not so different from the previous wood. The complaints of the soldiers were really aimed at me. That evening while I was dozing alone in my tent, slightly affected by malaria, I heard coming from the neighbouring tent the quarrelling voices of soldier who had probably had something to drink.

'I don't like the way the platoon leader is doing things'

The section leader was trying to calm him down saying, 'Well, the platoon leader has his own ideas.'

'What do you mean by platoon leader's ideas? If he is a good platoon leader he should be aware of how we soldiers feel. So far we have built five or six bridges, sweating our guts out. If our speed of building bridges is slow, I want him to tell us clearly that we are slow. If he wants us to finish the work five days earlier than the schedule he should say so. He is not being frank with us, bringing unknown men into our group to build the bridge a little bit early. If he tells us to drive piles from now on, I am ready to do it. I am disappointed in him this time. Why doesn't he understand our feelings after all the time he had spent with us since we left our country?'

His voice rose as he talked. I tried to pass off his talk as an irresponsible utterance under the influence of the local gin. But what the soldier had said came as a deep shock to me. The dissatisfaction that I had caused by adding the building unit just at the time when so many bridges were about to be completed by the unified efforts of all men in the platoon,

Illustration 3.11.1 Temporary wooden viaduct used for transportation of supplies. Rails were laid on the viaduct and light trains travelled over them. Later, the viaduct was filled with earth

Illustration 3.11.2   Curved viaduct at Kuriankurai (250 km), 17 metres high

was not felt by this soldier alone. It was evident that all the men, even the section leader who was trying to check him, had the same discontent. My idea of shortening the period by adding the extra workforce had been a hasty judgement made superficially without understanding the feelings of my soldiers. Many soldiers had succumbed to illness one by one due to the hard work at Matoma; it was not because I had ordered them to work until they broke down. It was natural that the order to work until they dropped had stimulated their determination to do their duty of their own free will, giving everything they had until they died. I needed to be grateful to the soldiers. Was it not I, the platoon leader, who had trampled upon and broken such noble determination, and betrayed my authority? I had reasoned to myself that the soldier's drunken complaint was not justified, but in my reasoning I should also have taken into consideration the soldier's feelings. It was inevitable that this kind of crude expression of dissatisfaction would be voiced in a military organisation.

All through the night I thought about it in my feverish head, and when morning came I called my section leaders and the sergeant of the building unit to my room and announced to them a change of duties. 'The bridge-building will be done under the former conditions. The building unit will work on the earth-moving for the embankment which had been done concurrently by the tool team.'

I was ashamed to have changed my order which was the most abhorrent thing for an army commander. However this was the result of my incompetence and I had to endure the shame. I was sorry for the sergeant, and expressed my regret for my discourteous behaviour to the men from the outside unit.

Everybody in my platoon was happy. This was clearly shown in their working all-out. And as the soldier had said, our work was completed five days ahead of the initial target date. In this sense my change of decision was not disastrous.

Konkoita (262 km) was the final meeting-point of the construction work which had been carried out from the Burmese side by the 5th Railway Regiment and from the Thai side by the 9th Railway Regiment. The 3rd Company that I belonged to was ordered to build the rail-bed embankment for the last 10 kilometres to Konkoita.

By the time our work at Matoma was finished the flooding had passed its peak and the weather was in a lull though it was still the monsoon season. When July came the platoon boarded boats bound for Konkoita. All the sections had some fever patients who walked unsteadily. The total numbers of the platoon had been reduced to two-thirds as the more seriously ill men had been sent to the base hospital.

When we were pile-driving for the last bridge, the PoW officer asked me, 'Shall we be sent behind the lines when this work is finished?' I answered, 'There is still a lot of work to be done.'

He sighed miserably, 'Ah, the rumour that we have to go to the Three Pagodas (located at the Burma–Thailand border) was true.' I sympathised with him, but it was not only the PoWs that were tired out by the work.

We had moved many times in the course of the construction of the railway: Ban Pong, Tamuang, Chungkai, Wan Tao Kien, Ban Kao, Non-purarai, 103 km and Matoma. In most of the places we had moved our tents several times in accordance with the progress of work. The soldiers were eager to know where our last work site would be. Their wish was to go on to the end of the construction work, when the current work was finished. Now they had the happy hope of going to the last work site. When we boarded the boats to Konkoita, one man cried, 'Now, this is the final move!' And everybody laughed.

On the way to Konkoita we stopped at Takunun (218 km) where the headquarters of our regiment and the Yanagida branch of the PoW camp were located. When my boat approached the pier, someone was waving his hands to me. It was Captain Alexander who had been with us at Chungkai as the leader of the blasting group. He asked me where we were going and then mentioned the names of several PoW officers one by one and asked me whether I had known them. He said, 'All of these men died of cholera. A great many died. Everybody. . . .'

He must have had fond memories of those old scenes, and his half-formed words died on his lips.

3.12   Celebrating the completion of the Railway

Captain Saburo Hasegawa, Adjutant, 5th Railway Regiment, 2nd Railway Command Group, Southern Army

The headquarters of the 5th Railway Regiment moved from Thanbyuzayat to Kyando (95 km Camp) in the middle of August 1943. The heavy rain had eased off from late July and the monsoon season seemed to have ended earlier than the previous year. Our soldiers worked harder to build the embankment and lay the rails.

We found out that lime had been used in Burma for dressing the surface of pagodas, and by urging the kiln owners to increase production, more lime was made available for disinfection against cholera. With intensive effort on the part of the disease-prevention teams, the outbreak of cholera eased from early August and was terminated by the end of August.

On 17 October 1943 the railway extended from Burma by the 5th Railway Regiment and that extended from Thailand by the 9th Railway Regiment met at Konkoita (262.8 kilometres from the zero mile post at Nong Pladuk). However as there were still many places that had to be reinforced to allow steam locomotives to travel along the railway, it was decided to hold a ceremony of completion at 10 a.m. on 25 October, at Konkoita. In order to share the glorious moment with all who had worked hard in the construction I had asked the commander to permit a few representatives from all the companies to attend the ceremony, but this was not granted. Only the few soldiers who were needed at the ceremony were left behind, and all the others in the regiment were ordered to move to north Burma where the rail transportation had to be safeguarded urgently for the coming operations against India.

The ceremony was attended by the chief of staff of the Southern Army, Lieutenant-General Shimizu, deputing for the commander-in-chief, Field Marshal Terauchi, and Lieutenant-General Nakamura, commander of the Thai army, who came in light trains. Also the battalion commanders of the two railway regiments and the independent units who had taken part in the construction work were present.

On the command 'Start the work', selected soldiers of our regiment who were in full uniforms and carrying rifles pushed forward a wagon and dropped two rails on to the bed, and at the same time soldiers and PoWs of the 9th Railway Regiment who wore only shirts or were bare-chested, without rifles, did the same thing from the other side. I felt it was a pity that the soldiers of our regiment were too formal, with everybody carrying rifles, but the soldiers from the Thai side were too casual, and I felt that the group headquarters should have instructed them to unify their dress, especially as the ceremony was filmed for news release and for showing to the emperor.

Then came the key event of the ceremony. Colonel Sasaki, commander of the 5th Railway Regiment, and Colonel Imai, commander of the 9th Railway Regiment, stood facing each other with hammers in their hands. Colonel Sasaki drove in the last steel spike on the sleeper as I held the spike with a supporter, while Colonel Imai drove in the last spike on the Thai side. Thus the railway was formally connected. Then from the Thai side a Japanese steam locomotive – C5631 – decorated with crossed Rising Sun flags and pulling ten wagons travelled over the meeting point, and then from the Burmese side a train pulled by a Burmese Type KS

Illustration 3.12.1 The completion ceremony of the railway at Konkoita (262km) on 25 October 1943. The railway regiment commanders, Colonels Imai (saluting) and Sasaki reported the completion to General Ishida, commander of the Railway Group

Illustration 3.12.2 Locomotive no. C5631. The first train to pass through the ceremony towards Burma was pulled by locomotive number C5631[1]

steam locomotive did the same, to loud cries of 'Banzai' (hurrah) from everybody. A wooden commemorative post five metres high, with the words 'Finishing point of the work, Burma–Thailand Railway' in black ink, was erected at the meeting-point.

Then a memorial service for those who had died during the construction was held in front of a wooden altar covered with a white cloth and wild flowers. General Ishida, commander of the 2nd Railway Command Group, conducted the service, saying 'In the hard construction work we lost two former commanders, General Shimoda and General Takasaki, one thousand Japanese soldiers, twelve thousand prisoners of war and eight thousand and four hundred workers from Burma, Thailand and Malaya. May their souls rest in peace.'

While the band of the Southern Army played a military requiem, representatives of the Japanese soldiers, the PoWs and the workers prayed at the altar. Then a simple banquet was held outdoors and field rations and *sake* were served to everybody.

Note

1 The type C56 steam locomotive which took part in the completion ceremony was used by the Thailand State Railways after the war, and is now displayed in the garden of the Yasukuni Shrine in Tokyo. The locomotive was one of the eighty Type C56 steam locomotives brought from Japan to Burma and Thailand during the War.

3.13 A thief of tins

Corporal Yukichi Ishii, 8th Company, 9th Railway Regiment, 2nd Railway Command Group, Southern Army

In the middle of May 1943 we were in the jungle at Tampi (147 kilometres from the zero-mile post). I was the chief of the mess, with five young soldiers. Our company was doing rush construction work with many British PoWs and local coolies (whom we called *romusha*), who were working to build an earth embankment for the railway. Four of them formed a group and dug and carried earth up to the quota of one cubic metre per day, and when the daily quota was finished they went back to the camps, some as early as noon but some at 8 p.m. As a Japanese soldier had to check the progress of the work group by group and to prepare for the next day's work for 200, he worked much longer hours than the PoWs. Though we tried to prepare good meals for the hard-working soldiers, it was not easy to come up with a suitable menu every day. Other than rice, which was our staple food, we had only powdered *miso* (for soup), powdered soyabean sauce and a few tins. The only vegetables available were bean sprouts, which we grew ourselves. One day Senior Private Takumi came to me and reported, 'Some tins have been stolen.' Hearing it, I thought instantly that Japanese soldiers had stolen the tins. When I checked the storeroom, 50 tins of cooked beef, which were our luxury, and ten tins of bacon which we had captured in Singapore were missing. So I kept an eye on the stock.

Several days later we found that ten tins of bacon were again missing. As we judged that must have been done by a thief from outside, I decided that we should stand on night watch in rotation. I stood on watch on the first night and Takumi on the second night, but nothing happened. On the fourth night at about 1 o'clock we heard the sharp sound of a whistle being blown by Private Abe who was on watch. It was raining. As we rushed to the tent, Abe came back to it covered in mud and reported that a thief had got in by rolling up the bottom of the tent. He had chased the thief but had lost him in the dark night.

When we checked the stock nothing was stolen, but a muddy jute bag was left there. Next morning, when we washed the bag and looked at it, we could read an English name faintly. Now it was the turn of a Japanese Sherlock Holmes to go to work, and Takumi and I went to the PoW camp which was about one kilometre away. There were about five hundred British PoWs there guarded by Korean soldiers under a Japanese commander. We talked to the guard, who looked disagreeable. At that time the Japanese soldiers and Korean guards were at odds with each other and there was often trouble over the transfer of the PoWs. After we had explained the situation at length, the guard allowed us to enter, and the two of us with the Korean guard looked around the camp. After searching for more than two hours we located the owner of the bag. But he was suffering from malaria and was not in a condition to go out and steal. He had a perfect alibi. The only way to discover the identity of the criminal was to extract it from him, but there was no way we could get him to tell us. We gradually raised our voices, and many of his comrades gathered round us; the situation began to take on a serious aspect. I thought of making my exit at that point, but then a tall man with something of an aristocratic look about him came forward and announced 'I took his bag to go and steal.' I felt relieved and took him to the camp commander, who took the matter calmly and said to me, 'Deal with him as you think fit.'

His words disappointed me as well as displeasing me. Anyway we had to take the PoW to our tent for investigation. He told us without reluctance, 'I have done all the stealing so far and gave the tins to the sick men. I am willing to accept any punishment here. Please don't make the case public (and official).' We were impressed by him, and thought that if we had been in his position we might not have confessed a crime which might be followed by punishment. However as we had to give some warning to the PoWs not to repeat the stealing, we could not release him and leave the matter as it was. The five of us discussed what we should do and decided that we should hit him on the backside 50 times. When we told him, he answered, 'OK, thank you.'

We all took turns and hit his backside with our fists 50 times as promised, and watched him. He fell to his knees and toppled forward. I ran to him and held him.

'Brace up! Punishment is over.'

He said one word: 'Thank you.'

We had not expected this kind of answer. 'Don't you feel resentful, after being beaten so much?'

'As I committed a crime, it was natural I should be punished. I'm grateful to you for not making it public.'

Hearing this, we were all moved in our hearts, and as a result we gave him a drink of the local gin we had with us to console him.

I could not forget what he told us when we chatted then. He was a reservist, born in Birmingham, and had children and parents to whom he wanted to return whatever happened. We deeply sympathised with his yearning to go home though we were provoked by his remark, 'The Allied forces will win in the long run.' Before we released him we ended up giving him ten tins of bacon, bean sprouts and cigarettes, which he received with the greatest joy, and he shook hands with me. I still remember the scene well. Later when I met him at the work site he came running up to me and wanted to shake my hand.

I do not know what happened to him after that, but I imagine that as he was such an impressive person he must have returned to England and been a good father to his family.

Thinking of the state of things when we later became prisoners, we felt deeply that the British have the fine character of a country of gentlemen. I think that we also lost the war in terms of humanity.

3.14   A private and prisoners

Private Tokuzo Sato, Headquarters, 4th Battalion, 9th Railway Regiment, 2nd Railway Command Group, Southern Army

In late 1942, I was transferred from being general affairs assistant in the battalion headquarters at Wang Yai (124 km) to being ordnance assistant in the tool and supply depot at Kanchanaburi and worked under Sergeant Katagiri.

The sergeant received plenty of materials for the construction of the railway from the regimental depot every day. My job was to divide up the materials received, store them in our depot for the time being, ship them by truck in accordance with the requests from the work units at the front, and record their movement in and out. The workers for the railway construction were supplied from the 2nd branch of the Malaya PoW camp, to which I went every morning at 8 o'clock and received forty to fifty men. I found that British soldiers were as human as any others, tending to loaf on the job and neglect their duties. So after observing the way they worked for several days, I set up a quota system such as: 'Today this team is to finish this part of the work, the second team that part, and that is all the work for today.' The result was as I expected; their efficiency went up and by 2 o'clock all the work, which previously had not been finished until 4 o'clock, was done.

When I asked what they would like to do they all wanted to bathe in the river. My broken English was somehow or other understood by them, and they complimented me, saying 'Speaking very good.' They were pleased that a mutual understanding could be found with me and became friendly.

The PoWs were not allowed to go out of the camp individually, but they could go out without any restrictions if escorted by a Japanese soldier. At around 2.30 p.m. I took all of them to the big river Mac Khlong by the town of Kanchanaburi, and let them do what they wanted for an hour, so some swam and some relaxed on the riverside. When they had worked hard I presented them with my own private soap. They lathered the foam on their hair, faces and bodies and themselves gaily jumped into the river. I was happy to see them enjoying themselves and felt I had done a good deed. Sometimes I gave them sugar which I got from a friend – a mess-kit full. I sent them back to the camp at 4 o'clock sharp. They waved to me saying, 'Thank you, thank you. Good-bye, tomorrow.'

As I treated them like this, they worked hard to match my kind intentions, resulting in a high efficiency. In reciprocating such friendship and working happily, they hoped to continue working at our depot, and the numbers sent to us were always exactly fifty, though at an early stage sometimes less than forty had come to us. Every morning when I went to meet them they were waiting for me and waving.

I worked with them as man to man, not as a enemy to enemy. The job was a pleasant one for me as I could do as I wanted with the PoWs, though I was a private from the reserves, who had often been scolded by my superiors for retaining an unmilitary civilian attitude. One of them who was good at painting gave me a postcard-size painting of Kanchanaburi as a token of their thanks. I sent this home as a picture postcard. It arrived safely. I still display it on my bookshelf as the only memento of that time.

After six months the battalion depot was moved to Wang Yai, as the construction front had advanced after breaking through the hard rocks to make the cuttings. I had to be parted from the familiar PoWs. I hoped that they had felt some of my samurai spirit (feudal warrior's code) through six months' contact.

At Wang Yai most of the work was done by local coolies and only two PoWs were assigned to us. The depot also acted as the liaison office of the battalion where many Japanese soldiers dropped in from time to time. Eventually the two PoWs got Japanese nicknames: George who was tall with glasses was called Taro, and Henry, who was short with a little moustache, Jiro. (Taro is the common name for the eldest son and Jiro for the second son in a Japanese family.)

The liaison office always kept four or five servings of meals until a certain hour, so that messengers who came unexpectedly could be fed. And when that time had passed Taro and Jiro could eat the leftover meals, and whatever they were not able to eat, they put in their mess kits, and took back to their camp to give to sick patients and to hungry friends. Sometimes they borrowed my container when their kits were full. They came to me without eating breakfast, so that their friends could get a little bit more. They stayed until late in the evening to take the leftover meals, while they helped me in loading supplies and taking stock. Taro was a tailor in London and had ably repaired the holes in my uniform. When I gave him some cloth which I had got from civilian friends as a token of thanks, he made trousers with it for himself and his friends in his spare time. At Kanchanaburi I had not given things individually to fifty men, but at Wangyai, with two men exclusively assigned to me, I was able to give them cigarettes, soap, loincloths and anything I could buy.

After three months at Wangyai the depot moved to Brankassi (208 km) where there were no PoWs and I worked only with local coolies.

I have vivid memories of George and Henry as they were regularly assigned to me. Their comments on our leader Katagiri and me are unforgettable. 'Leader Katagiri always good'; 'Private Saito sometimes very good, sometimes very bad.'

The personality of Sergeant Katagiri was good and amiable; he never scolded his men, and he went out to collect tools and materials, and was not in the depot very much. On the other hand, I was always at the depot and ordered them to work; I took good care of them but I thundered at them when they were idle or negligent. This scolding was the reason why they commented on me as being very bad, disregarding what was wrong with themselves. In this sense I felt the men from the 'country of gentlemen' and we Japanese were just the same, unfortunately.

Later I lived with the coolies exclusively assigned to me in the depot and treated them in the same way as I did the PoWs. I had human feelings towards the coolies and the PoWs who had to be commanded by superiors like me, more than I had towards Japanese officers and non-commissioned officers. I hope some of the PoWs still remember that there was a warm-hearted Japanese.

3.15   Korean guards

Army civilian employee Lee Han-ne, 3rd Section, 4th Branch, Thai PoW Accommodation HQ, Southern Army

I was born at Hojou village in Cholla-namdo, Korea, in 1925. I went to a primary school in the village where we Korean children were all forced to speak Japanese in school. If any one spoke his own language in school he had to stand at the back of the classroom as a punishment. After the annexation of Korea by Japan in 1910, extensive Japanisation measures were forced throughout Korea.

Japan entered the war in December 1941, and it was thought inevitable that Korean young men would be conscripted in the Japanese military service in the near future, as a volunteer system for the service had already been started. At that time the Japanese police in the village told me of the recruitment of guards for PoWs. The guards did not fight in the front line and it was safer than being a soldier, and the contract period of two years and the monthly salary of 50 yen were attractive, so I applied, and after an interview and a written test, I was accepted. The recruitment was really compulsory as the number of men from each area had been set by the Japanese government, and a failure to accept the recommendation by the powerful police could result in a decrease in the food allocation to my family, which would be critical.

From June 1942, about 3,223 Korean young men underwent strict military training at the temporary civilian training unit (the so-called Noguchi Butai) in Pusan. The training was the same as that for the infantry privates, including marching, rifle shooting and bayonet drill, and the most remarkable thing for us was that we were slapped on the cheek ('binta' in military slang) very often for even a minor error or misconduct. Sometimes everybody in the group was slapped for a mistake made by one person, or we had to stand in two lines facing each other and slap the comrade in front of us under strict supervision. These persistent practices implanted in us a feeling that the slapping was a common and acceptable form of penalty, and after being slapped the mistake would be forgiven.

We had no lessons on the culture, habits and food of the expected PoWs, which we thought necessary if we were to be the guards. We all signed an agreement that the military civilian's code would be strictly obeyed, and that orders from superiors would be carried out in all circumstances. In late September all of us, except a hundred men who remained in Korea, left Pusan in four separate groups, bound for Malaya, Java, Sumatra and Thailand. About a thousand men disembarked at Bangkok, and I was assigned to the 3rd section, 4th branch of the Thai PoW accommodation, which was then located at Bangkok. In February 1943 I and six other Korean guards were ordered to go to Hintok with about five hundred PoWs, as a sub-section of the 3rd section. The PoWs consisted of about two hundred each of British and Australians and about one hundred Dutch.

Hintok was deep in the jungle 100 kilometres from Kanchanaburi, on the planned route of the Burma–Thailand Railway. Seven of us had to organise the building of shacks for ourselves and the PoWs. We cut and pulled out big bamboo stems for the framework, which was a lot of work. The roofs were made of dried palm leaves but they leaked in the rain and the shacks were not good places to sleep in. The food was poor, consisting of low-quality rice, beans and dried or salted fish, and no vegetables were supplied at all. Even if vegetables had been forwarded to us they would have all rotted on the way in the tropical heat. We were told that meat and flour were not available in Thailand where the Japanese army procured its food.

The barracks of a platoon of the Japanese railway regiment, commanded by Lieutenant Eiji Hirota of the 9th Railway Regiment, were close to our PoW camp and we had to try to supply the numbers of men needed by them. However, due to the poor food and unsuitable living conditions, more and more PoWs got sick and it became impossible to send only healthy men for the work, and slightly sick men had to be pulled out and sent out for the work. We were ordered by the camp commander to supply as many workers as possible in accordance with the request of the railway regiment, as the construction of the railway for the Japanese army was urgent. The section commander, Lieutenant Usuki, was a spirited young officer who did not show any discrimination between the Japanese and the Koreans, and he had been the instructor of my group at Pusan. I was made the guard in charge of labour who had to plan the supply of workers to the railway unit. The railway commander, Lieutenant Hirota, came to me once and asked whether more PoWs could be sent for the railway construction work. I found it very difficult to fulfil the requirements for manpower in a reasonable manner.

Every evening the railway platoon sent over a messenger, telling us how many workers they needed the next day. If they needed 300 workers, and we had only 270 fit to work, what choice did we have? We had to send 30 men from the 'mildly ill' category off to the hard work. Whatever our feelings, they did not count.

Though the PoWs were handed over to the railway men at the gate of the camp, I escorted them to the worksites in order to prevent them from escaping and to encourage them to do their best while they were working under the supervision of the railway men.

Around June 1943, our commander told us that we had to comply with the request of the railway unit at all costs. As the railway unit was bound by a strict schedule to complete the railway by the set date, more men were needed, and this meant that we would have to send even sick men to work to comply with the request, as many PoWs were now sick. It was hard for me to tell sick men that they had to go to work. At the work site a daily quota system was operated. For example, those drilling holes in the hard rock had to bore a hole more than one metre deep with a hand chisel. It was hard labour, especially for the sick and weak men, but they had to work until the hole was completed, often working beyond the standard eight hours, and they came back to the camp really exhausted. Even so I still had to send such men to work on the following day.

As for the food which was essential to maintain the strength of the men, rice was supplied in sufficient quantity in the early stages, partly because they were not accustomed to eating rice. But when the monsoon season came, the quantity of food was reduced, as transportation by river boat was disturbed by the turbulence of the river.

There was little that we guards could do to help the PoWs. Our job was to keep watch on them, even though our numbers were too small even for carrying out the daily routines. There was a small camp shop run by a PoW but there was not much to sell. Greedy Chinese or Thai merchants came up by boat and sold fried bananas, noodles and other things at exorbitant prices. The PoWs could only buy a small bit of fried banana with their meagre pay. Though the PoWs were not allowed to contact outside persons, we tolerated their buying and sometimes helped them to get a better deal. Things could have been better if they had kept and carried personal items with them as far as Hintok, so that they could have exchanged these favourably for essential food, but most of the things had already been exchanged for luxury items, cigarettes or food on the way. I sometimes bought eggs with my salary and gave them to sick and weakened men, but that was too little to be of any help.

Because of the bad living conditions and the rain, infectious diseases spread among the weakened men, but there was no medicine available except for quinine tablets for malaria. All we could do was to let them rest under the care of a PoW doctor. Their situation was miserable, and many met with a tragic death.

In such a poor environment some of them tended to behave unreasonably, disobeying orders, dodging work, stealing supplies or quarrelling among themselves. As we, young men only seventeen years old, had to maintain good order among 500 men of mixed character, we had to slap the disorderly and ill-natured ones. As we did not speak English, it was not possible to call on them to reflect and amend their action with our limited vocabulary and sign language. It was inevitable that we should slap them, especially as we had been indoctrinated in our training in Pusan with the idea that slapping was a preferable instrument of education as well as a desirable method of instant punishment.

The PoWs were taller than us and were better built, so we looked on them with a kind of awe. There were only seven of us in the camp most of the time as against 500 PoWs, as our commander Usui and the NCO in charge of supplies came from the main camp to our place about once in two or three days and stayed only a few hours. So we were always afraid that we might lose control of these sturdy and numerous PoWs and that we might be overwhelmed by them, so the only way for us to control them was to attack and punish them quickly before they started a mass resistance. One morning at the assembly I saw a man was whistling and inattentive, so I warned him, but he went on whistling. As he did not obey my instructions I slapped him in the face, a bad habit we had got into during our training, but then not only he did not stop it but he assumed a hostile attitude. I realised that my slapping was not effective and regretted my conduct. Then two of my comrade guards recognised the situation, pulled him out of the line and beat him hard until he fell to the ground. They told me that we always had to make a PoW obey us instantly, whatever we did, so that he would never disobey. I could not disagree, as the seven guards were of the same rank as myself, and I was not in a position to stop their action.

From January 1944 I was transferred to the 4th branch camp for PoWs at Wang Yai (124 km). On June 1944, my term of two years was up but there was no mention of sending us back home. We were complaining about it among the guards, but we could not request our superiors for our discharge as we were told that one man who requested it had been beaten up badly by a Japanese staff sergeant. Probably to ease our complaints, some of us, including myself, were later promoted one rank from 'yonin' to 'koin', which meant that the position of my badge of rank was moved from the upper arm to the neck. Although we army civilian employees had a low opinion of ourselves as being even less highly regarded than carrier-pigeons, the promotion was a little bit of prestige to me in the army hierarchy.

3.16   The relationship between the Railway Regiment and the PoW camps

Kazuo Tamayama

On 20 June 1942, soon after the complete defeat of the Japanese navy at Midway, the Japanese imperial headquarters issued an order to build the Burma–Thailand Railway, and to employ about fifty thousand PoWs in its construction. It is important to note that the imperial headquarters, the highest Japanese military authority, ordered the use of PoWs for the project.

Accordingly, the Thailand PoW Accommodation (Camp) headquarters, a military administration organisation, was set up on 15 August, in order to house and feed the large number of PoWs at the work sites, and this became operational on 1 October 1942, as it took some time to train its new staff. On 16 August the Southern Army issued the order to start moving the PoWs from Singapore to the construction sites, and 3,000 PoWs arrived at Nong Pladuk, and 1,240 at Thanbyuzayat. These PoWs were temporarily put under the command of the railway regiments until 1 October, when they were transferred to the Thailand PoW Accommodation.

The Thailand PoW Accommodation had six branches, each with seven officers, 17 NCOs and about thirty clerical military employees, to administer six to eleven thousand PoWs, who were divided among many camps (sections and sub-sections) along the line. In addition to the above, about one thousand Korean guards were allocated to the branches, the numbers varying with their size. The Thailand PoW Accommodation had to do everything concerned with the living conditions of the PoWs, including building barracks, the procurement of food, clothing and supplies, and their transportation, with the support from the Southern Army headquarters.

The PoW camps (sections or sub-sections), mostly with 500 to 2,000 PoWs each, were organised as self-contained units. While they were supervised by Japanese commanders, the internal administration was carried out by the PoWs themselves. Sick persons were treated by PoW medical staff.

Labourers (coolies) for work on the railway were recruited from Malaya, Burma and Thailand on a voluntary basis for a short term of three months or less. Unlike the PoWs, they were directly under the supervision of the railway regiments, who were responsible for their accommodation as well as for most of their internal administration. Many men of the railway regiments were needed in employing the labourers, of whom the numbers actually at work did not exceed ten thousand at any time, as many of them escaped from the camps. So the PoWs were the major force in the construction work.

As shown in Illustration 3.16.1 the Thailand PoW Accommodation reported directly to the commander of the Southern Army. The 2nd Railway Command Group, responsible for the construction of the Railway, also reported to the commander. So these two organisations were independent of each other. The PoW Accommodation despatched PoWs to the construction work on a daily basis taking into account the requests of the railway units, who wanted as many men as possible to achieve their goal, while the Thailand PoW Accommodation tried to look after the well-being of the PoWs. The PoW Accommodation was responsible for feeding and clothing the PoWs even while they were working under the direction of the railway units. A few guards came to the work sites accompanying the PoWs to see that they did not escape.

Every morning, men from the work unit came to the PoW camp and received PoWs and took them to the work sites. They worked under the supervision of the working units (mostly railway platoons) and were returned to the camp by the set time. So the railway units borrowed PoWs under the conditions set by the camp. To take the example described in part 3, section 3, the commander of the 2nd branch, Lieutenant-Colonel Yanagida, issued a strong notice about the handling of PoWs to all work units, which included 'never beat the PoWs, and never make

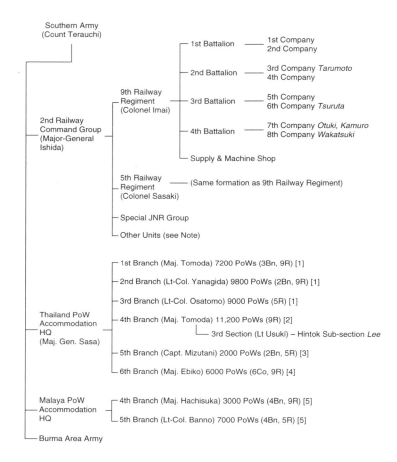

NOTE Approximate date of arrival at the line:
[1] October 1942 [2] November 1942 [3] February 1943 [4] April 1943 [5] May 1943

Other Units include: Imperial Guard Engineering Regiment, 54th Engineering Regiment,
41st Independent Infantry Battalion, two truck companies, 16th Patient Transport Unit,
four field hospitals and one base hospital

Illustration 3.16.1 Organisation of the Southern Army at the construction of the
Burma–Thailand Railway

them work beyond the set working time.' He even stopped supplying PoWs to a unit where men slapped them in disregard of the notice. As the work units explained the content of the notice to all the men (as described in part 3, section 2, p. 82), the notice was fairly well observed by the work units, though they were not happy with many of the restrictions in employing PoWs. But when the report of the unfortunate Featherston Incident was conveyed to the PoW camps in April 1943 (see part 3, section 19) the camps then allowed PoWs to work over the set time of eight hours. Japan had not ratified the Geneva Convention, but had been respecting its rules on the basis of reciprocity. However as it was clear that the Allied forces had killed Japanese prisoners against the rules at Featherstone, it was thought that some of the restrictions should be lifted as a reciprocal measure. Conceding to the strong requests from the railway regiments, who wanted to complete the day's allocation of work to PoWs whatever happened, the camps allowed overtime work for PoWs. The longer working hours, combined with the shortage of food and supplies, were extremely injurious to the health of the PoWs.

As has been described above, the Railway Regiments and the PoW camps belonged to separate organisations. So even an officer of a railway regiment could not give orders to an NCO of the PoW camp. The officer could only negotiate with the NCO when he wanted to employ PoWs in a different way. This relationship between the railway officers and the PoW camps was made clear, in the war-crimes court held at Singapore after the war, by Juji Tarumoto (see part 6, section 3) with the aid of his legal background and English ability. After his case no railway officers were sentenced to death, while a total of 33 men from the PoW camps were hanged, as the PoW camps were deemed responsible for most of the ill-treatment of PoWs. (From the railway regiments, Captain Eiji Hirota whose regiment was responsible for forcing weak, underfed PoWs each to drive a hole of 1.2 metres deep in rock, was the only one hanged.)

Most of the food and supplies for the PoW camps were carried in boats on the river. However at the peak of the monsoon season, the river was flooded with many floating tree stems, which made the passage of boats very difficult. And when the construction went deep into the mountains, food had to be carried quite a long distance by land, since roads in the rainy season were too muddy to allow lorries to go through. Even under such adverse conditions the PoW Accommodation was responsible for feeding the PoWs.

At the same time the railway regiments were responsible for forcing the weak and sick underfed PoWs to complete the daily quota of earth-moving allocated to the normal healthy prisoners. The quota for the prisoners, from 1.1 to 3 cubic metres per man, was less than that for Japanese soldiers, which was 4 to 5 cubic metres.

The Japanese thought it reasonable to give the PoWs the same amount of food as the Japanese soldiers, which was mostly rice. However the rice was not liked by the PoWs, yet bread was not available for them as the wheat needed to make bread was not available in Southeast Asia. As for meat, the Southern Army authorised an allotment of 150 grams of beef a day per PoW, and the purchase of oxen was begun in Thailand. However, after about one thousand oxen had been bought, the Thai government strongly objected to the purchase, as oxen were used for agricultural cultivation purposes only; with no beef cattle, the decrease in oxen would be detrimental to the agricultural production of the country. So the Japanese had to discontinue the buying of oxen, and the PoWs were given beef for only a few weeks in the early stages.

As it was not possible to get supplies from other countries, with sea transport disrupted by the efficient American submarines, the PoW Accommodation had to feed the PoWs with what they could get locally, which was mainly rice and small dried fish. Their food situation was the same as that of the soldiers of the railway regiments.

3.17 View of the PoWs

The hard times that the PoWs went through during the construction of the Burma–Thailand Railway is well described in the books they wrote which are listed below:

In the library of the National Army Museum (Royal Hospital Road, London):

1. Blair, Clay, *Return from the River Kwai* (Macdonald, London, 1979)
2. Chalker, Jack, and Leo Cooper, *Burma Railway Artist: the War Drawings of Jack Chalker* (private publication, Barnsley, 1994)
3. Coast, John, *Railway of Death* (Commodore Press, London, 1946)
4. Dunlop, E. E., *War Diaries of Weary Dunlop* (Nelson, Melbourne, 1986)
5. Franz, Harry, *Bamboo Treadmill* (private publication, Wootton, 1999)
6. Kershaw, G. F., *Track of Death: Burma–Siam Railroad* (Book Guild, Lewes, Sussex, 1992)
7. McCowran, Tom, *Beyond the Bamboo Screen: Scottish Prisoners of War under the Japanese* (Cualann Press, Dunfermline, 1999)
8. Parkin, Ray, *Into the Smother: a Journal of the Burma–Siam Railway* (Hogarth Press, London, 1963)

9. Peacock, Basil, and Cedric Chivers, *Prisoner on the Kwai* (Blackwood, London, 1966)
10. Shuttle, Jack, *Destination Kwai* (Tucann Books, Lincoln, 1994)
11. Watford, Van, *Prisoners of the Japanese in World War II* (McFarland, 1970)
12. Wood Higgs, Stanley, *Bamboo and Barbed Wire* (Roman Press, Bournemouth, 1988)

Other titles:

13. Lomax, Eric, *Railway Man* (Jonathan Cape, London, 1995). This book received the 1995 Waterstones/Esquire Non-Fiction Award and the J. R. Ackerley Prize.
14. Elliott, Alan, *In the Shadow of the Bridge* (An Grian'an, Daven Calais, 1995)
15. Boyle, James, *Railroad to Burma* (London: Allen & Unwin, 1990)
16. Goodman, Arthur, *The Will to Survive* (Spellmount, Staplehurst, 2002)
17. Thompson, Claude, *Into the Sun* (private publication, Warkworth, New Zealand, 1996)
    [Claude Thompson was a New Zealander who worked on the Trans-Sumatra Railway.]
18. Power, F.W.G, *Kurrah* (private publication, Victoria, Australia, 1991)

3.18 Extract from *History of 'F' Force*

by Lt-Col. S. W. Harris OBE, RA (Commanding 18 Division P.W Area, Changi)

Shortage of stores

In No. 3 Camp (400 Australians), which was small and compact, close to its water supply with a cookhouse near the sleeping quarters, this lack of containers was a serious inconvenience. In Nos 2 (1,600 British) and 5 (700 British) Camps it was a disaster. The former had a cookhouse a quarter of a mile from the camp, and as the sick figure rose there was no efficient means of carrying food thence 800 yards to the main hospital and to the isolation hospital yet another 400 yards. Through the never-ending rain parts of meals were ferried day by parties of officers and convalescents in the few buckets and containers available. No containers would be spared for use in the hospital for boiling water for sterilisation of utensils anywhere in camp, thus further ensuring the spread of disease.

In No. 5 Camp the special difficulty was not the distance from the cookhouse but the fact that water had to be carried from one well over a long and bad patch to the hospital cookhouse and the camp – the results being much the same as in No. 2 Camp. Sufficient containers were never issued by the I.J.A. (Imperial Japanese Army) even up to the end. There were few available in the 'F' Force I.J.A. stores, and, in spite of pressure from our side, no attempt was made to obtain them from the Engineers, who had plenty. One hundred ordinary buckets would have eliminated most of our serious difficulties in this regard.

As regards tools, a few were carried by each marching party but, as in the case of containers, the later trains were denuded of those at staging camps. The I.J.A. brought up practically no tools for 'F' Force, which greatly hampered improvement work in camp. In some camps it eventually became possible to borrow some tools from the Engineers, but then the process was so hedged with restrictions, that it lost a great deal of its potential value – until late September, by which time the damage had been done.

Interpreters

Two of the four prisoner interpreters with the force were arbitrarily retained by N.C.O.s of the I.J.A. organisation controlling the march at unimportant staging camps, and their services were lost to the force until it re-assembled in Kanburi [abbreviation of Kanchanaburi] in December.

Working parties

In all camps the I.J.A. Engineers demanded maximum numbers to work. The I.J.A. prisoners administration adopted as a principle the calculation of figures as follows:

Other Ranks

A = Hospital Patients
    Hospital Staff
    Camp Duties
    Total A

B = Total Camp strength
B minus A = figures ordered for outside work.

This did not allow for any sick in lines or convalescent. They had therefore to be kept in hospital if they were not to go out to work. The keeping of these men in hospital produced a delicate position; for the I.J.A. would not recognise debility, weakness, malaria, beri-beri and trench feet, as being incapacitating diseases.

It became our task therefore on the one side to struggle to obtain agreement to the lowest possible figure and, on the other, to select men best able to stand a day's work to go out from the convalescents and 'lines sick'.

The duties allowed in camp, apart from a small office, comprised men for cremation or burial sanitation, cookhouse, wood-collecting and cutting. As those were essentially jobs which required a particular aptitude and a considerable proficiency combined with health and strength (especially in view of the minimum numbers allowed) in no camp was it found possible to organise any system of a day-to-day changeover to relieve men going out to work every day. As a result, men working outside worked on day after day until they fell sick and went to hospital. As already described, there was continual selection from convalescents to replace those going sick. As a result, there was no half-way; in effect a man was ill in bed or out at work, and the deterioration in health was rapid, general and very quickly complete.

In camp also, multifarious duties had to be performed both for the I.J.A. and for ourselves. Ration drawing, path making, road construction in camp, latrine digging, fence making, draining, continual building for the I.J.A., but repairing (the huts were rotten and constantly collapsing), double-bunking, basket making, collecting firewood for I.J.A. cookhouse and guardroom, and many casual tasks. All these had perforce to be done by convalescents and by malaria patients on their better days, thus retarding and indeed often preventing recovery.

The situation would have been desperate enough even if the outside work had been a fair day's work, but the inhuman slave-driving to which the outside working men were continually subjected made the situation hopeless.

Outside work for I.J.A. engineers

The working day started with reveille and breakfast in darkness at about 0600–0700 hrs. Movement to and from meals and for purposes of nature were all in pouring rain about the muddy, ill-sited camp. Breakfast consisted of 3/4 pint of plain rice. Parade for work was at first light and then the I.J.A. Engineers took over. If the numbers were not up to demand there was a scene on parade, sometimes ending with the striking of officers in charge. The daily task of selecting the last few men to go out from a number of convalescents really all unfit to go was heartbreaking; and a tremendous strain on those to whose lot it fell.

The party would be marched off to draw tools and then to the scene of work. This often entailed a considerable march of 5–10 km. Many men (in June up to 80%) were without usable boots. Marching was always through deep mud with many snags in the way of rocks and sharp bamboo roots. Without boots it was difficult for men to keep their feet in many places.

The work itself was mostly very heavy – beyond the strength of an average fully fit man and far beyond the capacity of our starved and debilitated men. Particularly severe was the portaging of logs from the mountainside to the roadway and the pile-driving and tree hauling for the big bridge at Sonkrai, which often entailed working in swift cold water up to the waist, sometimes even to the armpits. Obviously obeying instructions from their officers, the Engineer other ranks in charge of parties drove the prisoners savagely with blows from fists, boots, sticks and wire whips.

Protests by our officers out on the work site often resulted in their being hit too. Visible resentment or objection were treated as mutinous and savagely punished.

It is necessary to emphasise that most of this continual beating was not disciplinary but was used to drive men as beasts to efforts beyond their strength.

All the time rain poured down, making conditions more unpleasant and work more difficult, On some tasks men were often kept actively working (i.e. continually plying shovels, adzes, axes etc) for three hours at a stretch without a second's break. A short interval, sometimes only a few minutes, was allowed for the midday meal – a pint of rice with a few beans.

Work continued until long after dark and then tools were collected and the march back began – a nightmare performance in the mud, rain and darkness. Tools had to be checked in and this was frequently made an excuse for further harsh treatment and delay. With the best will in the world it was very difficult to collect or check tools in the darkness at the scene or work where small parties were distributed over a large jungle area.

At last the party would arrive back in camp at 2200 hrs or even later, tired, worn out and dispirited. Numbers had again to be checked before they were dismissed to eat their evening meal (1 pint of rice and usually 1/2 pint of some form of vegetable stew) and turn in to their sleeping quarters – 2 ft by 6 ft or less per man – to get what sleep they could before the next day's agony started.

Those who were sick had to be examined by firelight. With these working conditions, starvation diet and with cholera, dysentery, diarrhoea, malaria, beri-beri, tropical ulcers and trench feet rife, it was not long (by the end of June) before the total number of men working outside camps from the whole force (originally 7000 strong) was 700 men.

In May, railway construction was several months behind schedule and the orders from Tokyo for its speedy finish entailed working through the monsoon, mid-May to mid-September. By 20 May the road south of Shimo-Nieke had ceased to be practicable for motor transport or bullock carts and there was no hope of re-establishing it for use.

In order to maintain a railway labour force of PWs and coolies in 'F' Force area it was therefore essential to keep open the road thence northwards into Burma. In May this road was merely a track cleared through the jungle. Through lack of foresight no steps had been taken to weatherproof it before the monsoon broke.

3.19   The Featherston Incident and its effect on PoWs

Kazuo Tamayama

During the war in the Pacific, the Americans gained an important foothold at Guadalcanal in early August 1942, and captured a large number of Japanese PoWs. On 11 September, 450 of them arrived in New Zealand at short notice and were accommodated in an old army training ground at Featherston, which was 60 kilometres north of Wellington, the capital of New Zealand. Featherston was the first PoW camp in the British Empire to hold Japanese PoWs.

The first intake of prisoners was largely non-military – Japanese labour forces engaged in building the airfield in Guadalcanal. Japanese military personnel began arriving in significant numbers in November 1942, including many men from the Japanese cruiser *Furutaka*, which was sunk near Guadalcanal. By mid-February 1943, more than eight hundred PoWs were under confinement, including 248 military PoWs who were in compound no. 2. Many of the military men were in extremely poor health. Some had hidden in caves for days without food before being captured by the Americans. Naval men were adrift for days on rafts at sea. At first, only a few men were required to work because of their poor state of health. But when their health improved, and Lieutenant-Colonel Donald H. Donaldson, who was a career Army officer in the English military tradition, arrived as the camp's commanding officer, more demands were made on PoWs. On 24 February the commander requested 105 men from compound 2 to join work parties the following day, whereas only 45 men had been working up to then. But next morning, 25 February, the Japanese PoWs refused to provide work parties and sought a meeting with Donaldson on the matter. The camp adjutant, Lieutenant James Malcolm, tried in vain to persuade the PoWs, and increased the armed guard to 47 men who took up positions at ground level and on hut roofs, virtually encircling the PoWs at close range. He wanted to capture the PoW spokesman, Lieutenant Adachi, as the man responsible for the disobedience. But the PoWs surrounded him tightly and the guards were not able to remove him. Tension mounted among the guards, who had their arms at the ready. The adjutant took out his pistol, aimed at Lt Adachi and told him to come out. But Adachi bluntly refused. Incensed, the adjutant fired a shot at him which only grazed his upper arm, so he fired a second shot which caused him to fall. Hearing the second shot the guards started shooting the PoWs who were seated close together in a quadrangular area. Many PoWs fell, until the senior NCO cried 'Stop shooting!' In less than a half minute, 31 Japanese were dead and 91 injured. Seventeen of these died later. Also one New Zealand guard died from a ricochet wound, and nine were wounded.[1]

The armed guards had been told to start shooting when the commander fired two shots. However, the adjutant in command forgot this, furious at having missed the first shot, and fired the second trying to hit Adachi. The Japanese did not do any rioting; they were just on a 'sit-down strike', but they were shot like sitting ducks while only a few were able to escape into nearby huts.[2]

Ambulances summoned from as far away as Wellington carried the seriously wounded to hospitals. Then wild stories spread in the area that Japanese prisoners had staged a breakout from the camp and some had escaped into the Tararua Range.

In the mid-afternoon the news was sent to the two men in charge of surveillance of the camp's operations, one representing Japanese interests and the other the International Committee of the Red Cross (ICRC) in Geneva. They were, respectively, Dr Walter Schmid, the Swiss consul-general in Wellington, and Dr Leon Bossard, a Swiss-born scientist involved in oil exploration in New Zealand. The two men went to Featherston immediately. Dr Bossard cabled an authentic outline of the incident to the ICRC in Geneva before any public announcement was made by the New Zealand government.[3] Also Dr Schmid cabled full details of the incident and of the 48 men killed to the Swiss legation in London. These reports were forwarded to Japan by the ICRC.

The New Zealand prime minister sent the news by top-secret cable to the United Kingdom government's Secretary of State for Dominion Affairs in London,[4] who responded swiftly, saying that

> It is essential in our opinion that this affair should be treated as normally as possible: anything at this stage which gives the impression that the authorities concerned feel they were at fault would be 'fatal' and setting up of an ad hoc civil tribunal would only suggest to the enemy that something abnormal had happened and that New Zealand Government have a guilty conscience.[5]

Based on this, the first statement to the public was made on 1 March, to the effect that the Japanese prisoners armed with stones, tools and other improvised weapons had rushed and attacked the guards, and it had been necessary to quell the riot and restore order. Thus the New Zealand government thought that they could cover up the facts by blaming the PoWs on the grounds of a faked riot, despite the fact that the reports placing the blame on the deliberate shooting by the guards had been forwarded to Japan by the two sources.

The first official reaction of the Japanese government to the incident, which reached Wellington via Whitehall on 16 March 1943, termed the shooting 'an unpardonable violation of humanity' and stated: 'The guards made no effort to avoid a serious consequence but wantonly opened fire on a trifling cause or pretext.'[6] The Japanese propaganda broadcast maintained that the prisoners had been fired on deliberately and that 'If the enemy resorts to barbarous action, Japan is prepared to retaliate.'[7]

The New Zealand government's replies to the Japanese reaction, after consultation with Whitehall, stressed that the provisions of the Geneva PoW Convention were being scrupulously observed, and the camp official would not be punished.[8] The Japanese government regarded Britain and New Zealand as one, and this obstinate attitude on the part of the governments in not admitting the facts had an unfortunate effect on all the PoWs in the hands of the Japanese. As the Japanese PoWs had been killed by the careless order of the officer in charge, the Japanese government got the impression that the Allied forces thought nothing of killing PoWs, and were disregarding the Geneva Convention.

Disappointed and angered by the British attitude, the Japanese Prisoner of War Control Bureau in Tokyo sent the details of the killing at Featherston to all Japanese PoW camps and brought the news to the notice of Allied PoWs in camps.[9] The Japanese camp staff read between the lines of the notice, and decided that, as the allied forces were not adhering to the Geneva Convention, they need no longer be bound by the spirit of the Convention, though, in January 1942, the Japanese had told the allies that she would respect the rules on the basis of reciprocity. Japan had signed the Prisoners of War Convention of 1929 but had never ratified it.

The British, Australian and Dutch PoWs were engaged in the construction of the Burma–Thailand Railway from the autumn of 1942. At the initial stage of construction, the Japanese PoW camp commander prepared detailed instructions on how to treat PoWs, and issued them to all railway and other units employing PoWs in their work. (See part 3, sections 2 and 3.) Accordingly the officers in the railway regiment ordered their men to follow the instructions. The PoW camp was strict in enforcing the instructions on the work units, and once refused to supply PoWs to a unit which had made PoWs work over the limited time. Under these circumstances the railway soldiers seldom reprimanded the PoWs, in contrast to the Korean guards at the PoW camps.

This attitude on the part of those at the PoW camps, who had been trying to live up to the spirit of the Convention, changed drastically after they received the official notice of the Featherston incident. They lifted the restrictions for overtime work. So the PoWs had to work long hours until the designated work was completed even during the worst conditions of the railway construction. And the PoWs' complaints citing the rules of the Convention, were turned down without any discussion, saying 'Do you know what your country did to our prisoners?'

The New Zealand government feared that severe reprisals might be taken by the Japanese on the prisoners in Japanese hands. (There were only 112 New Zealander PoWs captured by Japanese.) But the incident had a much wider effect on all British, Australian, Dutch and American prisoners.[10]

Notes

1. Owen Sanders, *Incident at Featherston* (Heinemann, New Zealand, 1996) p. 18; Mike Nicolaide, *The Featherston Chronicles – A Legacy of War* (HarperCollins, New Zealand, 1999).
2. Testimony of Lieutenant Adachi (*Bungei Shinju*, Tokyo, March 1963).
3. FO916/791, KW66/4–14, UK Public Record Office.
4. FO916/791, KW66/4–1, Public Record Office. This cable starts 'Regret having to report unfortunate happening....'
5. FO916/791, KW66/4–4, Public Record Office, also AD 1310/11/3 vol.1 (National Archives Head Office, Wellington, NZ); Cable: UK Secretary of State for Dominion Affairs to NZ Prime Minister. Though New Zealand became independent in 1925, it was usual for the government to get the advice of the UK Secretary of State on important matters. The US government was informed the same day, via the New Zealand Minister in Washington.
6. FO916/791, KW66/4–28, Public Record Office.
7. FO916/791, KW66/4 Report from Government of India, re-broadcast from Singapore on 4 March, to Tokyo on 5 March, to Batavia on 6 March.
8. FO916/791, KW66/4–29, Public Record Office.
9. Claude Thompson RNZHF, *Scars on the Heart* (David Batemen, New Zealand, 1996), p. 264. At the Jaarmarkt camp in Java, for example, a notice was posted stating that the New Zealand prime minister had announced that there had been 111 casualties, of whom 48 were killed by machine-gun fire, due to the prisoners disobeying of orders in a prisoner-of-war camp in New Zealand. If satisfactory explanations were not forthcoming, reprisals would be taken.
10. All the PoWs in the Featherston camp had been captured by the American forces. So the USA should also be responsible for the handling of men they captured.

Part 4   Struggle at the Myitkyina Line

4.1 Myitkyina Line

Captain Saburo Hasegawa, 3rd Battalion, 5th Railway Regiment

I was transferred to the command of 3rd Battalion from regimental adjutant, and arrived at Kotanpo on 17 February 1944. Four battalions of 5th Railway Regiment were spread along 586 kilometres of the Myitkyina line after finishing the construction of the Burma–Thailand Railway. My 3rd Battalion was responsible for the section from Kanbalu to Naba.

As our airforce located at Shwebo airfield had been badly damaged by the large-scale bombardment of British planes in mid-January, the railway was very often attacked by the British planes. Three days after I arrived at my new post, no. 171 bridge, which was 100 metres long, located around the middle of Shwebo and Kanbalu, was bombed and its girder was knocked down. It was in the territory of the 1st Battalion, but they were very busy repairing damage at Sagaing. So we decided that we should repair it. As I went there with major part of 5th Company, there were two unexploded bombs under the bridge stuck in a waterless sandy beach.

I told the soldiers to go far away, and dug sand around the bombs quietly. To my surprise one was a Japanese bomb marked 'type 95, 200 kilograms' in Japanese. The enemy seemed to have some supply shortage and used a captured bomb, or it might have been dropped by a Japanese plane in their advance in 1942.

A soldier who had experience in assembling bombs was able to take off the detonator fuse of the Japanese one but not the British one. If we kept it there it might explode and cause bigger damage at the next bombardment. As I was discussing with the company commander what to do with the bomb, Platoon Leader Kanno and ten men came with a long log and rope and told me that they would move the bomb to a safer place. I said, 'I cannot allow it. What happens if the bomb explodes on the way? It's too dangerous.' But the company commander wanted to move the bomb right now.

While we were arguing, more than ten British planes were seen in the western sky. I thought the situation was getting worse. The platoon leader said, 'If we do not act now, all of us and the bridge will be blown up. So I will do it now.' And he started to put the rope around the bomb. So I said, 'OK, do it!'

They hung the bomb by the rope under the crossed log, told us to keep off and carefully started to walk calling, 'One, two, one, two.' It was a dangerous job and a soldier joked that 'You must keep far away from us so that you can hold our funeral ceremony'.

We dug a deep hole in the middle of the river and laid the bomb by it, and then we dropped the bomb into the hole with a rope pulled from a trench 100 metres away. The bomb slid deep down into the hole but did not explode. Everybody cheered 'Banzai!'.

The plane we saw did not come around to us and we completed the repair of the bridge by evening of the next day. I returned to the billet of the command unit of 5th Company located at one kilometre north of Teyapin station.

Next morning I was walking with Company Commander Watanabe and a survey team to decide on a diversion for bridge No. 225. As the bridge was often bombed, it was essential to build an additional bridge in case the original one was destroyed in order to keep the trains moving. We heard an air-raid warning and hid ourselves in the nearby jungle. Two B25 planes came and dropped bombs near the bridge and then swept around with machine-guns and also shot shells (or bombs) at the bridge which exploded on the river beach blowing up sand smoke. Fortunately none of them hit the bridge, to our relief. But their machine-guns sprayed shot all around indiscriminately trying to kill us. As sometimes the bullets hit the ground just in front of me, I was afraid that I might be shot any time, and, though the air attack lasted only for thirty minutes, I felt as if I was continuously attacked for half a day.

After the approximate route was decided, I went back to the barracks and ate a late lunch, during which a telephone from Kotanpo station warned of the approach of a group of planes. Within five minutes a B25 plane came circling above us at an altitude of 300 metres, aiming at wagons at Teyabin station. As I watched with my binoculars, the plane came from the north at the third attack at a low altitude of 100 metres spraying machine-gun shells.

As I heard ten or so shots from the station air-raid shelter, the plane changed direction towards the west and went behind trees, and soon a big explosion was heard. As I was wondering what had happened, the telephone rang from the station.

'We shot down the enemy plane, at two kilometres west. Please send men there immediately.'

The company commander went with an armed platoon and an ox-cart, and asked me to come with them. It took about an hour to get there as it was in a dense teak forest with a lot of undergrowth. The plane had mowed down big trees and lost its wings while gliding in the forest, and the engines had sunk into the ground. The crew were scattered on the ground half burnt, and one was hanging down from a high tree on a parachute.

A mob of about thirty Burmese were already around the plane and were rummaging in the debris. I posted a cordon and kept off the Burmese. The five crew on the ground were all dead. I thought the one in the tree might be alive and ordered the village headman to ask someone to climb up the tree and cut the rope. But he told me that this man had been killed by his shotgun. I asked him why, and he answered that as the plane machine-gunned the village heavily they had had to kill him as revenge. So we lost a chance to interrogate him.

As we were searching the debris one lady's sandal was found. I thought probably one of the crew must have carried his girlfriend's shoe just for fun. But a Burmese came to us saying that a little distance from there was an English woman. She was a white, blonde sergeant shot through the head. We carefully buried her under Buddhist rites with deep sympathy of railway soldiers for the patriotic lady.

Out of thirteen 13-mm machine-guns on the plane, five were in good condition and seemed usable. I sent these to the regimental workshop asking for them to be modified for ground use. About ten days later three guns were returned to us, together with tripods. These became our useful anti-aircraft weapons as we had collected 500 bullets from the plane.

As we found out from the downed plane, the underneath of the pilot seat was protected by a steel sheet, which could not be penetrated by rifle bullets. But as the plane came very low it was shot at from our shelter almost horizontally and one bullet must have hit the pilot who opened the windshield to look down. This must be the only case that a medium bomber was shot down by 18 rifle bullets.

4.2 Fight with Chindits at Mawlu (White City)

Lieutenant Bun-ichiro Asazuma, 6th Company, 3rd Battalion, 5th Railway Regiment

On 5 March 1944, I was watching the sky from the roundabout bridge over the Meza river, which we were building during the night. I saw a kind of train in the sky pulled by a big plane with a blinking green light flying successively from the direction of India to China. I thought they might be sending supplies or reinforcements to China.

A big group of the same planes flew in the following night. On the morning of the 7th, two soldiers who went to Katha to recruit local labourers came back urgently. They reported that many planes without propellers landed on the sand beach of the River Irrawaddy, south of Katha, and sometimes fighter planes took off from there. According to the locals many Englishmen came and went in the mountains. They waited until the few remaining British had gone and then burnt the planes and baggage, helped by Burmese locals.

This was an emergency situation. The men working on repairing the bridge were recalled, and defensive positions were built around the station and the bridge. As it was the tradition of 5th Railway Regiment to fight while learning, I carried out fighting drill for all the men in the company. Though we sent out many scouts and spies in all directions, no information was obtained about the whereabouts of the enemy. However more enemy planes flew even in the night, and we saw many red and green signal flares shoot up from the ground. Also they dropped many incendiary bombs along the railway to burn the cut wood for locomotives, so the fire spread easily to the forests at the end of the dry season, causing wild animals to run around, and we could do nothing about it. On the 9th, the station building and empty wagons at Ponchan station, south of Meza, were blasted and the enemy fought with a unit passing by there, but no railway soldiers were injured as no man was stationed there. After that the enemy attacked only stations to which no men were attached, or unguarded bridges.

A scout led by Warrant Officer Murakami found ten or so enemy bathing in a small stream at Katha branch and captured one American soldier He was a 19-year-old glider pilot recruited from the University of Michigan. From his story we knew that the propellerless plane was a glider capable of carrying 20 armed men and more than a thousand soldiers had been flown in.

On 13 March we received a report from the 1st Company at Naba that about three hundred men of the air-lifted enemy came north-east of Naba and blasted bridge no. 535 north of Naba station, and they were concentrating on the nearby hill. Their purpose seemed to be the obstruction of railway transport.

Our regimental commander came and had an operation meeting at Meza in the morning of 15 March. Though it was common sense that the enemy should be attacked before they settled down, 15 Army gave us no information about sending forces to attack them. So it was inevitable that the regiment would attack the enemy in order to perform the duty of transporting troops and materials for the on-going Imphal operation, though we had no instruction from the Army. However the regiment was fully stretched over the length of 750 kilometres (which in itself was an over-capacity as the standard coverage for a regiment was 400 kilometres) and the supply had to be kept moving to 15 and 31 Divisions. It was decided that a major part of the 6th Company and a platoon of the 1st Company were all that could be spared from the on-going jobs. Captain Hasegawa, commander of the 3rd Battalion, requested the command of the attacking group but this was not granted as he had been injured ten days previously and was not able to run.

The attacking group commanded by the Colonel left Naba by a light train led by a motor-car in the morning of 17 March and arrived two kilometres south of Mawlu station. As the advance scouts found beehive-like positions on the hill two kilometres north-west of Mawlu station, and as fighter planes were taking off from behind the position, the commander decided to attack the positions soon after sunset, and all of us hid in the jungle. The fighter planes circled over us and tried to shoot us.

Soon after noon, a bloodstained messenger came from an infantry platoon (led by Second Lieutenant Kiyomizu of the 2nd battalion of 51st Infantry Regiment), with this message: 'As we were advancing without knowing the situation, we were attacked by an enemy from the hill north of the station. But the enemy is strong and persistent, and we suffered high casualties and are not able to accommodate our injured men. Please help us!'

The commander decided to attack the enemy to help our infantry in a critical situation. The group spread out north of the station – my 6th Company on the east advanced by creeping towards the enemy positions and Sato platoon of the 1st Company went along the railway. The enemy fighters' repeated attacks, and concentrated fire from three ranks of machine-guns and mortars made it difficult for us to advance.

We stayed this side of Henu River and concealed ourselves by lying in dead ground or in tall grass.

As we found gaps in their shooting range, we renewed our advance skilfully. When we reached 100 metres in front of the first line position, the commander ordered us to charge. At that moment a mortar shell exploded behind him, its splinter cut through his helmet and he fell down unconscious. As his messenger came to help him and called his name, his senses came back. He bandaged the wound with the help of the messenger and continued the advance. Toyota platoon circled half of the enemy position from the left, and the enemy retreated to the second line position. While the platoon threw hand grenades and rushed into the second line position, an enemy grenade exploded near the platoon leader who died bravely.

Ito platoon who went in the centre was not able to advance as the front of the second line was a sharp cliff, so they moved to the right and charged into the position together with Abe platoon and the infantry platoon. Owing to our concentrated attack the enemy retreated, and we circled the position on the hilltop. Meanwhile the infantry rescued their injured men and we took care of theirs and our own. In a short break in the fighting I gave the order to eat our biscuit ration. Our men also gave biscuits to the infantry men who said that they were refreshed by the biscuit which tasted especially good.

The enemy started to attack us at 16:30 while their fighters strafed us. In the severe fighting more men were injured. As we had almost used up the ammunition and it was difficult to continue fighting, the commander ordered us to retreat at 17:00. It was fortunate that we could disengage as the enemy did not pursue us, staying in their positions. We retreated along the railway and gradually gathered at a village east of Mawlu station. After sunset at 18:30 the train pulled by a steam locomotive commanded by Lieutenant Harada bravely came to Mawlu, which was close to the enemy, and took us and the dead back to Naba, where the heavily wounded men were put in Naba base hospital and other injured were taken care of.

In the early morning of 18 March, my company returned to Meza by a light train. We lined up and I reported to Battalion Commander Captain Hasegawa: 'Among one hundred men including company commander, fourteen men were killed including Platoon Leader Toyota. Forty-one men were hospitalised at Naba. So forty-five men have arrived back here. It was my great regret that so many men were killed.'

While I was reporting several men fell down from extreme fatigue. The commander just said, 'It was a great work you have accomplished,' and ordered us to get medical care and to rest. After the soldiers were dismissed, I went with the battalion commander to the temple in the village where the bodies of our men were provisionally enshrined and prayed a requiem in front of them. Then I felt severe pain, and blood came out of my shoulder. As the medical officer was busy taking care of the many injured, the commander took off my bandage and found two pieces of splinters stuck in my shoulder. He took off the splinters with a knife and pincette, which he had sterilised himself, and put on a temporary bandage with germicide. Then in distress I reported to him the detail of the battle. He told me with tears in his eyes, 'Don't be discouraged. It is inevitable to lose many men in the battle. As the damage of the railway is great due to the attack of the enemy airborne troop, you should work hard to restore the railway encouraging your men.' He might have been worried that I might commit suicide, with the heavy responsibility for the loss of many men of my company. To me the fact that 14 men were killed and only 45 out of 100 had returned, while most of the 45 men were somehow injured, was a sad and shocking experience, and more miserable as we could not achieve our objective of destroying the enemy.

The regimental commander, who was heavily bandaged around the head, stopped at Meza on his return from Naba by a light train. The battalion commander and I reported to him the status of the injured men, and asked for an additional supply of machine guns and bullets, and a cannon to destroy the fortified (with concrete) position of the enemy.

Hearing of our failure to capture Mawlu, Army headquarters sent two infantry companies commanded by Lt-Colonel Nagahashi. But as three weeks had passed since the enemy came to Mawlu, their positions had been reinforced to become a semi-permanent stronghold. The two companies were badly damaged and retreated while the commander was seriously injured. The Army then sent a mixed brigade composed of four infantry battalions and two field-gun companies commanded by Major-General Hayashi. But as most of them had to come from the Moulmein area, 1,200 kilometres to the south, it took a long time for them to arrive despite the hard work of the railway units, for the railway had been broken to pieces by the superior British airforce. The headquarters first arrived on 25 March and all the brigade gathered by 3 April. They attacked using the field guns on 6 April but could make only little progress. A night attack on 9 April did not go well, with the loss of 60 men. The final attack starting on the night of 14 April lasted for three days but the brigade could take none of the enemy strongholds. As about a third of their men were lost and a part of the enemy came out of the position and attacked our rear, Commander Hayashi decided to retreat, and the brigade left the area quietly by 18 April, though their object had not been achieved.

The departure of the mixed brigade put us in a very difficult situation, as the enemy could advance from their position freely. Our railway regiment had to cope with the enemy with our limited force only. Enemy air-raids were stepped up on the bridges and rails. Though we tried hard to repair them, they were often destroyed again within three days or so. To cope with this situation the railway group commander moved the Akabori battalion of 7th Railway Regiment to our area to repair the destruction caused by enemy aircraft. So with our 1st, 3rd, 4th, 5th and 6th Companies, seven companies, a total of 1,500 men, gathered around south of Noba, I told our men that it was good that the enemy came out of their position, so that we could fight on equal terms or better with the co-operation of local people. We had organised an extensive information-gathering system based on the experience of the war in China, in order to cope with the guerrilla movements of the enemy. We had asked the village headman of the surrounding area to report any movements of the British troops as soon as they were seen, and some incentives were distributed in advance. This was augmented by a close network of spies and sentries.

At 08:00 on 18 April, information was sent to me that many enemy soldiers were walking on both sides of the railway one kilometre south of Naba station. With a few men and a medium machine-gun, I hurried to the edge of the hill, and we shot them up from a distance of 300 metres. The enemy was surprised and ran into the jungle chaotically carrying their wounded. The machine-gun was a water-cooled one which we had captured in Singapore.

4.3 The battle near Ponchan

Lieutenant Shigehiro Asakura, 4th Company, 2nd Battalion, 5th Railway Regiment

Around noon on 14 April 1944, we heard a big thunder-like explosion to the south. The bridge near Ponchan station, which the 6th Company had repaired a few days ago, had been blown up. The 4th Company, who were moving north on a light train, attacked the enemy who were in position to the east of the unmanned station. The enemy resisted strongly until the next day when our two platoons charged into them, and they then retreated into the jungle to the west. In the battle

19 men were killed including a platoon leader who led the charge bran-
dishing his Japanese sword.

Our 3rd Company and the other part of the 2nd Battalion gathered
on the south bank of the Meza river and prepared for the attack. On the
morning of 16 April Warrant Officer Kinoshita, who went out as a
scout, returned blood-stained and injured and reported that the enemy
was found. My company and men from battalion headquarters went
out to look for them, and in the evening found an enemy advance post
at the foot of the western hills. I talked with the battalion commander
and gave orders as follows: The 1st and 2nd platoons were to go to the
northern slope of the hill under the direct command of the battalion
commander. The 3rd and 4th platoons and 1st and 2nd light machine-
gun sections were to attack from the front under my command. The 3rd
light machine-gun section and the medium machine-gun section were
to climb to the top of the hill for a pincer operation under the command of 2nd Lieutenant Nishimura.

The two platoons under me spread out in the forest and advanced
quietly towards the enemy. I walked 20 metres ahead of them. When
I took out my binoculars I saw about fifty enemy soldiers who were just
starting to move. I saw clearly men trying to pick up knapsacks or
putting on helmets. I immediately ordered, 'Target! Enemy fifty metres
in front of us. Fire!'

The enemy countered with automatic rifles and the volleys of shooting continued back and forth. Suddenly five mortar shells exploded
nearby, and Platoon Leader Fujisawa was lightly wounded by a splinter.
Our men seemed disturbed and awaited my order. I guessed instantly
that the mortar must be firing blindly at the sound of our shooting. So
if we got closer to the enemy, they would have to stop firing to avoid
killing their own men. So I ordered both platoons to advance 15 metres.
As we moved forward the mortar stopped firing. Influenced by the
quick shooting of the enemy automatic rifles, our machine-guns kept
firing and used up all their ammunition.

Twenty minutes passed with no sound came from Nishimura's
machine-guns. The sun was just going to set, and I saw many blue flashes
made by enemy tracer bullets. As our machine-guns kept silence, the
enemy seemed to be gradually advancing towards us. I thought it was
a good time to charge with bayonets. As I cried, 'Be ready to charge! Take
out hand grenades! Advance to the front elevation by crawling!'
Nishimura's machine-guns started shooting.

'Advance ten metres, and throw hand grenades'. The explosion of our
grenades echoed in the jungle, and the enemy seemed confused at

being attacked from both sides. I thought it was a good chance to charge in, but I had to wait as we would be shot by our own machine-guns. We could not chase them.

'Stop advance! Shout loudly!'

'Wah! Wah!' we cried as if we were charging but did not advance. The enemy retreated very quickly and disappeared from our vision. The sun went down and the battlefield became dark and quite unearthly. We saw a lot of bloodstains around the enemy's position, but no dead soldiers. All they left was a dead horse, though we thought that we must have inflicted a lot of damage. We captured ten horses; some had no harness on them, some had saddles but no bridles and some were tied to trees. They must have left in great haste. We had not noticed that there were horses. The reason was that the vocal chords of the horses had been removed so that they did not neigh. I was impressed by their thorough preparation.

Our other two platoons and headquarters fighting unit commanded by the battalion commander climbed up to the top of the hill and found several hundred enemy men with horses resting in the western valley. As the two platoons were advancing to encircle them from side, my company started shooting. Hearing that, the resting men jumped up in a hurry to prepare for the fighting. The commander ordered the two platoons to shoot rapidly, and the headquarters fighting unit led by Lieutenant Sugiyama to charge. Fifteen men of this unit went close to the enemy, threw many hand grenades from higher ground and rushed into the enemy ranks with bayonets. The surprised enemy escaped into the jungle in confusion leaving behind their belongings. As it got darker the commander gave up pursuing them after some chasing shots.

We all assembled and our company camped there fully armed. The battalion commander went back to Meza, together with the 4th Company who just arrived to reinforce us.

In this battle we captured ten horses, six radio-telephones, explosives, rifle bullets and many canned rations.

4.4 Keep the trains running

Captain Saburo Hasegawa 3rd Battalion, 5th Railway Regiment

In the later part of April, we were told by our information network that two enemy groups, each of fifty men, were moving around in the mountains near Wuntho and Kotanpo. Information sent from the village headmen was correct, and we had not yet been surprised by the enemy (Chindit). Our doctor, Medical Captain Tsuchida, volunteered to go out with a patrol, and found three British soldiers near to death in a forestry official's hut in Minbu village, 12 kilometres west of Kotanpo. The railway soldiers who went with him wanted to stab them with bayonets, but the doctor stopped them.

'Wait! Don't kill the dying men. Enemy who are incapable of fighting should not be killed. Anyway they will not live long.'

The doctor showed the red cross badge to them, and then explained in English that he was going to treat them, and injected them with some medicine. Before the doctor left, one of the British soldiers slightly opened his eyes and expressed his thanks to him.

In the hut there was electric wire for blasting and other material, which the soldiers cut up and threw into the jungle. They left milk for the patients and took the other food back to our barracks. The airborne troops were not active, probably as they were watched by Burmese people. They did not attack the railway stations, which were only defended by a few railway soldiers, and they did not attack trains which were running regularly at night. They must have respected the fighting capability of the railway soldiers.

In the morning of 5 May, Major General Kiyoe Yamamoto, commander of the Burma Railway, arrived at our headquarters at Kotanpo on a light train. I reported to him the enemy situation, the damage from air-raids and our positions, and served him lunch. Soon after lunch we heard the sound of a big explosion and shooting from the direction of no. 285 bridge which was located two kilometres south of Kotanpo. It could not be an air-raid as we saw no plane. So we sent a patrol in a truck to the bridge. The bridge was 50 metres long and had not been bombed. The water depth of the river was less than half a metre. Near the bridge was a pump and a water tank for steam locomotives, camouflaged with tree branches.

Later the truck came back with Lance Corporal Wakita, who reported:

I was guarding the feed pump with a Burmese railway employee. I saw a group of thirty men with wire and explosive approaching from the other side of the bridge. I went into the shelter with the assistant and waited. The enemy crawled onto the bridge and advanced towards the centre. I aimed carefully and shot at the first man and then at the second man. Both shots seemed effective and the two men retreated holding their hands on wounds. Then I shot at men at the end of the bridge. They could not come closer and started to fire their rifles but the bullets did not penetrate the shelter. They abandoned their plan, blasted some rails on the track and ran away. I shot at the retreating enemy until I had used up the thirty bullets that I had.

I was told that Lance Corporal Wakita was an excellent shot who had once hit a flying sparrow with a bullet from his rifle. I got Wakita to report directly to the commander. He was happy to hear what was said to me, that 'your 5th Regiment has good soldiers.' And he gave Wakita two packs of British cigarettes, which we could not get in the mountains, as a token of praise.

The commander, Yamamoto, had planned to send supplies, urgently needed for 18 (Kiku) Division, to Mogaung by forcing a way through with heavy trains on the Myitkyina line. The Division had not been supplied for the past two months, while struggling with American and Chinese forces in the Hukuawng valley, as the railway had been cut by the enemy.

Four trains pulled by steam locomotives, each with 20 wagons fully loaded with supplies, arrived at Kanbalu station in the night of 9 May. From here my battalion took over the operation and protection of the trains, while the 2nd Battalion advanced repairing the damaged rail track, and the 1st Company watched and tried to clear the enemy position at Mawlu.

On the morning of 11 May, the trains approached Mawlu station where the 1st Company commander reported that the enemy had just retreated. While the trains waited under the jungle trees, the 2nd Battalion urgently repaired the damaged bridge over the Hess river and the rail track. The trains started to move northwards while the two companies leap-frogged forward, urgently repairing the damaged sections. When we came to Namkuin, which was close to our goal, Mogaung, we encountered the enemy. I watched the enemy on the western hill from the locomotive of the first train, while Asakura Company worked hard to repair the rails even though they were in full view of the enemy. I told the train driver to drive as fast as possible following the rail-tractor in front of us. The trains steamed on while mortar bombs fell around them, but fortunately none were hit. In the late evening of 11 May, the trains arrived at Mogaung where we were welcomed by the staff of 18 Division, who were seriously affected by lack of ammunition and food. Our mission was completed.

We knew that the Japanese airforce had provided air cover on our route with their full complement of fighters, and so we were not bombed even though we ran over the last stretch during the daytime.

In order to keep trains running under heavy air-attack, I made two diversion routes at all the important bridges: so there was a main bridge, a detour (second) bridge and a light bridge. The light bridge could be built in a night, making use of the footings which had previously been built under the water, over which a light train of up to four wagons pulled by a rail truck could pass. Wagons were separated from the heavy train, pulled by a steam locomotive, and were moved over the light bridge, sometimes even being pushed by hand. Sturdy shelters for the steam locomotives were built in hillsides or in the jungle.

A detour telephone line was installed far apart from the bridges or stations, which were often bombed. Using this I could talk to my regimental commander at Shwebo at any time. I should have provided this earlier than I did.

Despite the rainy season, enemy planes continued to attack the bridges. However, even when their bombs destroyed a main bridge, at least one of the diversion bridges was not damaged and trains moved every night.

Early in June, an independent anti-aircraft gun company (four type 88, 75 mm guns and four anti-aircraft machine-guns, total 200 men), and five days later two 40 mm Bofors guns (captured from the British) were sent to us and placed under my command. Together with the three 13 mm machine-guns acquired from the B25 (see part 4, section 1), we had a strong anti-aircraft system to guard the Meza bridge.

Later in June, when the sun shone for an hour, four British fighter bombers came each carrying two 100-kilogram bombs. As they came close to the bridge, our AA guns started firing and two of the planes exploded before they reached the bridge. The railway soldiers cheered to see the planes shot down. After we thought they had retreated, another 12 planes came towards our AA guns. When they came within range, our first volley caused one plane to drop out of formation, but the others pressed home the attack. The gun at the south end of the bridge was attacked more often and one shell killed two gunners. Though our machine-gun positions were also shot up by the planes, the machine-guns kept firing effectively. One plane caught fire and fell in the hills. I imagined that some of the damaged planes were unable to return to their base. After thirty minutes the fighting was over and the bridge and the station remained undamaged. Our anti-air defence system had proved to be effective.

4.5 Transportation of provisions

Ordinance Lieutenant Kenji Hamazaki, Provision Section, 3rd Battalion, 5th Railway Regiment

I was at Kotanpo, where the headquarters of the 3rd Battalion had been, and was in charge of collecting food and other supplies for the two companies, who were mostly in the Meza area. I went around the neighbouring area and got some rice by barter as our military banknotes were not accepted by the local people.

On about 5 July 1944, I left Kotanpo on a light train which carried rice and pork for Meza. I wanted to report to the battalion commander at Meza on the supply situation and wanted to see how the soldiers were faring for food. As the track was damaged we stayed at Namkan that night and left the next evening. When the train arrived at Meza, a crowd of men came hurrying towards the train.

'Let me get on!'

'Please, I beg as a favour.'

These were more than five hundred of these soldiers. All of them had no rifles and caps, and were only carrying mess kits and canteens.

All of them came almost crawling towards us, with pale swollen faces. They looked like a crowd of ghosts. They were undoubtedly survivors from the troops defeated in the Imphal area, and nearly all were suffering from malaria and under-nourishment. They begged, almost weeping, 'Dear railway soldiers! Please help me!' They cried to railway soldiers who were their countrymen, 'I beg you!' regardless of military rank. These were crowds of men who had completely given up being soldiers. Why were there no commanders? Where were the irresponsible commanders who could not look after their men? I was amazed and felt broken-hearted.

I asked some of the more active soldiers, 'What is the matter? How is the Imphal operation going?' They told me that they started out carrying two weeks' rations and ammunition on their backs. Though they reached their objectives, there was no re-supply of food and ammunition, which should have been sent across the steep mountain range. With no food and no ammunition, the starving troops were obliged to retreat in the heavy rain. There were a great many retreating soldiers along the railway north of Meza; many of them used up all of their strength and collapsed, and their corpses were scattered along the line. Already white bones were all that remained of some of them. I met the battalion commander. He appreciated the pork I brought, valuable nourishment for the sick soldiers, who now amounted to about half of the battalion. He agreed that most of the rice I brought should be used for feeding the retreating soldiers. As the retreating men were in such a miserable state, the battalion had been issuing 300 grams of rice per person from their own stock, although supplying them was outside the mission of the railway unit. With the rice that I brought, one kilogram of rice was to be given to each person. This should last two days until they reached the next supply point. The regiment was running two heavy trains every night to carry back retreating men.

When I returned to the light train the wagons were filled with sick soldiers. I sat by the driver of the rail-tractor pulling the train and ordered him to set off. I was obliged to disregard the many soldiers who were begging to get on, and hoped that the next heavy train would come on time and pick them up.

4.6   Annihilated at Myitkyina

Lieutenant Takao Yoshikawa, 2nd Company, 1st Battalion, 5th Railway Regiment

I had been the leader of the 2nd platoon of the 2nd Company responsible for train operation in the northern part of the Myitkyina line until May 1944, when I was appointed commander of the 1st Company. Before I started in my new post I went back to Myitkyina to wind up any unfinished business and to collect my personal belongings. And by an irony of fate I happened to be at Myitkyina on 17 May 1944.

It was a clear fine day from the start. We were used to the enemy air-raids which arrived almost to a set timetable every day. On this day enemy fighters came in successive waves, one group after another, circling above us and then diving down and firing their machine-guns whenever they saw any men. At about 3 p.m. I received an urgent telephone call from the headquarters of the 114th Infantry Regiment, who were responsible for the defence of the town: 'Enemy attack! Myitkyina airport captured by the enemy.'

At that time the following railway units were at Myitkyina:

Part of the operation platoon (Lieutenant Yoshikawa and about 15 men).
The major part of the engine-shed platoon (Sergeant Hagiwara and about 50 men – the platoon leader was on a trip to Mogaung).
A part of the rail maintenance platoon (Second Lieutenant Asai and about 5 men).

By evening all the railwaymen gathered at the station, and a messenger came back from the headquarters and told us that an enemy penetration group had captured the airport supported by fighter planes, and moreover that major reinforcements were arriving by plane. Our airport battalion could not help feeling overwhelmed by the vast difference in numbers. The enemy must be trying to capture Myitkyina. Then I received the following orders:

1. All railway units are to come under the command of Lieutenant Yoshikawa, who is to report to the commander of the 114th Infantry Regiment for the defence of Myitkyina.
2. The combined railway unit will move to the northern part of the town where regimental headquarters are located, except for a small force to watch the station and engine-shed.

During the nights of 17–19 May, neither we nor the enemy made any moves, but we spent the nights worrying what was going to happen, sometimes glad, sometimes sad, and influenced by every trifle of information or speculation.

Around 7 a.m. on 20 May, about a regiment of the Chinese army broke through the southern position held by our military police, and came rushing to the area around the station and engine-shed. Our few watchmen had to retreat, overwhelmed by their numbers. We were told that there were only 400 men available for fighting in the area including our railway unit. As Myitkyina could not be defended unless we recaptured the town area, it was decided that all available troops of the 114th Infantry Regiment would counter-attack from the early morning of 21 May, and our unit was to be in reserve. Our unit came under the command of Captain Yamazaki of the signal company.

After sunset we were ordered to recover a regimental gun (a 75-mm mountain gun) which the infantry had left behind in the southern area, and which was essential for the counter-attack. I was very unhappy that the railwaymen, who had not been trained as a fighting unit, were ordered to get the gun out of the enemy area. But I controlled my anger and ordered Sergeant Hiraoka to take a patrol and go and recover it. He went out with four men, came back safely after an hour and reported as follows:

> In the southern area, all the houses were lit up and, filled with Chinese soldiers who were talking loudly. In the dark we advanced and found the house where the gun was. This typical Burmese house

had the living space on the first floor, and the ground space was open and used for storage. Although the Chinese soldiers were upstairs, there was no sentry on the ground; they never expected that a Japanese patrol would come. So I thought that we could do the recovery by ourselves, and we pulled the gun, with ropes rattling, through the enemy area, and have brought the gun back here.

I was amazed by the bold action of Hiraoka Section, and reported this marvellous achievement to Captain Yamazaki, who praised the section as superior to the infantry. The morale of our unit became very high.

On 21 May our infantry made a daring counter-attack on the Chinese in the south, supported by fire from the recovered gun. The Chinese troops were taken by surprise and ran away in confusion. Our attack proved to be a big success, and we recaptured the area. Captain Yamazaki told me that confirmed enemy dead were more than 300, while we only lost three men.

Next day we were ordered to take up a position on the western side of the town, which was about two kilometres from the edge of the airport. We were fired on by machine-guns and mortars but their aim was poor. In the ten days we were there, only two soldiers were wounded and were sent to field hospital.

By the end of May, the 3rd Battalion of the 114th Regiment broke through the enemy and arrived to join us, to our delight, and accordingly the positions of units were changed. We were moved to defend a front of 1.5 kilometres, stretching west from the engine-shed and facing south. We were also allocated two medium machine-guns. One section, led by Corporal Komatsu of the transport unit, whose men had no fighting experience, was added to us. We had a total of about 80 men at this stage including 65 railwaymen. In the early part of June, we had a relatively quiet time as the enemy was seen only occasionally, and we had enough food on hand.

We were told that 53 (An) Division, who were heading north after breaking through Mawlu, would be coming to rescue us, and in co-operation with them we were to start attacking the enemy in two days. The morale of our men was high. But unfortunately it was suddenly decided that instead of rescuing us 53 Division should go to rescue 18 Division who were in a serious situation at Kamaing. We were all very much disappointed.

One day in early June, several Japanese planes came flying over us. All our men, forgetting that they were facing the enemy, came out of the trenches and welcomed the planes. The planes then dived on the airstrip to our west through a fierce burst of enemy anti-aircraft shells. We prayed for their safety.

During early June we had little contact with enemy troops, but their mortars kept firing on our positions and planes machine-gunned and bombed us. High-velocity shells from anti-aircraft guns on the airfield bothered us, as the time between the gun firing and the shell exploding was short, and gave us little time to get into the shelters. The shelling was fierce: several hundred shells on even a section position. Even our sturdy defences were damaged one by one by the repeated shelling. From mid-June on, fighting continued every day. It was an effort to defend our positions, as well as becoming a war of attrition. Every day we were shelled in this life-or-death struggle. Men began to wonder what their fate would be tomorrow, to die early or late. The effect of shower-like shelling on human beings is terrifying. At that time we had an allocation of only four shells a day for our 70-mm battalion gun. Even those four shells had some effect on enemy action for a while.

One day a group of enemy came advancing through the bush and took up a position between our Asai Platoon and the Komatsu Section. The soldiers of the Komatsu Section, who had not previously been in a battle, were afraid of the enemy and retreated. I scolded the leader and had the section go back to their original position, and prepared a counter-attack. In the afternoon two sections lead by Lieutenant Asai from the left, and Hagiwara Section led by me from the right, attacked the enemy. After a heavy burst of shooting from both sides, we charged the enemy, shouting loudly. They ran away without engaging us with the bayonet, and the counter-attack succeeded. The enemy left 25 dead bodies, all young Chinese. We captured three light machine-guns and ten automatic rifles. But unfortunately Sergeant Hagiwara and a lance corporal were killed in the fight.

In the later part of June the enemy, by digging a trench across an open field, gradually approached the position of Nakata Section. From our position we could clearly see the enemy soldiers swinging up their hoes for digging. We threw a grenade as hard as we could and saw it blow up a soldier, but they did not stop digging. A few days later Nakata Section was subjected to repeated and concentrated bombing and machine-gunning by fighter planes. I was watching the severe attack from a nearby trench, but there was nothing I could do.

In the evening, when the attack ended, I ran to the position. All I saw was many big bomb craters, but no trace of the Nakata Section at all: nothing remained of the position, no man, not even a piece of their belongings. I stood there tearfully, gulping down sobs.

In July the enemy attack became more fierce on all our positions. By that time we could tell what they were going to do. First the target position was subjected to concentrated shelling by artillery and mortars for about an hour. At the same time they also shelled the sides and back of the position to prevent reinforcement. It is difficult to describe how severe this shelling was. After the shelling stopped, Chinese soldiers advanced on the position and attacked by throwing grenades. As we fought back, the soldiers retreated, and again the concentrated shelling of guns and mortars began. As heavy shells were used, our position was gradually demolished, and one or two men were killed in the repeated attack. The medium machine-guns which had been sent to reinforce us fought effectively and killed many Chinese by shooting at close range. However these were heavily shelled and both were destroyed in due course. When the position of Yamauchi Section was eventually taken by the enemy, we counter-attacked with the help of an infantry platoon and three grenade launchers from the headquarters, successfully recovering the position and establishing a new trench just behind it. In the counter-attack, one railwayman was killed, and out of ten men in the position only two survived.

In the later part of July, a letter of citation was forwarded from general headquarters in Tokyo to Myitkyina defence forces, and this was a boost to the morale of the soldiers. By this time we had some small-arms ammunition left but no shells for our guns. The only grenades left were the ones that each of us kept to kill ourselves with at the last moment. The food allocated to us was one rice ball of fist size per day and was not enough to maintain our strength. We ate anything edible: jungle grasses, cores of banana stems, dogs and cats. As we had lost Nakata and Yamauchi Sections, it became difficult to defend our line systematically, as headquarters had no more men to spare for us. Around the end of July, Asai Platoon, Komatsu Section and Hasegawa Section were decimated and the remaining 20 men formed the last defence line around the trench where I had been. One day after an hour's concentrated shelling, the sound of the explosions changed. I thought it must mean they were using hand-grenades and ordered everyone to get into the outside trenches. There I saw several Chinese soldiers crawling to about 30 metres in front of me. I fired my pistol and the bullet hit the foot of the leading Chinese who uttered a yell and retreated, dragging his foot. At the same time my men drove off the attackers with a machine-gun and rifles. This was the first time I had seen an enemy so close. The enemy repeated their attack many times but we drove them off; at best they advanced to about 50 metres in front of us. In these fights we lost two men, and I was wounded in the left side of my chest by a splinter from a mortar shell. Fortunately the piece was small and struck my rib, so I was able to continue commanding the railway unit.

At about noon in the early part of August, we received the order: 'Tonight at (such and such) hours, we retreat from Myitkyina and move to the east bank of the Irrawaddy. Crossing should be done by rafts.'

I asked Sergeant Hiraoka to make a raft, and in the evening we (a total of nine men including myself) gathered at our cookhouse. As I was talking with Private Ito under the eaves, a mortar shell suddenly exploded in front of me and Ito fell down, killed instantly. So we were reduced to eight. After dark, we went north to the river-crossing point, where we ate plenty of rice mixed with canned beef which was supplied by the kind consideration of headquarters. The River Irrawaddy was in full flood, it being the rainy season. We saw many rafts floating down with a loud shout, 'Ya-ho!' They seemed to be carrying the soldiers of the 114th Infantry Regiment. But further downstream, enemy flares started to light up the river and the rafts were clearly seen. Flares were fired continuously and were followed by shelling. Then we heard a peculiar sound which could only mean that a raft had been hit by a shell. It sounded diabolic to us. It was clear that the enemy were trying to hit the rafts on the river. If we went on a raft now we would surely be an easy prey for the enemy. Someone told me that the commander and most of 114th Infantry Regiment had already crossed the river. So I told my men: 'All we have to do is finished. As our commander has retreated, there is no point in our staying here to be annihilated. I will break through the enemy front line toward Namkwi and then go down a branch of the Irrawaddy. As I am suffering badly from beriberi, I am unable to swim. But those who want to swim across the river may do so.'

After discussion three men decided to go on land with me. The other four wanted to cross the river by raft, and stayed at the river bank. I never heard what happened to them, and assume that they did not survive.

Those who decided to go on land, myself and three men, stayed near the river the following day. In the evening, to be ready for departure, we started to eat our last supper, which we had reserved from the previous night. Then a mortar shell burst close by and our precious supper in the canteens was all lost, mixed with mud and sand blown up by the explosion. A splinter from this bomb hit Private Sugawara in the neck and he died instantly.

The three of us who were left headed towards the west and entered a grassy plain. Though it was the rainy season, the moon vaguely lit our way. We heard the sound of men walking from the south, so we lay flat in the grass. In the moonlight we saw many figures advancing north. We waited quietly and were not discovered. After they went away, we continued westwards along a little stream for a kilometre and climbed up a hill on the left, where there was a long stretch of triangular tents. We went through the forest to one side of them hiding ourselves as best we could. Suddenly a tall figure rose up in front of us – an enemy sentry! We held our breath and lay down. As the enemy seemed not to have noticed us, we made a detour and arrived in a forest close to the railway. Private Negishi did not arrive as he must have lost the way. As we were in enemy territory we could not call his name. There was no way of finding him. So we became only two, Private Wada and I. As it was a good place to hide, we decided to rest during the daytime.

When the night came, we started to walk alongside the railway. As both sides of the railway were like lakes due to the rainy season and it was impossible to walk there, we had no choice but to walk on the side of the embankment. But soon we were detected by the enemy. Though we hid ourselves in a bush by the embankment, the sound of footsteps came closer. As we had no chance of escape, we charged the approaching soldiers. When Private Wada attacked an enemy soldier with a war-cry, I felt a tremendous shock as if my body had knocked hard into a concrete wall, and I lost consciousness.

When I came to myself, I was in an unfamiliar tent. I shuddered as I came to realise that I had become a shameful prisoner.

Postscript

As I wrote about the terrible fight at Myitkyina, my heart was too full for words and my body trembled. From the time of the battle until several years after the surrender of Japan, what tormented me was the deep regret that I was not able to die together with my men. The scenes of the hard-fought battles and the figures of the men who died in the fighting came before my eyes often, and I spent sleepless nights as they appeared and vanished in my dreams many times. Since the war our society has changed very much and people's thinking has changed, but it was not possible for me to change my way of thinking and my moral beliefs, and I spent many days in immense mental agony. I cannot get over the fact that I am alive, and am not able to die. The true reason that I wanted again to be in the military service (in the Japanese Self Defence Force) was because I wanted to find a chance to die honourably. It was a faint desire but this was the way I thought. As I grew older and time passed my thinking gradually changed, perhaps due to my subconscious desires that said: 'Let it be forgotten; I want to be free of it. I do not wish to remember that time any more,' and inspired by the wish of my good friend Mr Ootosiro, who had been a fellow platoon leader in the 2nd Company, I wrote this article mainly for the repose of the souls of the deceased, as well as trying to record the fact that the railway soldiers fought bravely and even favourably compared with our infantry. I told myself that my personal feelings should be extinguished.

4.7   The retreat from the Myitkyina line

Lance Corporal Kenji Koshikawa, Headquarters, 3rd Battalion, 5th Railway Regiment

On 6 September 1944, the full moon came up in a clear sky after a long spell of rain. Though it was easy to work in the moonlight, enemy planes came attacking the trains, bridges and trucks. As the enemy usually came before midnight, the soldiers were allowed to rest until midnight at the work site, but their sleep was often disturbed by the sound of planes. We had to work hard even in the rainy season, when we were wet to the skin. Furthermore we were constantly attacked by malarial mosquitos, which were even more dangerous than the enemy planes. We were forced to take anti-malaria drugs which affected our stomachs and appetite, and so we could not take enough nourishment and our physical strength became weaker and weaker. We kept going only through our feeling of responsibility for the honour of railway soldiers.

We knew that the enemy was approaching closer to us day by day, and I wondered how long we would have to continue repairing the bomb damage. But as long as the 1st Battalion was operating north of us, we had to keep the line open.

Just by a sheet of call-up paper, the war had brought us here, to a strange land far away from home, into a situation where our lives might be terminated at any time. We had not received any mail from home after the Imphal operation became critical, so we took out sweat-stained wrinkled-up old letters and read them over and over, and were reminded of our parents, wives and children. 'My old mother has ceased drinking her favourite tea as an ascetic gesture to wish me good luck. I hope both my parents are well.'

While I forgot myself in nostalgic memories, suddenly machine-gun tracer bullets swept in front of my eyes and the sentry shouted 'Air-raid!'

Startled, I came to myself. The enemy plane shot up the moonlit railway for a while and then went away over the Namkan mountains showing its red and green wing lights.

From September the stream of starving and defeated soldiers became less and organised fighting units appeared, retreating from the front line. So there was now no confusion and begging by soldiers to get on trains as before. As many units who passed along the railway had eaten up the local vegetables on the way, we could not now get vegetables for our meals. We could not even get the tasteless white gourd-melons, so we lacked nourishment.

In the early part of September the regimental commander came to Meza in the night. The battalion commander led the way to our head-quarters building which was in the jungle 500 metres east of the station. When he came to the narrow bridge, he asked the regimental commander to go ahead, and I took his hand to cross the bridge as his sight at night was poor. The regimental commander said, 'Hasegawa, your vision seems very bad.'

The battalion commander replied, 'I am not night-blind, but I cannot see well.'

'I am sorry to see a battalion commander in such a situation, so I see and I realise that the men in the 3rd Battalion are weakened physically.'

When the regimental commander left, he promised to send garlic which is good for the recovery of sight.

A few days later two big bags of onions and a packet of garlic were sent by the regimental commander. The battalion commander ate the garlic as ordered and his sight recovered in ten days. The onions were divided between the two companies. I planted about ten onions in the ground, ate the buds twice and then ate the bulbs according to his instruction. The onions tasted particularly good as we had not had vegetables for so long.

In the evening of 9 October 1944, the battalion commander left Meza on a light train for Shwebo, and I accompanied him as his messenger. On the way we had to wait for the repair of bomb damage and it was morning when we reached Kanbalu. As the commander was in a hurry to attend the regimental meeting planned for that evening, we continued our journey as most of the way was through forests. Once an enemy plane came over and shot up the railway in front of us, but fortunately our train was not hit, and we arrived at the regimental headquarters in Shwebo in the late morning.

As I had nothing to do until the evening I went to see my friend at headquarters. He was happy to see me in good shape and gave me a little bit of fried banana and black sugar which I saved until I returned to Meza and shared with our comrades. He told me in a low voice, 'It seems that the regiment is going to retreat to Mandalay. Already some of the patients in the hospitals have been sent back. It is a pity that our army has been defeated at Imphal. Though we worked extremely hard and built the Burma–Thailand Railway, many of the materials sent from Japan and moved up the railway to this line have not been delivered to the front, and are still lying around in the forests near the terminal stations. This is because of the irritating enemy air-raids on the narrow roads to the front. But don't be discouraged; we will have to work harder than ever as train-transportation will be essential in the retreat. Take good care of yourself and we will meet again.'

The important meeting attended by all battalion commanders was held in the evening and at around midnight Captain Hasegawa came back with a tense look and we headed back to Meza. As the Japanese troops were ordered to retreat from the Myitkyina line, many trains went south carrying patients, troops, weapons and ammunition.

One morning, a corporal wearing a sword and carrying two chickens in his hand came to the railway station. 'I am Corporal Takayama of Army ordnance depot. We request three wagons to send back about one thousand rifles. But about half of them need repairing, so these can be discarded'.

Hearing this, the commander said, 'Don't be foolish! Weapons are valuable. Even the broken one may be useful later. Carry them all back. The patients who have been evacuated did not have rifles, so they will be needed soon. This is the order of 5th Railway Regiment who is responsible for the transportation.'

The corporal thanked us and gave us the two chickens, after we refused to allow his men to eat them on their journey. The commander also asked for a magazine for our light machine-gun, which we needed badly. He sent four magazines to us later.

On 28 October the retreating 2nd Battalion passed through Meza towards the south, followed by the 1st Battalion who passed Meza on 30 October. We were now at the tail end of the railway. On 2 November the fighting came close to us and we heard the explosion of enemy shells and the sound of our medium machine-guns clearly.

Next morning we all lined up and said farewell to 47 dead comrades by presenting arms accompanied by a bugle call, and then the commander ordered us to blow up the Meza bridge which we had repaired many times. The two diversion wooden bridges had been dismantled earlier. Then we retreated step by step demolishing the railway facilities. When we came to Kotanpo on 3 December and were lifting rails, local people came and asked what we were doing. We explained, 'As a lot of track has been damaged by the English bombardment at Mandalay, we are taking these there for repairs. When that is finished we shall return and put them back.' We gave them the same answer whatever we were asked, and continued the work. The local people offered to help us, but we firmly declined their offer.

The following night when we were working near the next station, many villagers of Kotanpo came, each carrying a hand lamp or a pine-torch. Everybody brought and offered us dumplings wrapped in banana leaves, a speciality of Kotanpo, or red rice baked in bamboo stalks, or freshly rolled local cigars, saying, 'Master. We have come to see you off.' We were embarrassed and wondering what to do, when company commander Watanabe arrived with some empty wagons. A man who looked like the village headman, together with some local people, surrounded him and asked him to accept the offerings. A woman who spoke some Japanese greeted him with tears. 'Watanabe master and everybody going. We all feel lonely.' As we were worried that their many lights might attract an air-raid, we accepted their kind offer, and told them through an interpreter, 'Please tell the village headman to come to where we are working tomorrow night with an ox-cart.' The villagers left expressing regret at parting and waving their lights, which was a delightful scene for us. We were happy to be liked by the local people.

Next night, the village headman who wore a pink cap or headband, which is a sign of formal wear in Burma, came with an assistant and gave us some presents similar to those the day before, which filled five bamboo flat-baskets. In return we gave him a big bag of salt and several bottles of creosote tablets and iodine tincture, which we had brought with us from the rear. Salt is a valuable commodity in an area far from the sea, so he thanked us for our presents with great delight, put them on the cart and left swinging the lights.

When we first came to Kotanpo, we vaccinated all the villagers and employed many men and women for building wooden bridges, cooking and other jobs. At the fire festival and the water festival, annual events in the village, we danced with them and made money offerings to a local deity. Our doctor Tsuchiya visited critically ill local patients. So the villagers were on intimate terms with us. It was nice of them to come to see us off when we were defeated and retreating. However it was heart-breaking to tell a lie about our destruction work to Burmese people who trusted us.

After our surrender in August 1945, Japanese railway regiments were ordered by the British to work on the recovery of the railways. When my friend in 9th Railway Regiment went to the area to re-lay rails on the southern part of the Myitkyina line, the local people were very happy to see the railway and offered coffee and cigars to the working Japanese railway soldiers (JSP) saying, 'Japanese kept their promise and came back to repair the railway.'

4.8 Maintenance of locomotives

Sergeant Hideo Hattori, Maintenance Unit, 4th Battalion, 5th Railway Regiment

After the construction of the Burma–Thailand Railway was completed, our battalion moved to north Burma and was ordered to operate the Ye line and the southern part of the Myitkyina line. Our maintenance unit was established at the Ywataung locomotive depot under the command of Second Lieutenant Gen-ichi Sato, and was composed of 60 men with various skills, such as train driver, assembler (fitter), stoker, blacksmith, carpenter and wagon inspector. I was made the leader of a repair team. We took over from 5th JNR Railway Unit, which was composed of employees of the Japanese National Railways. Our team worked with local craftsmen. The head of the local employees, Mr U-tanbe graduated from Rangoon railway school and spoke good Japanese. Also four locals and two young Indians acted as interpreters. These men were useful, as none of us spoke Burmese, having been in China and the mountains of Thailand until then.

We worked from early morning to 11:00 and from 15:00 to sunset, avoiding the time when enemy planes usually came. Within these short working hours we had to work hard on maintenance work and repair, so that the steam locomotives could be used during the night. The train drivers did a very dangerous job, as they ran their trains during the night without lights and were sometimes machine-gunned or bombed by planes, so they were celebrities. In contrast the work of our repair team was inconspicuous and modest. Every day the team repaired the dilapidated locomotives, sometimes crawling into hot boilers, and repairing the wheels and the many broken parts.

The local people were really pro-Japanese and honestly co-operated with us. In the evening coffee stands and sales stalls were opened in the street in front of the station, which we soldiers called Ginza Street (named after the best shopping area of Tokyo).

One day Mr U-tanbe opened a Janjamama show at a plaza in front of a temple, with the permission of our commander. Many local people came and were in high spirits, whistling and clapping hands. Janjamama players who came from Mandalay danced merrily to the rhythm of Japanese songs and the Patriotic March (a popular wartime song). It was a peaceful time. In the middle of the show names of contributors were announced, and I was surprised that my name was included in them. I asked Mr U-tanbe why and he told me, 'Kesansibu' (don't worry). They knew that we soldiers were paid little but working at the risk of our lives for the independence of Burma in the Great Asia Co-prosperity Sphere.

In March 1944 we heard that the Japanese army were advancing towards Imphal, and a rumour came round that our railway regiment was to go to the Assam–Bengal Railway. This led me to entertain apprehensions about how long the war would last if I was really going to India. I left Japan in 1939 and was in China, Thailand and Burma, far away from the home country. At that time our commander Sato called all the leaders and explained that British airborne troops had landed near Mawlu and Mohan on the Myitkyina line and our 2nd and 3rd Battalions were fighting against heavy odds. We should be prepared for landings in our area.

Enemy planes now came more often and damaged locomotives were brought to us almost every day, which made us very busy. Our locomotive depot was also attacked. A machine-gun section, led by Sergeant Shimada, was in Ywataung and fought back against the planes, but it was soon moved to defend no. 35 bridge at Nyuyapin, and then the planes came at will at low altitude. One day three Lockheeds suddenly appeared and I slipped into a foxhole. A Burmese interpreter who was in the next foxhole got out, trying to move to the shelter when the first plane left, but he was shot through the head by the second plane. Though his brother ran to help him he was already dead. This was the first victim in our maintenance unit. We performed a religious service for him and sent the corpse to his home in Sagaing, with a letter of mourning for the dead.

One night we received an emergency call, and all the men of the unit left on a light train for Kekka, an unmanned station 40 kilometres north, because of information that airborne troops had landed there. Though we went there ready to fight, it was found to be incorrect information. However, we found there some wrecked type YC and YD locomotives, and parts taken away from these proved very useful for our repair work.

We were using a covered wagon (box car) as our office. One morning at 10 o'clock, while I was making arrangements for the repair of a loco-motive with a private, an air-raid warning bell rang violently. At the same time two planes came towards the depot firing their machine guns. I had no time to get to the shelter. As I got out of the wagon, I felt a blow on my left foot and fell down. The two planes flew away just above my head. I looked down and saw that a flying brick had hit my foot. While the planes were circling I ran into the shelter and was saved. The planes came around several times but the locomotives and our men were all safe. After the planes left, I went to the office and found a shot had pierced the roof and knocked my desk to the ground. If I had left the office a few seconds later I could have been shot through the head. A narrow escape from death! In May we heard that the situation of Myitkyina had become serious and the maintenance unit of 1st Battalion was in danger of being isolated. Yasu Division, whom we had sent north in our emergency transport to rescue them, encountered stiff resistance and could not reach Myitkyina, and the maintenance unit there suffered an honourable death. Two of my good friends who underwent training with me as privates were supposed to be among them. I prayed for the repose of their souls and at the same time felt conscious of the increased importance of our job, with its new need to compensate for the loss of the maintenance force of the regiment.

Just at that time the steam locomotive YC167 was sent to us badly damaged by air attack, with many scars from machine-gun fire. The chimney, one main steam pipe and the left-hand cylinder were badly broken. As the damage was too great for us to deal with, we sent the locomotive back to the regimental repair depot. Three days later we got a message that repair was impossible so the locomotive would be discarded. Hearing this I thought that we should try ourselves to repair it, as the loss of one steam locomotive decreased our transportation capacity, every bit of which was urgently needed for the on-going oper-ations. As the bridge over the Irrawaddy River had been destroyed it was not possible to transfer heavy locomotives from the main line to our northern lines. We had the damaged locomotive sent to us and put it on a siding in the jungle. That evening I went to Kekka with two soldiers and our local chief craftsman, and we tried to take off a main steam pipe and a left cylinder from the engine. But rusted nuts were hard to undo, so one by one we cut them off using hammers and cold chisels, making a lot of noise in the quiet deserted station. We finished the work just in time to load them on the last train of the night to Ywataung. Then we started the main repair. We hung a gantry from a big tree in the jungle and, using this, finished the major repair work in two or three days. We tested the boiler by filling it with water. All was well after we fixed some minor leakage. However, when we tried to drive the locomotive, it had no power. We found that this was caused by improper adjustment of the piston valve. Nobody, including the chief technician, knew how to adjust the valve. However, I found a textbook, which I had used three years before, and studied it for a whole day. I then worked on the valve and piston, and succeeded in getting it to run at full power.

Later the Hattori repair team got a letter of citation from the battalion commander, which was a great honour for troops in a rear area.

Though August is the peak rainy season in Burma, it showered only occasionally at Ywataung and the roads were dusty. However due to heavy rain up in the mountains, area, the River Chindwin flooded and the water came up to 100 metres west of the village, forming a kind of big lake.

At that time more than ten bombers dropped heavy bombs around our depot. Though we were in the shelter we jumped at the shock of the explosion and I felt that this might be the end of my life. When we got out of the shelter, the whole place smelled of explosives and the village was in ruin. A local technician came running and told us that the chief technician was buried in a shelter. We hurried there with shovels and dug the men out. The chief technician was pulled out unconscious, but we gave him artificial respiration and he recovered after a while. His wife had been to Mandalay that morning to visit a temple, and heard of the bombing on her return to Sagaing. She hurried back to her home, saw that their house and shelter were miserably destroyed, thought that her husband was dead, and came to me to learn that he was saved. She thanked me with her hands pressed together. I told her that as you prayed at the temple, Pyar god helped him, and we let the couple stay in our lodging for the night.

The scene around the village was peaceful with views of many small pagodas on the hill at Sagaing glittering to the east. The war caused great distress to the local people.

We were ordered to move to the main line linking Mandalay and Rangoon. On 8 January 1945, we left Ywataung and crossed the Irrawaddy River, and stayed at a military hotel for transit men. While we were eating supper, British planes made an attack. Though none of us was hurt, as we all went into the shelters, the whole of our meal on the table was covered by sand and dirt from the explosions, and we could hardly eat it. It was the beginning of the hardest days!

4.9 The British view: the battle at White City (Henu) on 17 March 1944

Kazuo Tamayama

Wingate's second expedition into Burma (code name: Thursday) was started on 5 March 1944. All the columns, except one brigade, were flown in by glider to their destination in the Japanese rear, and established strongholds and airstrips. All of Calvert's 77th Infantry Brigade flew in to 'Broadway', and moved fanwise towards the railway linking Sagaing and Myitkyina, in preparation for the establishment of a semi-permanent block between Hopin and Mawlu, where the railway and the road to the north run side by side.

One battalion, the Lancashire Fusiliers under Hugh Christie, was to harass communications and blow up bridges just south of Mohinyin, and thus slow up any enemy advancing from there. Another battalion, the South Staffords under Shuttleworth, was to do the same between Indaw and Mawlu. The 3/6 Gurkhas were in reserve with Brigade HQ.

Brigade HQ arrived first on the hilltop near Henu. Then two South Stafford columns and a Gurkha column (Degg) were ordered to establish the block at Henu and started to dig in with what they had. A heavy supply drop that they had asked for, consisting of barbed wire, picks and shovels, much ammunition and food, was dropped high up on the hillside, and could not be retrieved until a week later, by elephant.

Freddie Shaw's Gurkha column put in a holding attack at Nansiaung, and came back to rendezvous with HQ the next morning (17 March) rather shaken, as the Japanese had attacked them first during the night. But they held the Japanese while other British columns moved as planned.

As more firing was heard at the block, six platoons were moved forward, trying to attack the Japanese in the flank or rear. They contacted Degg by walkie-talkie, and by his guidance moved along the ridge and saw the Japanese milling around a small pagoda on top of a little knoll overlooking the paddy.

Quite a number of Japanese had penetrated between Degg's and Skone's column, and they appeared to be based on Pagoda Hill and the village of Henu. They had no heavy weapons other than mortars. The brigadier ordered a charge to capture Pagoda hill. Everybody who was on the hill joined in the charge: machine-gunners, mortar teams, and all officers.

At the top of the hill the Japanese got up and charged back. There, in a space about fifty yards square, severe hand-to-hand fighting took place. It was followed by a lull while both sides threw grenades over and around the pagoda. Fortunately the Japanese grenades made a lot of noise but did little damage. Shaw's two platoons now arrived on the scene. As the Japanese seemed to be running short of ammunition, the South Staffords, on the right, and the Gurkhas, on the left, pushed forward and gained ground around the pagoda and on the hill, thus forcing the Japanese to retreat into the village of Henu.

Three British officers and 20 other ranks were killed, and four British officers and 60 other ranks were wounded. Forty-two Japanese dead were counted. The Japanese attackers consisted of about one company of railway engineers (100 men, see part 4 section 2) and a platoon of infantry. Brigadier Calvert mentioned that the British had been fortunate to be blooded against comparatively untrained, although gallant troops.

The block was established, and was made secure by an air-drop of entrenching tools, wire and ammunition on the night of 18/19 March. A light plane airstrip was made between the railway embankment and Pagoda Hill, and all wounded were evacuated to Broadway, and thence to India by nightly Dakotas.

The block was named 'White City'. A Japanese attack on 21/22 March, by two hastily assembled infantry companies, was repelled but with the high casualties of six British officers, 26 British other ranks and two Gurkhas.

Japanese supplies to 18 Division in north Burma, which faced General Stilwell's US-equipped and trained Chinese divisions, were completely blocked by the stronghold 'White City', and the division was forced to retreat towards Myitkyina.

References

Louis Allen, *Burma, the Longest War* (Dent, London, 1984), p. 328–37.
Michael Calvert, *Prisoner of Hope* (Jonathan Cape, London, 1971), p. 46–53.

Part 5   Retreat

5.1   Move to Lashio line

Major Saburo Hasegawa, Commander, 3rd Battalion, 5th Railway Regiment

On the night of 11 January 1945, after finishing the hard work of the Myitkyina line, we crossed the River Irrawaddy and moved to the eastern part of Mandalay.

Next morning, although we were tired, we all dug air-raid shelters. At eight in the morning we saw a B25 bombing raid on the northern half of Mandalay. At 1.00 p.m. forty-eight big bombers in four formations came over and half of them dropped bombs around our area. Fortunately none of us were hit, but our rice warehouse caught fire. This was put out by our men.

In the morning of 13 January, I was called to regimental headquarters where the commander, and staff officer Enami, were waiting for me. I reported formally to the commander that, by the morning of the 12th the 3rd Battalion finished disposing of the rails which were stored near Ava bridge. He then told me that the situation had changed and invited me to sit down.

'Hasegawa, I must tell you that the French forces in French Indo-china have started to cause trouble and it has become necessary to move a railway regiment there. So our regiment is to take over responsibility for the Lashio line from the 7th Railway Regiment, so that they can be moved south, and your 3rd Battalion will be in charge of the Lashio line. It will be a tough assignment.'

This was an unexpected order. In the army an order should be accepted immediately, but this was contrary to what had been promised to us. I was thinking that our men would probably die of disease, as their health would not recover with no rest and not enough food. Regimental commander Hashimoto grew excited. 'Can't you answer?'

'Please let me say, the 3rd Battalion has been on the Myitkyina line, fighting against the airborne troops, and repairing the railway continuously. We expended every drop of energy that we had in the demolitions and retreat. Our men are exhausted beyond their limit. I would like to decline this order.'

I made this representation to my boss. In my mind, I thought my men would suffer badly by the unreasonable change of orders. However an order is absolute; I can only express my opinion.

'What! Do you make a complaint! 5th Railway Regiment was ordered by railway headquarters to be in charge there, and I selected your battalion as the most suitable.'

This put me in an angry mood. He had no feeling for his soldiers. There might be many alternatives to moving 7th Railway Regiment. Staff officer Enami noticed the tension and said to me: 'Well, Hasegawa. The commander has given this order as he relies on your battalion. I understand your feeling for your men. But the commander had no other choice due to the change of situation.' I kept silent. If I talked back any more, I would be charged with disobedience and court-martialled. If I did not obey the order, I would be sacked and some other person would replace me, and would be given the same order. Either way it was my men who would suffer. I did not want to see any more of my men killed. All I could do was to say nothing, so I stood still.

Staff officer Enami intervened saying, 'If you cannot answer immediately, take some time and think it over.' Though the regimental commander kept silence, I said, 'Please give me some time.'

I thought it over on my way back to my unit. It is the army principle that any order should be received without hesitation and should be carried out immediately. However in Burma where we had been defeated, the former style of the Japanese army had been lost. After the defeat at Imphal, some commanders ran away leaving behind their men. Those who lost their commander starved to death. What should I do?

I dropped in to the office of the 5th Company. The company commander looked at my face and asked me what had happened. 'I would like to consult with my two company commanders.'

When the commander of the 6th Company came, I explained the situation to them.

'If I reply, "Yes sir," our men will be worn out and they will be disheartened by the frequent change of orders. Other battalions have gone back south two months ago, and are relaxing without facing the enemy.

We have only just disengaged from the enemy and have suffered a lot of hardship. It is an outrageous order for us, who have come back for a rest, to go to the Lashio line which is already under attack at Mandalay. I would not like my battalion to perish but, after thinking about it deeply, I would like to hear how you feel.'

The two company commanders listened to me in silence, and then the senior, Watanabe, said, 'If the 3rd Battalion is trusted to such a degree, my men will go there happily. Don't you think so, Hashimoto?'

'I agree. As Watanabe commander said, we are trusted and have been selected. So why not do it willingly? If we are cut off at Mandalay we will command our men firmly and get away. Why not report at once to the regimental commander?'

So I was persuaded to return, and knocked on the door of the regimental commander. 'Hasegawa accepts the order. My companies have started to prepare for the move.'

The commander nodded smiling. 'What happened to you? You have never before opposed an order.'

I explained that, in the current situation, it was probable that the Lashio line would be cut off at Mandalay and we might perish. So I could not decide on my own and had asked the opinion of my company commanders, who were willing to accept the order and showed firm determination in case we were cut off. 'I was urged by them to go to you, and I apologise that I expressed my egoism.' The commander commented, 'You are lucky to have two such good company commanders.'

Then the staff officer explained to me the situation on the Lashio front and around Mandalay. Mandalay city, which is the junction for the Lashio line, could be broken into at any time, although 15 Division was defending its northern hills.

Once the decision had been made, our battalion was quick to take action, and departed on the night of 14 January to take over the operation of the 7th Regiment, the 5th Company from Mandalay to Maymyo, and the 6th Company from Maymyo to Chaume.

Soon after we had deployed on the Lashio line, from 18 February we urgently transported 2 and 18 Divisions. These two divisions were moved from the Lashio front to the south, using our trains via Mandalay to Myitnge. As the bridge at Myitnge was essential, it was defended by all the available planes – 26 fighters – for ten days. This was effective and the bridge was not destroyed. Our soldiers were happy to see the circling Japanese planes, and tried hard to speed up the transportation.

At the end of February we were told that the British armoured forces were attacking Meiktila, and all the forces around Maymyo should withdraw to south of the River Myitnge. As there was a big hospital at Maymyo, we moved the patients first by train, and this took five days. The 5th Company and battalion headquarters left Maymyo on 10 March on two trains as well as trucks. I was on the last train from Maymyo.

5.2 Defending Mandalay

Captain Kazushi Omori, Commander 7th Company, 4th Battalion, 5th Railway Regiment

The 15th Division, which had been in Malaya, retreated 25 kilometres to the north edge of Mandalay on 6 March. The divisional commander, Lt General Yamamoto, had been the commander of Burma railway headquarters, and decided to defend Mandalay by all means. As my company was in charge of the train service from Mandalay to the south, most of our men were in Mandalay. On 8 March, I received the order to defend the locomotive depot as a part of the overall defence line. As the commander well knew our specialist task, it was a reasonable order. We dug trenches at the north gate and nearby slope of Mandalay hill and took up positions.

Around noon on 9 March, many enemy soldiers came to our front and started shooting, and many shells exploded around us. Then four enemy heavy tanks came close to us and shelled us heavily. As we had only rifles and light machine-guns, we could do nothing to the tanks. The platoon leader close to me had his men make a feint as if they were going to attack them with anti-tank mines. The tanks took notice of this and did not advance any more but continued shelling heavily. We did not retreat and kept our heads down. Fortunately the shells passed over us, and we opened fire whenever enemy infantry came up. When the evening came, the enemy retreated, fearful of our fighting at close quarters. Six of our men were killed including Staff Sergeant Ohshima.

The next day, the 10th, the enemy attacked the north gate of the engine shed and heavy fighting continued for a while, but they retreated as our shooting was accurate and caused them casualties. Two of our men were killed. That evening we received an order to move to the south of the river Myitnge and to come under the command of the 3rd Battalion. We prepared to move our men and supplies to the south by five trains pulled by steam locomotives.

On the morning of 11 March, light trains of the 5th Company came from Maymyo to Mandalay under cover of the morning mist. At about 8 o'clock, two bombers successively dived down on the Tombo bridge to the east of Mandalay. When the bomb of the first plane exploded, the second plane was close behind and both planes blew up in the air, probably as the bomb of the second plane was detonated by the blast from the first bomb. The bridge was destroyed but the last trains of the retreating 3rd Battalion had already passed over it, and we were saved the trouble of blasting the bridge.

In the early morning of 12 March, our five heavy trains left Mandalay but movement was slow as some repair to the line was needed. We came close to Myitnge around noon and saw the central area of Mandalay being bombed by more than fifty bombers. Then several fighters came attacking our trains. The trains stopped and the men ran out and dispersed in the paddy fields. Our anti-aircraft guns fired at the fighters who were surprised and flew away. The trains started off and I was on the last train. Near the bridge I jumped off the train to greet Major Hasegawa who was waiting for us.

I reported to him that all the men of the company had arrived safely with ammunition, food and medical supplies, for which he expressed deep gratitude. Three light trains of the 5th Company arrived following us. The last wagon of the last train carried a 13-mm machine gun protected by sandbags as a rearguard. In the early morning of 14 March, we all moved to Kyaukse and burnt down the wooden Myitnge Bridge.

5.3   Retreat on the Mandalay line

Major Saburo Hasegawa, Commander, 3rd Battalion, 5th Railway Regiment

We retreated from the Myitnge bridge to Kyaukse on 14 March 1945. Then I wondered whether the track of the Mandalay line should be destroyed completely or not. We could make a rail-destroyer, pulled by a steam locomotive, which would pull off rails from their beds at the speed of 20 kilometres per hour. The pulled-off rails would be bent horizontally and could not be used again. However I came round to thinking that the Burmese people would suffer most if the rail was taken off as the Burmese had few trucks and their economy depended on the railway. The British army had a lot of lorries, as well as air supply, and would not be greatly disturbed by being unable to use the railway. So I decided not to destroy the rails.

The Japanese attack to recapture Meiktila failed, and on 20 March we retreated southwards along the Mandalay main line. On 22 March, I received a wireless message that the 3rd Battalion should retreat to Pegu and then maintain the line between Sittang and Pegu. That evening we left Toungoo in two light trains, each with six wagons, and also in two trucks.

When we arrived at Pyu station the sun came out, so we concealed ourselves in some nearby houses, cooked breakfast and slept during the morning. Around noon we saw a large group of tanks and trucks going south on the Mandalay road, which was two kilometres west of the railway. I consulted with my officers and decided to build a makeshift bridge over the River Pyu and to move the light trains through it. We had to hurry as we heard enemy shelling to the south. We were behind the enemy armoured troops. As we did not have the necessary timber, we sharpened some wooden sleepers at one end and used them as piles. As our 200 experienced soldiers worked efficiently, the construction progressed quickly and the wooden makeshift bridge of over 100 metres long was completed within two and a half hours. I thought this must be a record for speed in bridge building. We had rail-trucks pass through the bridge at their slowest speed and then pushed the wagons over by hand. We stopped at Kanikuin station to prepare supper and breakfast, and left there after dark.

When we came to the entrance of Indaigon station, there was a man with a green lamp to guide the train. I asked him to which unit he belonged. He was a stationmaster of 5th Special JNR Unit, who was staying at his post as he had not received the order to retreat.

I told him that this was the last train, and he should retreat by order of the commander of the last train. But he insisted that he could not retreat without the order from his superior, and instead he wanted us to give him some rifle bullets and also some medicine as two of his colleagues were suffering from malaria. So I told him the reason that I must take these men with us on the train. 'According to the army operation manual, Major Hasegawa, who is the commander of the rear guard train is responsible for all remaining railway units on the Mandalay line. So I order you and your men to retreat on the last train. I shall be blamed if you do not come with us. If you understand, be ready to depart immediately.'

I was impressed that these men, only three out of five, were proposing to defend the station with the bullets that we supplied. These men were employees of the Japan National Railway, and their spirit to conform with the five principles of railway soldiers was praiseworthy, and in the best military tradition. I like the Japanese National Railways, as my railway-soldier spirit had been pounded into me when I was despatched there for two years to be trained as a locomotive driver.

Illustration 5.1.1   Rail-destroyer attached to rails

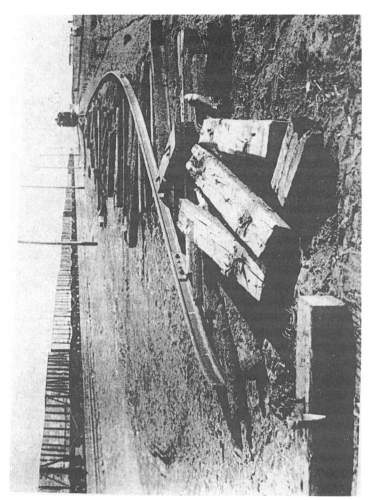

Illustration 5.1.2   Track smashed by the rail-destroyer

Our rear guard train took in these five men, and after repairing damage to the rails at several small stations, we arrived at Pegu on 25 April.

It took us 40 days to retreat 600 kilometres from the Myitnge bridge which we left on 14 March. We retreated repairing rails and racing against the British armoured troops, which were then halted by the Japanese defence line north of Pegu.

5.4 Destroy the C56 locomotive

Master Sergeant Hyogo Ito, Command Unit, 5th Company, 3rd Battalion, 5th Railway Regiment

After we left Thazi and Yamethin the Japanese defence weakened and we had to retreat faster. On the night of 18 April 1945, we were ordered to retreat after destroying the facilities of Pyinmana station. The rails in the station had been bombed almost every day and it was not necessary to destroy any more. So we just derailed a wagon at each set of points.

There were three steam locomotives. Two were British-made ones which we destroyed with hand-grenades. But the remaining one was a Japanese-made C56 which was in an excellent condition and was in the locomotive shelter, all fired up and ready to go. Engine drivers of the 5th Company insisted that they would like to drive it back south, rather than destroying it. This C56 had been mobilised in Japan, had come to Burma with us and had fought with us in the hard campaign. So everybody was eager for the engine to retreat with us. However the Suwa bridge south of Pyinmana was destroyed by bombing and it would take more than five days to repair the bridge for this heavy engine to pass through, while the rapid enemy advance did not allow us to wait so long.

Company commander Sato sent some soldiers to destroy the engine. When they came close to the shelter, nobody dared to throw the hand-grenades saying, 'You do it!' 'I can't. You do it.' They could not kill the living engine which had been regarded almost as one of our family. So he ordered me to supervise the destruction. However, when I saw the engine I thought that I could never destroy it. I returned to the commander and asked permission to repair the bridge and take the engine southwards.

The commander was moved by the eager wish of the soldiers and finally went to consult with the battalion commander, who said: 'It is hard for a commander to order the destruction of a familiar engine; it is like taking a comrade's life. It is even more painful for the men who have to do it. However, even if we were to repair the bridge, the defence of the station will give way sometime tomorrow. Then the enemy will come and attack us while repairing the bridge, and surely we, who do not have an anti-tank gun, will be smashed and the engine will be captured by the enemy unharmed. This C56 must be regarded as a soldier like us. As it is in the military code, so the engine should not fall into enemy hands alive. So we shall let the engine blow itself up just as soldiers commit suicide. I understand how you feel. But the enemy situation does not allow any delay. I will explain the matter to the soldiers and attend the destruction. Unless we act quickly the sun will come up and we shall be attacked by the enemy tanks.'

The destruction team went with the two commanders to the shelter. The C56 engine was five metres inside from the entrance of the well-made shelter tunnel. A thin smoke was coming out of its chimney. The driver in charge of the engine got permission to blow the last whistle and went into the cab. The whistle specific to the C56 sounded loudly in the narrow shelter. It was the sad end of the engine. My heart was full of emotion. The company commander ordered us to open the smokebox. Then came the order: 'Everybody withdraw!'

'Explosion team! Throw grenades!' With a huge roar, earth and steam blew out and the C56 came to an end. Out tears fell and I gave a prayer of thanks in my mind for the past performance of the engine. I said a sorrowful goodbye to the C56.

5.5 Evacuation from Rangoon

Civilian employee Shohichi Imagawa, Engineering Group,
5th Special JNR Unit

On 24 and 25 April 1945, we were busy destroying the facilities of Kamayo workshop, burning papers and packing necessaries for the long walk, having been ordered to move to Kuala Lumpur. Those despatched to Wanetchang and Insein came back to Kamayo, where the headquarters of our engineering group was located. On 24 April, Commander Kawano told the local employees that the workshop was closed and thanked them for their faithful help. We gave some of our belongings as a present to the local employees. On 26 April, when we gathered in the shop ready to leave, more than 160 employees came, lined up and started singing in chorus 'White noble Mount Fuji' in Japanese. And the Burmese leader stepped ahead and spoke to us: 'Even if Japan is defeated in the war, the friendship and courage that you Japanese have given us will remain in the hearts of the Burmese. We will never forget the spirit of the Japanese. We pray that you will arrive at your destination safely.' Though his Japanese was faltering, it was a greeting from the heart of the leader. There were tears came out from all of us, and we felt a strong tie with the Burmese employees.

We got on a train pulled by one C56 engine and pushed by a small engine (type MC) with a wagon carrying a tank, from which water was supplied by a hand-operated pump to the engine. We left in the evening, and took two hours to make the 20 kilometres to Rangoon, going slowly as the rails might be damaged by bombing.

At Rangoon many Japanese civilians, including many women and children, were waiting to get on the train, so we accommodated them as much as possible. They told us that one train had left a few hours ago but it was too full to get on. To their anger, the army headquarters and many officers had already escaped from Rangoon, leaving behind the civilians, and the city was in a chaotic state with no police protection.

However, our C56 engine by itself had to go up to Letpadan to take back men of the operation group of our unit, who had been held up as their engine was damaged by an air-attack. As it was dangerous to stay in Rangoon, which was likely to be bombed when the sun arose, our small shunting engine pulled thirty or more wagons and left in a hurry. After a tedious drive of 101 kilometres our train arrived at Waw, where railway soldiers told us, 'Everyone off! Watch your step! The train cannot go any further as the bridge ahead is down. Leave the train and take shelter before dawn.' We were relieved to see the railway soldiers organising the operation well. We had to cross the canal on a narrow footbridge and walk to the Sittang River.

5.6 The last train from Rangoon

Civilian employee Hidekichi Shimada, Engineering Group,
5th Special JNR Unit

On 27 April 1945, I was at Rangoon station waiting for the C56 engine which had gone to Letpadan. Around noon the train pulled by a YD engine, which left Rangoon the previous evening and went to Waw, came back. Also our C56 engine came back pulling a damaged C56 and wagons loaded with the operation group, who had left Letpadan on the evening of the 25th. They were delayed as the C56 was derailed and shot up by machine-gun fire from enemy planes, but the damage was light and it was thought possible to repair it. So 135 men were pulling the engine with ropes trying to take it to Rangoon, when our C56 came to their rescue and towed the damaged engine to Rangoon. By the evening a long train was formed, to carry us civilians and fighting troops to Pegu, pulled by the C56 and pushed by a YD engine. I drove the leading C56, helped by men of the operation group. After stopping at Dabein to fill the engine with water, the train was attacked by a fighter so we all had to take shelter. At about 49 km from Rangoon, we were shot up by guerrillas but the train ran through, while the troops on the latter half of the train shot back at the attackers. We passed many deserted stations where there were no railwaymen, even at Pegu where the troops got off. At one station, I found a badly damaged engine left on the track which we had to move to a siding. The train arrived at Waw in the early morning of 28 April. The bridge in front was blasted and the rails had dropped in the water. The train was on an embankment where there was no shelter. Suddenly we heard the sound of firing. As I looked back, I saw men were getting off the train, screaming and running in the other direction. Enemy attack! The situation was serious. A man in charge of recording meritorious deeds came into the engine room crying 'I will burn these important papers' and put a bundle of papers into the furnace. Though I was shocked and frightened by the sudden change of situation, I said to myself, 'Calm down, calm down!' and lit a cigarette, an imperial gift which had been given us at departure, and thought aloud, 'What should I do now?' I decided that I should make the engine unusable and burn the important supplies on the train. I took a bundle of trousers from a wagon and put it inside the furnace to ignite, and threw burning pairs of trousers into each of the wagons. Although I could not finish setting fire to the supplies right up to the tail end, I felt that this would be enough. Then suddenly I heard more shooting and was assailed by terrible fear. Now I had to run up a slope which was facing the enemy, for 100 metres, a suitable target for sniping. I ran as fast as I could and tumbled down the other side. Then I heard, 'Why are you so tardy?' As I looked, soldiers of 33 Division were taking position against the enemy. I was relieved. A soldier asked me, 'Have you eaten?'

'Not since yesterday.'

'Eat this.' He handed me without much ado a big ball of rice, while staring to the front. I was deeply grateful and took a large bite. I felt as if my brother, who had died in the war, might have been reborn into this soldier. Even though I was very hungry, I had no saliva, probably due to the excitement; I felt as if I was chewing sand.

When I had finished eating, I felt better and recovered my mental stability. My comrade, Mr Mizutani, came and handed me my equipment which I had left in the train. It was very nice of him; without it I should have been inconvenienced later. Before I could start to talk with him, an officer of the fighting soldiers ordered, 'Non-combatants must leave. The village four kilometres from here is pro-Japanese. Retreat up there.'

When I arrived at the village only half of our group were there. Commander Kawano gave orders on our further movement. At the end he said, 'I thank the man who burned our supplies on the train.' Hearing this, I was satisfied that what I had done was correct.

I boiled rice and planned to rest, but I had an uneasy feeling so I put on my equipment and went to the centre of village. The commander gave the order, 'That mountain is Sittang. Advance in that direction.' At the same time some soldiers on a jeep came and urged us to retreat urgently. 'Why are you so slow! The tanks will be here at any moment.'

The people of the village felt the danger by instinct, and ran towards the sounds of firing, waving a handkerchief in each hand. Though this village was pro-Japanese, this could be the last resort to protect them. It was a sad sight to see the young ladies running at the front of the crowd.

As we had to cross the river, commander Kawano gave all his personal items to his messenger and ordered, 'With these, find a boat.' The sun was about to set and we had to hurry. After some time the messenger found a boat which could carry five men. Its Burmese boatman did not carry a pole but pushed the boat walking in the water. A plane came over and we lay flat on the mud and tried to cover ourselves up with fallen leaves. The plane did not see us, but shot up the train we had just left as if it was on a shooting range.

After we crossed the river we moved in a group of five or six and walked. We hired an ox-cart for our wounded comrade. The driver was a boy of about 12 years old. We gave him a mosquito net as a token of thanks. He buried it under a tree, saying he would pick it up on his return. I was touched by this but didn't think him very wise.

It was a long way to Sittang. We saw a lone fire on a mountainside. The boy told us it was the crossing point of the River Sittang. It was a lighthouse showing the retreating route for the Japanese army. We walked steadily towards it. At the crossing-point, many thousands of soldiers were awaiting their turn. As it was an excellent target for British planes, the crossing was made only during the night, while the boats were dispersed and hidden during the daytime.

We awaited our turn; fortunately I was able to cross the turbulent river the next night as an assistant to the wounded, who were given priority. I had been under constant strain after I left Insein, including the hard driving for 130 kilometres. Much relieved to have crossed the river, I fell into a deep sleep in a shelter on a rocky mountain overlooking the crossing, when I was not disturbed by the buzz of enemy planes.

5.7   Over the Burma–Thailand Railway to Malaya

Civilian employee Yonezo Tomita, Engineering Group, 5th Special JNR Unit

After crossing the Sittang River, we slept well. When I woke up it was 29 April, the national holiday for the Emperor's birthday. But we had no celebration of the day, as we had to start a long march towards Moulmein. I was impressed by the speech from our commander at the departure. He said, 'Even if our unit should perish, no man should be left behind.'

We walked in a rubber forest to avoid air raids. To quench my thirst, I pushed down fallen leaves with my shoe, formed a puddle, and put the water into my canteen. As I drank it I felt some choking feeling in my throat. I spat it out and was surprised to find tadpoles on my palm. So I filtered the water with my towel and put creosote tablets in my canteen. Water was invaluable on a march. After we had walked for some time we heard from a passing soldier that a local train was operating from a place four kilometres ahead. So we were delighted to walk to that place, where soldiers of the 5th Railway Regiment told us that a train would leave in the evening. It was a light train pulling six wagons, and I got on the wagon second from the tail. After the train had run only a few hundred metres, it was derailed and fell on its side with a tremendous crash. It had hit a mine set by guerrillas, but fortunately I was not hurt being near the tail. Two drivers of the Special JNR Unit died and several others were injured. Since the tractor was destroyed we had to start walking again. Unfortunately the rainy season had started, so we marched every night in drenching rain covered only by our bivouac sheets. During the day we slept under the raised floors of local houses. We boiled rice in mess tins when there was no air raid. When we ran out of rice and vegetables, we got them by bartering with towels. The 12 towels that we were given at departure proved very useful. We walked towards the south, like sleep-walkers or tramps, and finally reached Martaban. The mountains there, which had been beautiful, were a miserable sight, having been reduced by the severe bombing to bare slopes covered only by dark burned tree-roots. I got on the ferry from Martaban to Moulmein, and saw a lot of shipping sunk by enemy planes. Fortunately our boat was not attacked.

The wide paved roads of Moulmein were clean and washed by the rain, but the surface was broken in many places by bomb craters. The doors of almost all the stores were closed and only a few people were walking on the streets. As we were to cross the mountains of the Burma–Thailand border, we bought ten days' supply of rice and salt in exchange for our military socks. We imagined on the way we might get some fruit or new buds to be eaten in place of vegetables, and some fish from the rivers in the valleys. As a trial we went to a nearby river and threw in a hand grenade. To our disappointment none of the fish came floating up, and our plan to prepare dried fish ended in an empty dream.

The Burma side of the Burma–Thailand Railway was maintained and operated by the 5th Railway Regiment. The regiment offered an automobile to our commander, Colonel Kawano, but he insisted that he would travel on the train together with us. Because of this we were able to get on the train earlier than expected. However as one box car was allocated to 40 of us, we had no room to lie down, only to sit huddled on our baggage. The train ran only during the night and we slept in the box car during the daytime. When we had to change trains, we had to sleep in an unpleasant jungle full of wild animals. At one river, the wooden rail bridge had been destroyed by bombing, but the railway soldiers fixed it in a day. They had prepared components beforehand, and replaced the broken ones quickly. As the bridges were built using standard-size components, repairing the wooden bridges was done much more easily than the steel ones.

After four days we came to the steel bridge over the River Kwai, which had been demolished by bombing. We crossed the river in boats operated by British prisoners of war who were naked to the waist. When patients got on the boat, the PoWs supported the sick men holding them tightly from both sides and were kind to them.

At Kanchanaburi I met Mr Wakabayashi, a good friend of mine who had worked in the same JNR factory in Japan. It was delightful to see him and we held hands together without talking for a while. He took me and my comrade, Mr Machida, to his place, and fussed around to boil water in a drum tub for us to have a bath, got a replacement for our broken shoes and prepared boiled sugar beans for us. After our hard live-or-die march, his kindness made a deep impression on me. I asked him to exchange a 100 yen note, which I kept with my thousand-stitch belt amulet, for Thai money so that I could buy food for our further trip.

After two days' rest, I thanked him for his kindness and left for Malaya. The trains on the Bangkok–Singapore line were operated by the Thai Railways, not by the Japanese army. The trains were very crowded, with people sitting even on the couplings and the roofs. As I was not able to get inside, I got on to the roof of a wagon. It was my first experience of sitting on the roof of a moving box car. The engine burnt wood as in other parts of the southern area. The worst part of this was that red-hot pieces of wood came flying out from the funnel onto the roofs. Even if I lay down, the fire-flakes fell on my back and neck. As they were so hot, I covered myself with my bivouac sheet which I held tight so that it would not be blown off, but it was burnt by the cinders sometimes.

Moreover there was only a small clearance between overhead structures and the wagon, and the steel roof was slippery. Consequently, I felt more dead than alive when the train went through a tunnel. I hung on to the roof desperately. Once after passing through a tunnel, I heard a cry: 'Someone is missing.' I immediately thought that someone must have dropped from the roof, and a thrill of horror shook my whole body.

Where bridges were demolished, we had to get off and walk to the next station. We moved our patients first, and then came back and carried our rations. As I repeated this several times, I got used to riding on the roof and came to feel that it was more comfortable than to sit squeezed in tight in the narrow wagons. I gained enough confidence to look around at the landscape and to talk to comrades.

As we came further south, we saw more soldiers in dirty uniforms, and felt that the war was coming to the Malayan peninsula. But we were worried not to see any artillery and we wondered how the army planned to defend the area.

We arrived at our hastily-built factory in the suburbs of Kuala Lumpur on 26 June, and started doing simple jobs there.

In August there was unrest around the factory, so we took turns in guard duty at the ration store. On the night of 17 August, when I was on sentry duty with a comrade, a car appeared, driving along the road at high speed. We stopped the car, and a Japanese employee of a trading company got out and abruptly told us, 'Don't you know? The Emperor's speech has been broadcast and Japan has surrendered unconditionally. I am in a hurry to settle our affairs.' As I heard of the defeat of our country so unexpectedly, I was completely amazed, and sat down on the grass totally overcome by the news.

Next day our commander Colonel Kawano came to the factory wearing the brand new rank badge of a major-general, ordered everybody together, and officially told us of the unconditional surrender of Japan. He added, 'As the Allied forces are sure to send all of us back to Japan, obey their orders and we will return to our home in high spirits.'

We all went back to the barracks and wept. We spent some days utterly depressed, until orders from the Allied forces were delivered to us. Then we had to start the miserable life of captured men.

5.8 To Sumatra

Sergeant Akira Kani, 7th Company, 4th Battalion, 9th Railway Regiment

When the Burma–Thailand Railway was almost completed, we were ordered to build a railway across the Kra isthmus to link both coasts of the Malayan peninsula. We completed the 60-kilometre line in two months and returned to Anakuin (369 km), on the Burmese side of the Burma–Thailand Railway, on 15 February 1944. Thanks to the railway, the trip from Kra isthmus to Anakuin took four days, but the railway needed constant repair and maintenance. We ran trains and did maintenance work between Ronsi (354 km) and Anakuin, often troubled by the British Mosquito planes which flew low and surprised us. We ran trains only during the night. After only a month on this new job, our 4th Battalion was ordered to move to Sumatra. We said good-bye to the railway, where we had worked so hard, and went to Singapore on several trains. At Singapore we stayed in a warehouse near the pier, loaded our tools and materials on several boats, embarked, crossed the Malacca Strait, and went up a wide river through a jungle. Next morning the boat was still going up the river at a slow speed. The width of the river was then about 300 metres and the colour of the water was reddish brown; some men called it a coffee colour. By noon, the morning mist had cleared and on both sides of the river there was jungle. We landed at Pekanbaru in Sumatra on 12 April 1944, and walked four kilometres to our hastily built barracks, while friendly native people watched us. My first impression of Pekanbaru was of a white town, where the white government building, marked by Japanese signs, stood surrounded by greenery. There was a movie theatre and a recreation centre for soldiers. A Japanese film was being shown at the theatre and we heard local people whistling its theme song on the street. Here our 4th Battalion, together with a Special JNR (Okamura) Unit and transportation units, was to build a railway between Pekanbaru and Muara, a length of 220 kilometres. The new railway was to be connected to the existing line at Muara, as it was essential to move natural resources from Sumatra to Singapore, and some of them on to Japan.

As we had only one battalion which consisted of two companies, we were split platoon by platoon, or sometimes section by section, and spread along the 220-kilometre length to build the railway. Our platoon worked on building an embankment at around 18 km from Pekanbaru, where the problem was the soft ground in a low marshy area, and where mud-turtles and big rock snakes lived. While we were still struggling to complete the work, our platoon was ordered to build an 18-kilometre branch line to Rogas coal mine from Kotabaru (100 km). Two days later we moved to Tapui, and built our own barracks of bamboo with palm-leaf roofs. Meanwhile, platoon leader Hirota and I walked along the route of the proposed line through the jungle, to prepare the work plan. The mining of coal had been started by military employees, and as the quality of coal was superior, the coke made from it was to be sent to Singapore along the railway which we were to build. While we were working hard on this branch line, platoon leader Hirota was suddenly transferred to become the battalion adjutant and left in a hurry. We missed him very much as we had worked together with him at some of the very difficult places on the Burma–Thailand Railway – for instance, the cutting at Hintok. We did not know that we would never see him again. Warrant Officer Yamada came as his replacement and we continued the construction.

Although the work of the railway soldiers was always very hard, we did not have the severe pressure from above to meet a deadline as had been the case in the construction of the Burma–Thailand Railway, and we worked on our own initiative. We had always enough food and time to rest to recover our strength. There were no air-raids. We felt that a soldiers' saying, 'Burma is a hell, Java/Sumatra is a paradise' really hit the nail on the head. One problem for the NCO in charge of the local workers was that they were not dependable; a large number of workers were sent to our work site but often many of them ran away the next morning.

The construction of the Rogas branch line was completed in February 1945, and our platoon moved to Muara and was in charge of rail transportation until the war ended.

5.9   The Trans-Sumatra Railway

Corporal Tatsuo Morohoshi, Command Unit, 7th Company, 4th Battalion, 9th Railway Regiment

In April 1944, our battalion moved to Sumatra, and the command unit of 7th Company settled down in Pekanbaru together with battalion headquarters, the machine shop and the supply depot. The 7th Company was building a railway from Pekanbaru towards the south, while the 8th Company was working on the line from the 38-kilometre point to 70 kilometres. In August 1944, our company moved to Muara to take over the task of the 1st Battalion of 8th Railway Regiment, which was transferred to the Philippines. Muara was at high altitude and the temperature was comfortable. But we had to be careful about malaria. A lorry transportation unit was stationed there, and I liaised with their medical doctor and took our patients there for treatment, as the doctor of our battalion was at battalion headquarters which was 70 kilometres away.

In late September, most of the command unit, together with two platoons, went to north Sumatra, to repair the important steel rail bridge which had been demolished by Allied guerrillas, and to build air-raid shelters. I remained in Muara but was kept busy as I had to prepare the daily report of the Company in addition to my medical work.

At that time I became acquainted with Sergeant Saito who was the senior NCO at a branch PoW camp. He came to Muara often to arrange transportation of supplies, and once for his own medical treatment when I arranged an appointment for him. I talked with him for some time while he was waiting for transport. From what he told me, and from what I saw, I sensed that the situation of the PoW camp in Sumatra was much better than that I had observed on the Burma–Thailand Railway. I sometimes visited the workplaces of the two platoons in our Company to check their health and to help patients.

The total length of the Trans-Sumatra Railway (TSR) was 215 kilometres, plus 18 kilometres for the Rogas branch, whereas that of the Burma–Thailand Railway (BTR) was 415 kilometres. The TSR went across level plains or gentle hills with only one rock-cutting at the Mukomuko

Valley, whereas the BTR went through steep mountains covered with tropical jungle, and needed much cutting through rocks such as at Hintok and Chughai.

The most important advantage in building the TSR was its good access, as there was a fair road almost parallel to the line and so the work could be started from both ends simultaneously, and light trains could be used to haul supplies. As the railway was almost flat, a rail-tractor could pull eight 10-ton wagons. Because of these advantages the PoWs were issued 900 grams of rice – the same amount as the Japanese soldiers – without fail all through the construction period. In contrast, on the BTR the rough road became muddy, and lorries could carry little in the rainy season, so the PoWs got only half of the specified amount of rice as the construction progressed deeply into the mountains during the rains. At TSR about two small fishes and ten grams of buffalo meat per day were issued, with some tapioca leaves as a vegetable. So the food situation on the TSR was much better than on the BTR, although PoWs at both places did not like rice.

Dutch PoWs still had some local money, guilders (probably because they were paid just before their surrender), and they bought food from the local people, whereas those working on the BTR did not have any local money. As cases of beriberi increased among PoWs on the TSR, unpolished rice (whole-grain rice) and beans were issued in place of a part of the ordinary rice. But the PoWs took this as a downgrading of the food and were reluctant to eat it. (Unpolished rice contains Vitamin B which cures or prevents beriberi, and beans contain essential protein.) Japanese soldiers cooked the rice for a long time and ate it as porridge – a digestible form of the food.

Another difference between the sites was that only those who were suitable for hard work and had been used to it came to the TSR construction, whereas even sick men were transferred from Singapore to the BTR. There were not many epidemics among local people in the area around the TSR, whereas the BTR went through one of the worst cholera-infected areas. There were some cases of amoebic dysentery at the TSR but the spread of this disease was controlled as it was much less contagious than cholera.

At the TSR all other-rank PoWs, except the sick and injured, went out to work and all the officers stayed in the camp to do the cooking and other work. But the soldiers complained that the officers were not good at cooking and they were not enthusiastic about serving the soldiers. So the unpolished rice and beans were not cooked adequately, unfortunately for the PoWs; for this reason later on some soldiers with cooking experience were transferred to the kitchen.

Japanese railway soldiers had learnt how to cope with the PoWs from their hard experience with the BTR, and each platoon using PoWs had about four interpreters. This improved communication between the two sides, compared with the BTR where only a few English-speaking men were available. The camps were run by the PoWs themselves, and there was no fence around the camp. Though they were not supposed to go outside the camp, they did go out in the evening to visit local people for entertainment. Some PoWs who were of mixed race (Dutch and locals), spoke the local language and established a good relationship with local residents. They were able to obtain food and other comforts. The guards did not prevent PoWs from going out of the camp.

As I heard at the construction site, the workload for PoWs was three cubic metres of earth per man per day, whereas the standard for Japanese soldiers was four. At the BTR the workload started at 1.1 cubic metres and went up to three. Two kilometres per day of rail was to be laid by 600 PoWs and one platoon of Japanese. But rail-laying was a highly technical job and the norm was seldom attained, but there was no over-time work after sunset for safety reasons. Since it was a flow operation, a single person's mistake could hold up the whole job, and it was hard to tell whether the mistake had been made intentionally or was an inevitable error due to lack of experience. So the person who made the mistake was often beaten up by an irritated railway soldier, while anyone who delayed the work could be regarded as a hero among the PoWs.

The commander of the PoW camp in this area was Lt-Colonel Banno who had been liked by the PoWs on the BTR (see part 3). So the PoWs were treated more reasonably on the TSR than on the BTR. The camp guards did not beat up PoWs as those on the BTR had done.

The death toll on the TSR was far lower than the 12,493 men who died on the BTR. I recorded the deaths of PoWs in the daily report of my company, which was roughly one every week or two.[1]

The body weight of all the PoWs went down drastically during the nine months; we concluded that the reason must have been that they were unable to digest rice physiologically as the Japanese do. We had hoped that the shortage of meat would have been supplemented partly by protein from the beans. I felt sorry for the PoWs who had to work while living on an unfamiliar diet. Unfortunately very little meat was available in the area.

When the war ended the relationship between us and the PoWs was reversed. They wore the formal uniforms that they had kept, and looked quite different. We wondered what they would do to us. I felt relieved to see that the PoWs became friendly to us. When they received food by parachute drop, they came and gave a chocolate bar to each of us. A friend of mine, Lance Corporal Ito, drove a light train to move Dutch people from Muara to Pekanbaru. When it was derailed and a few Dutch were injured, he was afraid that he would be beaten up because of the failure, as he would have been in the Japanese army, but the PoWs helped to put the train back on the line without any complaints, which he appreciated very much.

Note

The death toll of Dutch PoWs on the Trans-Sumatra Railway, by the end of the war on 15 August 1945, was 389 men. (Information provided by Mrs W. Adriaans, librarian of the Bronbeek Museum, Arnhem, The Netherlands).

5.10   The British view: advance to Rangoon

Ian Lyall Grant

After the Japanese had suffered a disastrous defeat in the Imphal area in the summer of 1944, the British XIV Army of seven divisions (divided into IV and XXXIII Corps) pursued them into Burma. While the independent XV Corps, of four divisions, worked its way down the west coast, the XXXIII Corps advanced to Kalewa, crossed the Chindwin in December 1944, and struck east through Shwebo. The Japanese 18th Army, opposing them, decided to hold the line of the Irrawaddy. The British forced three crossings of this river, and the 19th Indian Division entered Mandalay on 8 March.

Meanwhile the British IV Corps advanced south from Kalemyo down the Myittha valley, and crossed the Irrawaddy on 18 February near Pakokku. Its 17th Indian Division then struck east for 80 miles and seized Meiktila in the rear of the 18th Army. The Japanese rapidly built up a force to recapture Meiktila but, after heavy fighting, failed to do so, and the 18th Army was ordered to withdraw on 28 March. This was the last of the major battles.

Throughout these operations, the British had complete air superiority, and land and air activity was closely co-ordinated. Not only were Japanese front-line troops under constant threat of attack, but so were their lines of communication. Moreover XIV Army relied heavily on air supply, and increasingly so as the advance proceed. Hence it was essential to capture Rangoon before the monsoon expected in May, for then roads and forward airfields would be flooded. Supply from the north would become hazardous, and it would be imperative to receive seaborne supply through Rangoon.

After Meiktila, the British main thrust was made by IV Corps down the shortest route to Rangoon via Pyawbwe and Toungoo, while XXXIII Corps took the longer route via Yenangyaung and Prome. Although the Japanese continued to resist strongly, their formations were now greatly under strength and had lost most of their tanks and guns. Toungoo's two airfields were captured on 22 April by the 5th Indian Division, and after some severe fighting, Pegu, where the Japanese held a strong position to cover the evacuation of Rangoon, was captured on 1 May by the 17th Indian Division. However, the monsoon broke on 2 May, delaying any further advance.

The possibility of such a delay had been foreseen, and parachutists were dropped on 30 April to capture positions at the mouth of the Rangoon river. They were followed the next day by seaborne troops from 26th Indian Division of XV Corps, who entered Rangoon, from which the Japanese had already withdrawn, on 3 May.

Three months of sporadic fighting now followed as the scattered Japanese forces attempted to withdraw across the Sittang, through the hills and forests, and regroup in Tenasserim. However, serious naval defeats in the Pacific, the dropping of the two atomic bombs on Hiroshima and Nagasaki, and the entry of massive Russian forces into the war, forced Japan to sue for peace, and in August the war ended.

Part 6   Japanese Surrendered Personnel and the Military Court

6.1   We were defeated

Lieutenant Ken Iwai, Sumatra Detachment, Material Depot,
9th Railway Regiment

On 16 August 1945, two B24 bombers flew over the Rogas railway factory, where I was stationed. The planes came down low as if they were going to strafe us with their machine-guns, and as a reflex movement I ran towards the shelter. Then it came to me that hostilities must have been terminated, and I stood still on the spot and looked at the B24s wondering what they would do. A dark green B24 circled low around my head and opened the side door fully and the crew waved their hands in a wide-sweeping gesture. Then they started to drop packages by parachutes one by one onto the PoW camp for the Dutch, which was located close to us on the other side of a stream. While I was looking up at the sky in amazement, many parachutes came down, and after the whirring had faded away, the PoWs – no, the Dutch soldiers who had now become the victors – ran with great shouts of joy towards the dropped packages. I continued to watch them and muttered to myself so as to convince myself, 'We've been defeated.'

The Dutch soldiers, who were now free and had changed places with us, came up to us in clean uniforms, while we were standing waiting for further orders. Each time they brought us some of the chocolate or cigarettes supplied by air, and I was happy to see that good human relations existed between us and them.

After working on the construction and initial operation of the Burma–Thailand Railway, the 4th Battalion and part of the materials supply depot of the 9th Railway Regiment moved to Sumatra in April 1944, and worked on building the Trans–Sumatra railway between Pekanbaru and Muara. As the completion ceremony of the 210-kilometre railway was to be held on 15 August 1945, I went to the linking up point, 178 kilometres from Pekanbaru, where a simple ceremony was to be held attended by a few railwaymen. After the ceremony we drank toasts in small glasses of Japanese beer and then Colonel Kasamatsu gave us a guideline address: 'Whatever big changes fall to the lot of Japan, you must not be dismayed.'

From this and from some other information I had been receiving, I guessed that 'Japan is defeated, and the war is over.' It was the irony of fate that Japan was defeated on the day of the completion ceremony for the railway on which we had worked so hard. The thought came to me on impulse, 'What have I achieved in the end after being called up into the army?', and I could not control my unreassuring and inconsolable feelings.

After the ceremony I went back quickly to the Rogas factory. Late in the evening I received an urgent call from the battalion headquarters, as I had expected, and hurried to Muara. There I received the orders of the battalion commander on 'the termination of the war'. The officers of the 4th Battalion who were gathered there seemed to be calm but depressed.

Next morning I hurried back to the Rogas factory. The three of us in the car were in a gloomy, oppressed mood and did not say anything. At the factory I had all the men assemble in the automobile repair shop, and I carefully explained that Japan had surrendered unconditionally. When told of the defeat I was relieved to see that the men did not seem greatly shaken by the news, as I had feared they would be. What I had been thinking about alone in the car proved to be the result of over-anxiety, and I felt that my first difficulty had been overcome.

As evening came on, the Southern Cross shone brilliantly in the sky. I tried to convince myself that 'compared to the vast universe, what happens on the earth is trifling'. I breathed deeply and set my mind at rest for a moment, but still a wave of anxiety passed through my mind with the selfish whisper, 'Now the war is over, I don't have to worry about being injured or killed. But what do we do anyway from now on?'

According to the Potsdam Proclamation that Japan had accepted, our return to Japan from the war fronts was guaranteed. We would then engage in civil occupations. But we did not know how this would be carried out. Looking at the Southern Cross I felt that there must be more things I had not got as far as muttering about.

Five days after the surrender, the 25th Army, who were in charge of Sumatra and Java, ordered us to resume our operations. However we received information that the aggressive Indonesian people who had declared independence on 17 August might resort to force, and were planning to steal the weapons and ammunition of the defeated Japanese, in an effort to consolidate their power. Even though their direct objective was to seize our weapons and ammunition, there was a great fear that in the course of their action our lives would inevitably be in danger. So we could not move about freely without fear as we had before.

Accordingly, I sent an armed truck commanded by Staff Sergeant Fushimi with four men to the Rahat factory in south Sumatra, and I went to the Padang factory with three soldiers. That day we arrived at Padang safely without any trouble. I went to the Padang Hotel where I had stayed in the past, but the hotel as well as the Japanese Isetan store had already been closed. So we stayed at the house of Lieutenant Otake, the liaison officer of the railway unit.

Next day we talked with the staff of the factory, which was in fact controlled by the Indonesians who had declared independence. The discussions went smoothly and we recovered our materials which were being processed and settled all payments. Next day when we came back to Rogas, the Dutch PoWs who had worked with us had already departed leaving behind an empty barracks of palm-leaf huts.

According to the message from the 25th Army we were to be kept armed to maintain public order until our duties were taken over by the British forces who were to come to Sumatra. And the military organisation of the Japanese army was maintained as before. The Japanese military banknotes in guilders with designs of bananas and papayas continued in use as the local currency. One day later in August a group of Japanese landed at the railway bridge 60 kilometres north of Rogas. They proved to be about 15 navy men who had escaped from Singapore soon after the defeat, with food and weapons loaded on big steel boats. Their actions seemed amusing to us. But to our surprise, they claimed that they intended to continue fighting, joining up with the navy force at Padang. When they found out that our railway unit was not yet disarmed they made persistent demands for weapons, food, clothing and trucks. But the commander of the 4th Battalion made it clear that he would on no account co-operate with them even though they were our countrymen. It was obvious that a serious situation would arise if we indulged their wishes. So finding themselves isolated they seem to have gone to Padang on a local bus.

When the British forces came to Sumatra, we were supposed to leave the island. Even though we did not know where we were to go, we assumed that we would disembark from Pekanbaru port, and so it was necessary to maintain the just-completed Trans-Sumatra railway for our own transportation to the port. So we had a small number of men stationed at key points on the railway, and we had to ensure their safety in case the attitude of the local people changed.

At the end of August, our materials supply depot moved from Rogas to Muara, where the headquarters of the 4th Battalion was located. Muara was also the connecting point with the existing line. All of our lathes, drills, equipment, supplies and the blacksmith's shop were loaded on to three railway wagons and moved on light trains to Muara.

About a fortnight after our arrival, a branch of the 17th Military Hospital was opened in Muara in hurriedly built palm-leaf houses. We hoped that we would be able to stay here, and not go to the miserable Rempang Island. About 20 assistant nurses also came to the branch. These were Japanese ladies who had been in central Sumatra. They were designated assistant nurses as a measure to protect womenfolk from the troubles which might be caused by the defeat, as well as guaranteeing their living and status until their return to Japan. Among them were clerks of the Pakanbaru hotel and staff of the Isetan store whom I had met before.

At that time we were notified that the Allied forces had started to arrest those suspected of having maltreated PoWs and labourers. This was depressing news. We spent an anxious time worrying about how to cope with the situation. Measures were taken to cover up everybody's past by burning all the official papers as well as personal memoranda. I burnt the map in which I had punctiliously noted the dates of my journey from 18 September 1941 when I landed at Haiphong, and my diaries. I burnt my photographs after I had looked at each of them, recalling past memories.

Just at that time a British force in trucks passed through Muara, an event about which we had been notified by the army headquarters. The first British force I saw after the surrender was Gurkhas in greenish uniforms with tiger emblems. They did not stop at Muara but just ran through the village towards southern Sumatra.

In November the Indonesian independence movement became more active and radical, and the 25th Army wanted us to step up our peace-keeping role as an order from the British. The British may have thought it practical to use former Japanese forces whose command structure was still in operation, rather than to send more of their own troops to Sumatra, which was not desirable. However the aggressive local people wanted to get weapons by any possible means. Under these circumstances a peacekeeping meeting was held at the army headquarters at Pajakunbuh on 6 December, which my friend captain Somiya attended representing the 4th Battalion. Before his departure he came to me and borrowed my type-14 standard army-issue pistol, as his small palm-size Browning might not be effective in case of an emergency.

Next morning he left Pajakunbuh with three trucks carrying light machine-guns and ammunition issued to the battalion, and also clothing and vegetables. On the way his party met with two road blocks where big fallen trees covered the full width of the road. They cut the trees with a big saw to make way for the truck to pass. Then he saw a Japanese truck coming from the other direction driven by a native Indonesian. He guessed that the truck had been forcibly commandeered by the activists, but he did not try to inspect it, being afraid that his own trucks might also be stolen and his party annihilated, as he had only a small number of men, so he came back to Muara at top speed.

On hearing Somiya's report, one platoon went to look for the truck but in vain. Next day one company went out but could not find any trace of our 12 men who had been on the truck. Three days later some of the bodies were flown to Muara. All 12 men had been killed by hatchets or bamboo spears and thrown into the Inderagiri River. We called this the Bassankaru incident – a miserable memory.

In the middle of December some of the in-patients at the Muara branch hospital, together with the hospital staff including all the assistant nurses, left for Japan. Only the men were left in the Muara and Payakunbuh area without knowing how long they would stay there.

After celebrating the New Year of 1946, we got an order to prepare the papers related to demobilisation. Happily this kept the battalion headquarters and company command units very busy. In the middle of March, the 4th Battalion of the 9th Railway Regiment and our detachment at the materials supply depot were ordered to assemble at Pekanbaru port, which must surely be a step towards our return to Japan. At that point we received an order that Captain Hirota, Lieutenant Nagamachi and 2nd Lieutenant Ushiba were to stay in Sumatra as they were named as being suspected of maltreatment of PoWs and labourers in the construction of the Burma–Thailand Railway. This suddenly put all of us into a state of trepidation. But as we had no means of protecting them, the rest of us, excluding the three, left Muara for Pekanbaru by light trains operated by ourselves on the railway we had built with so much hard work.

While we waited for a week at the port, I had a high fever caused by malaria, but was able to get on a grey boat, a former Japanese submarine-chaser frigate, on 8 April. But this was not the journey to demobilisation which we had hoped for.

6.2 Days without pride

JSP Tatsuo Morohoshi, former sergeant, 7th Company, 4th Battalion, 9th Railway Regiment

After the completion of the Burma–Thailand Railway, our battalion was in charge of its maintenance and operation between Thanbyuzayat and Ronsi (354 km). In March 1944 our 4th Battalion was ordered to construct the Trans-Sumatra Railway and was moved to central Sumatra via Singapore. The railway was completed on 15 August 1945, on the day that Japan surrendered. We gathered at Muara and waited for the day when we could go back to Japan.

On 9 April 1946, we left Pakanbaru in Sumatra on board mine-sweepers of the former Japanese navy. When our boat came out into the Strait of Malacca, all of us gathered on the front deck and simply threw all our rifles in the sea. It was 'a farewell to arms', though we had been treating the rifles with the utmost care in the spirit of soldiers. Next morning we landed at Batu Pahat in southern Malaya. From that time on we felt the misery of being soldiers of a surrendered army (PoWs or JSP).

At first, we had only one sheet (one metre square) of tent to protect ourselves from the drenching rain, while we were not allowed to dig drainage trenches to protect ourselves from the invading rain on the grounds that they would damage the roots of the rubber trees. Second, our lives were threatened by the small allocation of food given to us. The breakfast given to us was only a small bowl of rice porridge, so we feared that we would suffer from extreme starvation. Those who went to work at the British camps were given lunch, which consisted of a small amount of rice and a tiny salted fish. By the time we arrived at the camp, almost all of the bottom of our mess kits for lunch were on view as the rice fitted in a side corner.

I was assigned to an office where a British soldier was working quietly. He did not say anything to me except to give instructions; perhaps he was prohibited from talking with PoWs except on official business.

My jobs were simple and easy such as cleaning the room, polishing his shoes and carrying clothes to the laundry in the camp. However it was uncomfortable to remain standing all the time as there was no chair. When the soldier went out with a friend, I sat down on the concrete floor, which made me feel miserable.

One day the soldier handed me a Japanese sword, which had perhaps been confiscated, and told me to polish it. Though I had practically no knowledge of Japanese swords, I gazed at the sword as if I knew it well. As I took off its handle, I saw an engraved signature. So I explained that a sword with such signature was highly valued in Japan. On hearing it he smiled; he had seldom smiled before. I felt that though he was not talkative he might be a good person. After a while he went out and came back with the friend, and told me to give the same explanation to him. He nodded. That day the soldier was in a good mood all day and gave me a packet of cigarettes for the first time.

As time passed, I came to feel extreme hunger. Though I had some Straits dollars which could be used in Malaya, I could not buy any food as I was not able to contact persons outside the camp.

One day the soldier brought a monkey to the room and tied it to a pole. The monkey seemed well trained and sat quietly holding a box of sweets in its hands. My senses were completely captivated by the sweets. When the soldier went out, I took the box from the monkey. As there were three sweets in it, I left one sweet in the box and let the monkey hold the box as before. I imagined that the monkey must be surprised to have met such an ill-mannered human being. In my mind I apologised to the monkey saying, 'Excuse me!' The well-known proverb 'Even when faced with death, one does not steal' came to my mind and I was ashamed of myself.

Several days later, as I was standing by the window as usual, a British officer happened to pass in the corridor. He was a lieutenant whom I had not seen before. I wondered whether I should salute him or not. As I had been given no instructions about saluting officers, I remained as I was. The officer came into the room quickly and hit my shoulder with his swagger stick saying 'Jap!' I felt intolerable humiliation and looked into his eyes, and he went away without more ado. I could not tell what had made him angry, my failure to salute him or a particular hatred of Japanese. If I had asked him, 'Why are you hitting me without giving a reason?' he might have got more angry and hit me more. It was wiser to put up with his unreasonable action as I was a JSP.

On 12 May, we moved to Kluang on foot, a distance of 70 kilometres. We left at 8 a.m. and walked 10 kilometres to a former naval camp and rested. We left there at midnight and walked 24 kilometres until the next stop. As we were tired because of the poor food and hard labour, many men dropped out. I was encouraged by a friend and struggled to keep walking. The soles of my feet had big blisters and I anticipated hard going for the rest of the walk of more than 30 kilometres. Though lorries came to carry our belongings, I staggered along the road and was finally picked up by a lorry from Kluang.

I wondered why there was a unwritten rule that PoWs should move on foot, as I had seen British and Australian PoWs walking along the construction site of the Burma–Thailand Railway. It would have been more efficient to have them moved in trucks so that their working power could be fully utilised rather than wasted on walking.

At Kluang we were given American field rations, Pacific Rations packed in a square can, half the quantity given to the British soldiers. This was a good nourishing meal, but it was like a confection to us (things like biscuits, oatmeal and chocolate bars), and the quantity was not enough for men suffering from chronic starvation.

On 24 May we arrived at Kemasik on the east coast of the Malay Peninsula and stayed in tents built on the sand. Our work was the repair of the road between Kemasik and Kuantan under the command of an Indian engineer unit. All the Pacific Rations we had were then taken away by the Indian soldiers and instead of these low-quality flour, dried vegetables, corn and mutton were issued to us. The flour was not liked by the Japanese, as some of them suffered diarrhoea, and later rice was issued instead.

About ten Indian soldiers, who were dark-coloured and almost the same height as Japanese, supervised our work. As they were not strict in controlling us, we thought that we should maintain our minimum health, preparing for the day when we might be able to go home, and so we worked slowly. Once or twice a day, when an Indian officer, a *jemadar* (second lieutenant) came around to our site in a jeep, we worked harder than usual. The Indian soldiers kenw this, but did not complain to us much. Due to our working attitude, the progress of the work fell behind schedule. The *jemadar* became impatient and reported on our slow progress in his accented English to our company commander, who did not take any action as he understood our feelings. So the *jemadar* became more excited and talked in high tones, and sometimes wreaked his anger on his own men, who then begged us to work, calling us 'Master'.

As the work was progressing far behind schedule, the *jemadar* got so angry that he allocated us rice mixed with a lot of sand, as a reprimand. We were really hard put to it to recover the rice; all of us had to spend all evening picking out the sand particles from the mixture under the dark lamp in the tent. We thought that he had not intentionally mixed sand in the rice, but must have allocated us a poor cattle feed. If the situation had been reversed it might have been possible to prosecute him as a war criminal. A corporal was in charge of our work. As he was under the orders of the strict *jemadar*, he was a trial to us. We called him 'copra' and avoided contact with him as much as we could.

About twice a week, a local bus with a wooden body, fully loaded with passengers and with luggage on the roof, passed along the road we were repairing. Chinese men among the passengers in the bus usually dropped two or three cigarettes from the window whenever they saw us working. This was a heavenly blessing for those who smoked. We were really impressed by this, as we had heard from the senior soldiers that their conduct in China had often been undesirable, and also in Malaya many Chinese had been killed by the Japanese army under suspicion of spying. We Japanese could not possibly have done same act of returning good for evil. It may be that the statement that Chinese president, Chiang Kai-Shek, published after our surrender, 'Overcome grudge with virtue', had spread through the southern area.

On 10 November, we moved to Kluang on the west coast, where all the men of our 4th Battalion had gathered. We lived in tents by the airstrip, where the electric lamps in our tents were a blessing to us. On the plateau south of the airfield were British barracks, from where camp announcements could be heard, depending on the wind. We were delighted to hear from time to time broadcasts of the Japanese popular song, 'The Apple Song'.

Our work was to build British barracks and a drainage system. The supervisor was a capable Indian engineer. He was very strict and sometimes we had to do the work again as it was unsatisfactory.

The investigation of war crimes was carried out relentlessly, and one day 2nd Lieutenant Rokuro Yokosuka was arrested at the workplace. We were told that our former platoon leader, Captain Eiji Hirota had been hanged in Changi prison.

About that time the control of our JSP camp was delegated to the former Japanese army organisation. So we had some flexibility, and Chinese merchants brought in whatever we wanted. We could get bread, cigarettes, Chinese liquor and daily necessities if we had money. But we had no money as the British did not pay for our work, since we were JSP (Japanese Surrendered Personnel, different from PoWs defined under the international convention). So those who were good at woodwork made furniture in the camp from the scrap wood collected on our way from work, and sold it to the town people. As Sunday was officially a rest day, almost all of us went out to work with surrounding Chinese farmers, who fed us plenty of rice for lunch and gave us an allowance of one Straits dollar per day.

One Sunday I went to the British camp on the hill in order to find out where the Apple Song was coming from. In a small building there were two British soldiers wearing insignia in the shape of the Japanese gate for a Shinto shrine. When I told them the purpose of my visit, they were delighted and talked about their pleasant days in Kure, Japan. We talked for two hours and they gave me two packets of cigarettes. The British soldiers there were friendly and knew Japan, unlike those at Batu Pahat when we landed in Malaya. I visited them several times.

At Kluang more than twenty thousand Japanese army and navy men were gathered, and gradually they left the camp and returned to Japan. However our unit was still designated as being suspected of war crimes, and we did not know when we would get home, which made us feel extremely anxious and dissatisfied. In order to console ourselves in our unsettled mood, various entertainment activities and a theatre were started and literary magazines were published.

In August 1947, we heard that the war-crimes investigation office had been closed and we realised our return home was coming soon. On 23 August a memorial service for six men who had died after the surrender was held, attended by all the men of the battalion, and captain Tosaku Kuribayashi, the battalion commander, delivered his final speech:

> You men have worked hard, from the formation of the regiment on September 1941; the Singapore and Burma operations, the construction of the Burma–Thailand Railway and the Trans-Sumatra Railway. And since the end of the war you have worked for two years under the command of the Allied forces. Now your loyal service to your country has came to an end.

He added with tears and in a sad voice: 'All of Japan, including Tokyo and all the big cities, is a wide expanse of burnt ruins. You are the pivotal persons for the recovery of our country. You are the warriors for the reconstruction of our fatherland.' We were deeply moved by his speech.

In September, we embarked at Singapore and arrived back in the port of Sasebo on 18 September 1947. I was so happy to see our beautiful home country dotted with pine trees and white sand. The 9th Railway Regiment was officially disbanded when we arrived at Sasebo.

6.3   Report to the jail

JSP Juji Tarumoto, former lieutenant, 9th Railway Regiment under the command of the Allied forces

On 28 September 1945, I was at the regimental headquarters located at Aparon which was 332 kilometres from the Thai end of the Burma–Thailand Railway. Our regiment was operating the railway on a limited scale. As I was finishing supper, Lieutenant Kiriyama, in charge of tele-communications, came in feverish haste and handed me a telegram. Officers gathered around me. 'By the orders of the allied forces, the following person is to report to the headquarters of the 18th Area Army soonest. Juji Tarumoto, Yoshida Unit.'

Everybody in the regiment had a gloomy foreboding that some kind of revenge would be taken on us because of the high casualties among the Allied PoWs in the construction of the railway, and was speculating what it would be. I was the first person in the regiment to be summoned. I did not know what would happen to me and imagined the worst possible case. I said forlornly 'I am ready to die.' My words completely silenced everybody around me.

In the morning of 9 October, I was standing at the gate of the 18th (Thailand) Army headquarters in Bangkok. Two British men came up to us and one of them called out 'Taramoto Jugi?' I answered 'Yes.' Then Captain Takei and Sergeant Tachibana were called. The British men gestured to us to follow and started walking, and we three followed the two men. Thus we were transferred very casually from the Japanese army to the British army. Several British soldiers followed us. We were put on a lorry, and were taken to Bangan Jail in a suburb of Bangkok. After waiting an hour in the dark entrance hall, we went through an inner door led by a British second lieutenant (who was adjutant to the commander of the prison) and our belongings were checked. They left me with a blanket, a mess kit, toothpaste, tissue paper, a mosquito net and a canteen. All other things – my shirts, pants, shaving gear, toothbrush, extra toothpaste, English–Japanese dictionary, several books, watch, rucksack and about 500 bahts in Thai money were taken away, and I was told they would be put in a store. Several days later I was given a receipt for the Thai money. (None of the things put in the storehouse were ever returned to me when I got out of the Bangan Jail. I do not know what happened to them.)

Then we were led through an inner gate into a small square around the side of which we could see several iron-grated rooms. To my surprise there were many Japanese crowded on the concrete floors and I felt somehow relieved to see so many of my fellow-countrymen there. Where we were going was not the rooms close to the entrance. We dropped in at a kitchen and had rice and soup put in our kits, passed through an irregularly shaped hole in the brick wall, and then came to a two-storeyed building surrounded by high walls. We three had our photographs taken individually and were led upstairs, where there was a corridor in the centre and cells on both sides. I saw the faces of many men staring at us newcomers through the iron bars facing the corridor. We were hustled into a cell and locked in, and the British lieutenant who led us left at a brisk pace. The cell was made of concrete and the area was about 200 square feet.

Soon a Japanese officer came and talked to us through the iron grid. 'A hard time you had, but don't worry. There are many in this building as you see. I am Captain Kakuta. I will help you in your daily life as you are confined.'

'Please take good care of us.'

'Have you had something to eat?'

'We got something in the kitchen.'

'Here the prisoners have been divided into groups from the 1st Company to the 7th Company, and only the 7th is separated from the other companies.'

The captain left us with the unanswered question why our 7th Company was isolated. A man in the opposite cell told us the reason across the corridor. 'You've come to an awful place. This is the felons' company. As everybody here is confined, Captain Kakuta comes from the 1st Company to help us.' I pushed aside the dust and laid my thin blanket on the concrete floor of cell number 16, 7th Company.

When I was put in the jail, there were already many men in the 7th Company who had been on the staff of the PoW camps connected with the Burma–Thailand Railway. There were many men in the goal, from military police and the Hikari organisation (who had helped the independence movement in India), but most of them were in the 1st and 2nd Companies. I could imagine how those connected with the railway were regarded by the Allied forces, and the men from the PoW camps were expecting more railwaymen to be coming in. Those from the PoW camps must have thought that they themselves had been compelled to force the PoWs to work on behalf of the railway regiments, who should really have been made responsible for the matter.

As I was sleeping on the concrete floor with a thin blanket, the cold was penetrating. We had two meals a day, the first at 11.00 a.m. about five ounces of boiled rice with a small amount of vegetable soup, and at 3.00 p.m. the same amount of rice and a portion of fish or a little sliced meat. From the first day in the jail I felt persistent hunger.

From mid-November the meals were improved, to our delight. This was done not by the jail but by a company of the Indian National Army who were moved to the jail and kindly gave us part of their rations. We were told that the INA soldiers stood proudly face-to-face with the jail guards and sang their independence anthem every morning in unison.

When the New Year of 1946 had passed, Captain Komai and two staff sergeants were flown from the jail to Singapore. Later we were shocked to hear from one of the jail staff, who had been a PoW, that the Captain had been sentenced to death. Then several more were sent to Singapore.

In the early morning of 18 April 1946, about 150 of us left the jail in lorries. We did not know where we were going but everybody imagined that our destination would be Singapore. We boarded a passenger ship of about 7,000 tons and were pushed into a room on the lowest level where it was very hot. The ship passed Singapore, went around the peninsula and arrived at Penang. We were taken to Pfai, on the coast opposite Penang and were put on a passenger train. Next morning the train arrived at Kuala Lumpur and we got off the train and walked about four kilometres to the Kuala Lumpur jail carrying our belongings. We got to the jail at 10.00 a.m. and were left in the strong sunshine. That day we did not have any breakfast or lunch, and at 3 o'clock were given British rations, which we devoured. Then in the evening we walked back to the station and boarded the same train. We did not know why we had had to walk to the jail. The next morning, on 28 April, we arrived at Singapore and were sent to Changi prison.

The Changi prison was guarded by Dutch soldiers, who confined us to a room and carried out a strict check on our personal belongings. The purpose of the check seemed to be to seize any attractive goods. If there was a good watch or good clothes, two or three of the guards dug them out. We were left with the minimum of daily necessities such as blankets and towels, and we Japanese were sent to A hall while the Koreans went to D hall. As we entered A hall, there was a roll-call, and then General Watari who was the chief of A hall cautioned us: 'Everything in Changi is strictly governed by many rules. If you violate any rule you will be punished mercilessly.' Then we were given a packet containing four crackers and were told that 'This is all you get for your meal today.' I saw several men who had been in the same jail in Bangan. Two meals were served to us, at 7 o'clock and 2 o'clock, but the quantity was much less than at Bangan. The morning meal was two

Indian biscuits with sometimes a scraping of butter or jam and some vegetable soup with little content. Supper was a porridge of ata powder. We suffered acute hunger every day. We had to do the jobs ordered by the jail. Also all of us had to do gymnastics every day after breakfast. This was very cruel for us when we were starving, but the guards forced us to do it and anyone who looked lazy had to run in the garden by himself. We called this 'torture drill'.

Those charged with crimes were transferred to C hall which was considered a hell at that time. So far the two former branch commanders of the Thai PoW camp had been sent to C hall. As I had been investigated only briefly at Bangan, I was somewhat relaxed. But on 20 May I was called to the investigation room. A British examining official, who spoke broken Japanese and was perhaps an American Nisei, looked through a thick file of typewritten papers and asked questions in the following way: 'You tortured PoW officers at Ban Kao? You employed PoW officers to do work?'

When I tried to explain the real situation, he often said, 'Don't lie! You are lying.' I was not sure how much he understood what I said.

Several days later he wanted me to sign the typewritten account of my interrogation. When I read it I found some important parts were omitted such as 'I went with my battalion commander and got the approval of the PoW camp commander.' Also 'I remember hitting him two or three times' was written as 'I hit him often.' So I made these corrections and signed it. This paper was perhaps intended to be submitted to the court by the prosecutors but this was not done.

On that day we were told that Captain Takahashi had been sentenced to death. This was a big shock for those of us who had been on the staff of the PoW camps. Taken together with Captain Komai who had been sentenced to death in February, this made two men from the Thai PoW camp who has been prosecuted, and sentenced to death. Everybody felt gloomy.

The fellows from the railway regiments wanted to hear how the examination had been carried out. I told them the situation in detail, as no one in the jail at that time had anything to do with my case – convenient for me. The reason that I had mentioned the name of the battalion commander in connection with the employment of PoW officers, was that he had been transferred back to Japan during the war and I thought that he would not be summoned from his home country by the nature of the case; whereas I did not mention the name of the company commander as he was being held in the Rangoon jail as a suspect.

On 28 May, just a month after I came to Changi, my name was called while I was doing grass cutting work, and I was immediately sent to C hall.

C hall: a prisoner awaiting trial

I was put in a solitary cell on the first floor of C hall. It was thought that C hall was a terrifying place, the next thing to death. Everybody there was to be prosecuted and then had to face the possibility of the death sentence. An interpreter in C hall explained to me: 'Men like you who have been prosecuted and are awaiting trial are called Solitary and are held in a cell. Solitary means lonely and cheerless. Anyway if we say solitary it means you.' The stone bed in the solitary cell at Changi reminded me of the stone stand at the entrance of my home cemetery deep in the mountains, on which coffins were placed for the last rite before they were buried. The shape of the stone bed in Changi was the same in style as the stand in my home village; though there was a difference in what was to be put on it – a dead man or a living man. The living man in this case was expecting the fate of being executed, just one step away from death. I slept on the stone bed and gradually got used to it, but I could not help being conscious of the connection between my fate and the coffin-stand back home.

In the middle of the night we would hear the violent footsteps of four to five men coming up to the first floor. With the loud sound of a key turning the door of a cell was opened. That sound alone was enough to wake me up, or make me jump out of bed, from my painful and light sleep in C hall. Everybody knew what was going to happen, and concentrated their ears sharply in the direction of the sound. It was the raid, the storming of a cell.

There was at least one raid every night. Those who were sentenced to death were sure to be raided on the day. Most of the raids were made on condemned criminals. The British guards' point of view must have been that those who were sentenced to death must be very unscrupulous men who had mercilessly killed their fellow-countrymen, and they could not hate them enough. They must have counted on the condemned men not having a mouth to speak up, however much they were abused. I looked around from the small peephole of my cell, my nerves frayed. When the guards were excited they might rush into my own cell any time. The previous night a drunken guard had thrown a dead mouse into my cell. Tonight I could not see the raided room from my narrow peephole. As I could not see where it was, I was more worried, and tried to judge their moves by my ears. Each of the dreadful sounds could not but make me shiver.

Several guards were shouting some words, sometimes mixed with scornful laughs. I could not make out what they were saying but sometimes I heard a kind of command: 'Stand up ... Sit down ... Come over here ... Stand up ... Sit down!' It seemed that they were forcing the man in the cell to repeat the same moves and enjoying watching him heartlessly. Then suddenly I heard a shrill scream 'Aa-ah!'

No laughing any more. Again I heard 'Aa-ah!' – the scream caused by the torture, try as the man might to endure it. It also tormented the men hearing it. After a while I heard the sound of hitting something with a stick. It sounded like some hard thing being hit, not a man. With the sound, an excruciating scream was heard breaking through the night in the hall. Then I heard sobbing; it must have beeen loud as it reached my cell far away. Sometimes the loud sounds of hitting and human cries were heard, with a higher-pitched scream, 'Aa-ah!' This then turned to weeping, which became louder and louder. I heard no more sounds of hitting. I did not know whether they had stopped hitting or were still tormenting his body with noiseless means. It was terrifying just to imagine what was going on. I felt more dead than alive. Suddenly I heard faint Japanese words, 'Kill me.' I stood still behind the door of my cell, like a man in a trance.

Next day when we were going into the dining room in single file as usual, I saw Mr M crouching by the entrance with his face swollen and blue all over. He had been tried in the court as one of the third group of the Burma–Thailand Railway, sentenced to death on the previous day and sent back to C hall. He was over 50 years old and I had known him from Bangan prison days. I tried to call to him but he was drooping his head as if trying not to be seen by us. Probably he did not want to show his ugly, beaten-up face to others. When I called in a low voice, 'Mr M' he raised his face and nodded slightly, and immediately bent his head low as before.

I went into the dining room with the rest of the file. He ate separately from the other condemned men and soon left with a guard. So I did not see him any more that day. However I could not help being reminded by his beaten-up face of the raid of the previous night. He had been tortured so much after receiving the death sentence.

On the following night and then again the next night Mr M kept weeping, tormented by the raids. His crying, which came up from deep in his soul, affected and greatly disturbed the men in C hall. I had chances just to get a glimpse of him; his face was swollen with weeping. I did not see him smile. He was timid and never talked to his neighbours.

Like other men in the same circumstance as myself, I felt that death itself was no longer much to be feared and the most dreadful thing was the torture by the guards which followed the death sentence.

Prosecution

There were many steel doors. I was following a guard who opened and closed each door and walked very quickly. As I had not been taking any exercise, being confined in a cell, I had a hard time following him. When I entered the examination room and stood in front of a small table, I felt almost as though I was suffocating, not only by walking quickly but also by a presentiment of doom. A short, fat middle-aged British man in front of me stood up slowly and started to read a type-written paper.

> You are charged...As a member of the 9th Railway Regiment who built the Burma–Thailand Railway, you are charged with disregarding international legal usage from October 1942 to August 1943, maltreating many Allied prisoners of war and hence causing them to die, and likewise encouraging your subordinates to maltreat and kill prisoners.

'Regarding this case, the prosecution is ready to submit many items of evidence which I have here. These will be handed to you later for you to read. I will just mention a few examples, such as that you beat the PoW soldiers, forced the PoW officers to work, forced sick men to work and killed PoW soldiers directly. I do not know whether this evidence is correct or not, as I have not seen the actual sites. However if it is correct, you are the cruellest man I've ever known.'

'I may add that you will be assigned a Japanese defence counsel and a British defence counsel at the court. Talk with them about what you would like to say. If you have anything you would like to say on this occasion you may say it as a special case. Is there anything you would like to say?'

My gloomy forebodings gradually took shape. When the fat man had ended his speech and looked at me through his glasses, these forebodings clearly indicated that a group behind this man was going to kill me. I stood still like a stone. My brain intuitively felt their intent to murder me. If there were words that I wanted to say then, it was 'You are going to kill me?' But what would be the good of that? I just said, 'I have nothing to say.'

Hearing this, the fat man left the room in a business-like manner. I was handed the indictment and an outline of the evidence.

Having read through the indictment, I lay on the stone bed utterly spent. The stone bed was cold, but at the same time sweat came out on my weakened body. Whether it was surprise at the unexpected indictment or anger against the underlying intent of revenge, or my excitement in trying to plead desperately against it, these things came into my mind together and confused me. The will to kill me that I felt when the indictment was read to me, the will to kill me that I felt when I was told 'You are the cruellest man I've ever known', the will to kill me became clearer and clearer as I read and re-read the indictment. I let myself be overpowered without a struggle by the will to kill me, and followed the line of least resistance, which was to be prepared for death. 'Mother, I cannot see you any more. I am going to die,' I muttered to myself. My eyes became hot as they formed the image of my mother. I felt that my tears somehow put me at my ease.

It was two days after I received the indictment that Mr Kawazoe, the counsel, came to see me. When I faced him in the reception room, I instinctively tried to judge my fate from his attitude. After my mental torture of two days in the solitary cell, I was looking for something from a man who might have a different way of thinking. But I did not dare to ask his opinion on my fate, and I knew that he would not be able to give a clear answer to such a question.

He gave me a general outline of the case with some discussion. He had graduated from the law college of Tokyo University in 1932, and had been my senior there; this senior–junior relationship in the same college seemed to help give him a favourable understanding of my case. He was sympathetic to my situation and I came to trust him.

'I know very little about the Burma–Thailand Railway. What was the actual situation?' he asked frankly in a kind voice. He also said, 'That was pretty hard work, but it was to be expected.'

I felt a breath of air untainted by the court after such a long time, and relaxed briefly even though I was in a serious situation. But the time was short. He got up saying, 'Please remember that they are in a hurry to open the court. I may be able to come twice more before then.'

He went to the door and then turned around to me unexpectedly. 'Ah, now, don't worry about the court, and keep your spirits up and don't indulge in needless worrying.' He said this as if he had recalled something that he should have told me, and went out. As he had said it casually, it gave me a renewed hope of life. I wondered why Mr Kawazoe had said it. Did he just want to console me, or did he have confidence in the outcome of the trial? But as he still knew very little about the case, he could not have any confidence in its outcome. I just imagined that he had perceived that I might be helped. Anyhow his last words were like a big flash of hope for me.

After returning to my cell in C hall I lay on my face and cried, 'Mother! I am still all right. I am sure to see you. Please stay alive until then.' My fear of death was not removed by this. The shadow of death still clung to the stone bed in the cell, as this meant that my chances between dying and living which had been nine to one had merely been improved to 50–50.

Once more I read the indictment and the evidential documents. The indictment said:

> The Accused is charged with committing a war crime in that between the 1st October 1942 and the 1st October 1943 while engaged in the construction and maintenance of the BURMA-SIAM railway, in violation of the laws and usage of war, he was concerned in the inhumane treatment of British, Australian and Dutch Prisoners of War resulting in the death of many of the said Prisoners of War and physical suffering by many others of the said Prisoners of War, together with similar acts committed by the subordinates of the Accused.

Many diverse facts were mentioned in the evidential documents attached to the indictment. Among them, most of the examples of my subordinates having caused the death of PoWs due to ill-treatment were acts committed by the Korean guards sent from the PoW camps. One example of a railway NCO or a soldier who had forced PoWs to build a bridge until late in the night while hungry, thereby causing one man to die later, was not of a man in my platoon but in another platoon. This might be a misunderstanding arising from the fact that the bridge was close to my area or because my position was deemed to be that of company commander or battalion commander. Throughout the evidence it was not recognised that I was simply a platoon leader; some parts clearly spoke of 'Battalion Commander Tarumoto'.

One reason for this misunderstanding was that the platoon leader had to cover a wide work area, and employed more than a thousand PoWs. Those who planned the work, the company commander or battalion commander, were not seen by the PoWs and it seemed to them that the platoon leader himself planned the work and carried it out.

During the construction I was in charge of three types of work: blasting, building bridges and constructing embankments. I remember a PoW officer telling me, 'Your job is that of a battalion commander. If you are a platoon leader you should be doing only one of these jobs.' In actual fact, in the construction of the railway, all those engaged in it, from regimental commander to private, had to perform heavy and wide-ranging duties. Otherwise the railway could not have been completed within the scheduled time. The misunderstanding on the part of the PoWs came from the excessive burden of the work. Up to this point the charges concerned my responsibility for the acts of my supposed subordinates, but all were wide of the mark.

The most important were the charges directly concerning my own actions. But much of the evidence consisted of mere abstract statement such as, 'Tarumoto is a cruel man. He used to hit men with a bamboo stick,' without showing the time and place. If one excluded such evidence, only three out of the fifty charges could be linked to actual incidents.

The first one was that I had forced PoW officers to work at Chungkai; the second was that I had driven the officers to work too hard; the third was that I had forced sick PoWs to work at Wang Lan.

On the first point, I had employed the officers in the construction work with the permission of the PoW camp. The employment of the officers was decided at a meeting attended by the Japanese camp commander, Lt-Colonel Yanagida, Colonel Williamson, the highest-ranking British PoW officer, and PoW company commanders. I thought it was reasonable for me, as a member of the railway regiment, to employ the PoWs offered with the permission of the camp.

The second point was abstract and no actual case was presented. However, three occasions occurred to me. I had requested a certificate from a Japanese medical officer for PoW officers who did not come to work; I had slapped the face of an officer who had shown a rebellious attitude in his work, or I had forced all officers to carry to the work site bolts and clamps that a group of PoW soldiers had neglected and laid aside in the bushes.

The third point had occurred when I visited the company command unit at Wang Lan. Platoon leader Takizawa who was in charge of the area, together with a Japanese medical doctor, checked the physical condition of those PoWs who claimed to be sick and ordered many of them to work. I relayed the message to the PoWs as interpreter. But I was thought to be responsible for all of this trouble.

It is worth noting that these three key cases took place in the early stages of construction when the transportation of supplies was relatively

easy and the PoWs' lodgings, meals and sanitary and working conditions were not so rough. In actual fact, most of the PoWs had died
during the rainy season in 1943 when the work was more severe. At that
time I was responsible for the work deep in the mountains, 100 kilometres from Chungkai or Wang Lan, where hard labour was required,
but there was no evidence submitted against me regarding the situation
there.

However, I wondered how useful such explanations would be. When
I heard more about the results of the courts which had been held in
February, I had grave doubts whether the trials were a fair means of
achieving justice, or simply a means of satisfying the desire for revenge.
The only acceptable excuse for my fate was that we had been defeated
in the war, and we had to give up all hope in the face of the decisive
fact of the defeat.

The trial

Mr Kawazoe, the counsel, came to me twice more before the trial. He
said, 'There will be no trouble if you are cleared of responsibility for the
administration of PoWs in such matters as food and sanitation. I think
that will be the key point.... Don't worry about the quantity of evidence,
as the more items there are, the more contradictions they may reveal
among themselves.... The prosecution seems to use written evidence
only, without calling witnesses. Witnesses can sometimes be very effective, and they may also render the evidence worthless. So in your case it
will be better if witnesses are present.' His words put me at my ease. At
the final meeting he said, 'They seem to be in a hurry to start the trial.'

On the morning of 10 June, I was suddenly told that I was to go to
the court, and after eating breakfast in a hurry, I was taken to the record
office where I joined my three witnesses. I took off my prisoner's
clothes and was given my military uniform and shoes. So I looked like
a former military man.

When we went out of the prison gate, a truck was waiting and the
suspect and three witnesses were pushed into it. There were six soldiers
guarding us. They asked persistently, 'What case?' We pretended that we
did not understand. Meanwhile one of the guards told me to say, 'I-am-
a-fucking-Japanese-bastard.' As I remained silent, he repeated it many
times. Finally when I said it in a low voice in a queer pronunciation as
I was told, they laughed. After that they did not talk to us, probably
because they were interested in the passing ladies as the truck came into
the streets of Singapore. The truck stopped in front of Autram prison,
and we were transferred to another truck. The guards were changed

from British to Indians. The court was very close, only five minutes' walk away. The truck passed through a gate marked 'Eighth War Crimes Court' and stopped at a sharp bend. I got out of the truck and found myself surrounded by more than ten Indian soldiers who were fully armed. 'This is the court that will decide my fate!' However the building was not the kind I had imagined from the name of the court. Many parts of the wooden building were rotten. The paint on the closed louvre windows was starting to come off. Surely it must be a deserted house where nobody had lived for a long time. We were led into the house and then to a small room which was the waiting and confinement room for suspects and witnesses.

There was a small table there and two benches on each side of the room. What caught my eyes were the words written everywhere in the room, such as '3 April 1946, death sentence' with a name. Almost all of them were just dates and names, unlike the ones with some comments in the solitary cell.

I ate the lunch that I had received at Autram jail before nine o'clock. I still had a good appetite. I ate all my meals after I received the indictment. The Indian, who was watching us outside the room, gave me a cigarette. A puff of it after a long time without cigarettes gave me a passing comfort. Then a British soldier who was not wearing a cap came in and sat on the desk and asked 'What case?' As I kept silent he said with a grin, 'Death march? I know.' As I still kept silent, he squeezed his throat with his hands, which meant death by hanging, and went out.

Then the door was opened and a guard signalled to me to come out. He wanted me to clean the upstairs room which was to be used as a court. I was handed a worn-out broom and cleaned the room from corner to corner and moved the tables and chairs back to where they were before. When I returned to the waiting room I was given a cigarette.

Mr Kawazoe came in hurriedly and told me the order of proceedings in the court. He especially mentioned that the first question asked by the judge would be 'guilty or not guilty', to which I should answer 'not guilty'. I saw through the glass window a group of court officials arrive in cars. Immediately I was called and had a piece of cardboard marked 'No. 1' hung on my chest, and went into the court room which I had just cleaned.

When the judge came in with two associate judges, everybody stood up. After I had sat down I was ordered to stand up again and the indictment was read. At that time the judge noticed that my first name was wrongly spelt as 'Jugi' and told this to the prosecutor, who nodded. As the house stood at the corner of a crossroads it was noisy outside and the judge ordered the louvres to be closed. So it became dark in the room.

The judge asked, 'Guilty or not guilty?' When I said 'not guilty', he nodded as if he was expecting it. Immediately the submission of the evidence by the prosecutor began. As there were many items of evidence, reading them took all morning. I understood the contents to the extent of the written outline I had received, but the prosecutor stressed certain words such as 'inhumane', 'cruel' and 'slave-driving'.

At last the reading was finished and I returned to the waiting room accompanied by the guards. As I had already eaten my lunch I had nothing to do. Luckily an Indian guard gave us cigarettes, which tasted very good. Mr Kawazoe just dropped in for a second and told me that I was to take the stand as a witness in the afternoon.

In the afternoon session, Mr Kawazoe applied for me to take the stand as a witness. I was called in front of the judge. The associate judge asked me whether I was a Christian or a Buddhist. After I had taken an oath I went into the witness stand. The first part was the questioning by Mr Kawazoe, which was no problem as he asked questions to help defend me, such as, 'Who was in charge of the meals and sanitation for the PoWs?'; 'Were the guards of the PoW camp, the military employees, under your command?'; 'What was your rank at that time?'; 'What were your duties?'; 'Who was in command of you?'; 'Did you tell the PoWs at that time that you were only an interpreter?'; 'Who was responsible for checking the sick PoWs and telling them to work?' So these questions were easy to answer. Then he suddenly asked, 'What university did you graduate from?'

This question had not been discussed. I answered, 'Tokyo Imperial University.' He asked again, 'What college?'

'The college of law.' Hearing this the judge grinned and had some conversation with the associate judges.

Questions in the court must not be leading questions which could be answered by yes or no. But when Mr Kawazoe put a leading question, the judge asked him, 'What has your occupation been?' 'I was a judicial official in Malaya.' I imagined that the British system of putting questions to the witness could not be easy for him, and the full details might not be entered as he wished.

The cross-examination by the prosecutor began. He stood up and checked the period during which I had worked and the place. Then he asked about the volume of earth-moving work allocated per PoW per day. I answered, 'One and a tenth cubic metre at Chungkai, which was very easy, as the standard for Japanese engineer soldiers is five cubic metres.'

I ventured to request them to change the expression used by the interpreter from 'not so difficult' to 'very easy', which the judge granted.

The most important point occurring in the cross examination concerned the 'orders'. He asked, 'When an officer gives an order to a non-commissioned officer, the latter has to obey the order, right?'

'That is so generally.'

'If you yourself give an order to a non-commissioned officer or a military employee of a PoW camp, they have to obey the order. Is this correct?'

'They do not have to obey the order as I have no authority to command them.'

The prosecutor seemed startled to hear my statement. In many of the past cases the defendant had perhaps stressed the 'absolute obedience to an order', so he wanted to apply this to my case. But he did not understand the chain of command. He repeated,

'In such case a subordinate does not obey his superior, is that correct?'

'That is correct.'

I needed to explained the system of command in detail, but unfortunately I could not do it properly. I was not sure whether the prosecutor or the judge had understood what I said on this point. I thought that as the prosecutor and the judge were originally military men and as the strict obedience to orders required in the British army seemed not too different from that in the Japanese army, they should have easily understood the point. But I wondered, was there a basic difference in the conception of orders between the two countries, or were they prejudiced on this matter? The cross-examination finished in about an hour.

In the afternoon of the second day, Mr Yanagida and Mr Higuchi took the stand as witnesses. Mr Kawazoe tried to get proof from Mr Yanagida that would clear me of responsibility for the control, feeding and sanitation of the PoWs, and would explain how the officers came to be engaged in the construction work. Though Mr Yanagida was old he testified clearly in a loud voice during the lengthy cross-examination.

After Mr Yanagida had finished his testimony, the judge said to Mr Kawazoe, 'I fully understand what the counsel for the defence has intended to prove by the testimony of the witness Yanagida. If what you plan to prove by the witness to follow is the same as this, there will be no need to obtain further testimony. However I do not object to your asking further witnesses if you wish.' Mr Kawazoe came over to me and asked me what I would like to do. Finally we decided to ask Mr Higuchi to stand as witness.

The testimony of Mr Higuchi exceeded my expectations. He added that I had been kind to the PoWs. There was no cross-examination by the prosecutor. The final presentations of the defence and the prosecution were to be made two days later.

At that time the defendants and witnesses summoned to attend the court were transferred from Changi prison to Autram prison in the city of Singapore from where they commuted to the court. However I was taken back to Changi prison after the first day of the trial was finished.

At Changi I was taken to the upstairs part of A hall, not C hall where I had been. The guards there took me into their recreation room and asked me the details of my case. I kept silent. Then they body-searched me and pulled out the indictment from my pocket. After they had read it, the guards looked at me with their bloodshot eyes and shouted all kind of abuses, but they did not touch me. Then I was put into a solitary cell at the end, and soon taken to the bathing facilities on the ground floor. Though it was pretty dark I could see lying beyond the screen suspects with whom I had shared the jail before being moved to C hall. Several people who knew me came close to the screen and called out to me, 'Are you all right?'

The guard chased me out to the stairs where an unfamiliar sergeant came from B hall and hit my left ear with his big fist. It was a heavy blow; I thought my eardrum had been broken and the pain became stronger as time passed. Later three guards came into my cell and asked, 'How many men did you kill? How did you kill them?' They swore at me in many words and took away the two blankets that had been given to me. I had a hard time trying to sleep on the stone bed.

Next morning I requested them to return the indictment that they had taken away but my request was turned down on the grounds of it not being necessary for me. During the lunch break I told Mr Otake, the assistant to the interpreter what had happened the previous night.

After the day's court was finished I was called over to the judge who welcomed me with a smile and asked, 'Do you have any appeal that you would like to make?' So I gave him an outline of what I had undergone. Then he wrote something on a piece of note paper and gave it to me, saying, 'Take this with you and hand it to the director of Changi prison. Because of this you may be tortured more; in such a case telephone me.' I was very much moved by this. I was happy that I had made a proper petition and felt that the British court was reasonable, and hence a fair judgement would be made.

Unexpectedly, I was not sent back to Changi prison and was accommodated with Mr Yanagida and Mr Higuchi in Autram prison. Later in the evening a medical doctor came to the prison and checked my ear, which was still aching.

On 15 June, the day of the final presentations and the judgement, Mr Kawazoe came to me in the waiting room and explained the course to be taken by the defence and added, 'I will plead that you are not guilty. However I do not expect a verdict of not guilty. But my personal feeling tells me that you will not be sentenced to death. I myself will suffer for having said this if the worst comes to the worst.'

A verdict of not guilty cannot be expected; my sweetest dreams had been broken. I was still hovering between innocence and death.

The court opened and Mr Kawazoe began his oral proceedings. The presentation written by him was translated into English and was read by a British adviser. He debated clearly on each item, the responsibility for the control of the PoWs, the work, the compelling of sick men to work and the ill treatment. It seemed that the judge was unsettled in his mind as the proceedings were read. The oral proceeding of the prosecutor tried to refute the points raised by the defence, which were in fact a summary of the evidence presented to the court.

After this the judge and the associate judges withdrew to a room to decide whether I was guilty or not guilty. The other men in the court room seemed relaxed and many started smoking. I sat still on my seat and considered that the die had been cast, and I was not composed enough to estimate the result. I was experiencing the temporary pleasure of having been released from a kind of spiritual strain.

Soon the judges came into the room and the chief judge ordered me to stand up, and pronounced their verdict: 'Guilty of inhumane malicious treatment of PoWs, excluding causing their death.' I could not clearly understand what he meant, but was relieved to feel that I had clearly been saved from the death penalty, though at the same time I was disappointed that I had been found guilty. After a recess of about five minutes the judges came in and asked, 'Is there anything that the defendant would like to say?'

I stood up and said, 'I trust the British laws and the British court procedure that I studied at university. This conception has not changed even now when I have been found guilty. I wish for a fair sentence to be passed.' Soon the judge told me to stand up again. 'You are sentenced to life imprisonment.' I received this without emotion though I had a feeling that the penalty was heavy.

Soon the judge left. He had to go to Kuala Lumpur by train that same day. The prosecutor and clerks gathered the papers on the table and left. The court room emptied. I was the last to leave and went down to the waiting-room guarded by Indian soldiers. Mr Yanagida and Mr Higuchi made haste to ask me the sentence. Hearing it both lamented, 'It is a very heavy penalty.'

I thanked them and sat down feebly. As I looked at the names on the wall of those who had been sentenced to death, I sighed with happiness that at least the death sentence had been avoided. Mr Kawazoe and Mr Otake came in and encouraged me, 'Do not be discouraged. Things could change for the better in due course, now you have not been sentenced to death.'

The truck with its guard of many soldiers carried me, a life-term convict, through the streets of Singapore and then the rubber plantations. I, and also Mr Higuchi and Mr Yanagida, remained grimly silent all through the drive. The truck passed through the heavy gates of Changi prison. After the gates were closed, I was made to run towards the cells for the convicted prisoners.

6.4   A Korean war criminal and a Japanese officer

Former Japanese Army Civilian Employee, Lee Han-ne (Japanese name: Hiromura Kakurai)

When Japan surrendered I was working in the Hintok sub-section, 3rd Section, 4th branch of the Thailand PoW Accommodation Headquarters. When Japan was defeated, the PoWs took over the administration of the camps, and we Korean guards (civilian employees) were simply released from the camp without any formal procedure. About twenty of us lived in a temple and waited for instructions from the Allied forces.

On 28 September 1945, all the Korean civilian employees were ordered by the Allied forces to come to the Korean camp located in Bangkok. When we got there, we were made to file past a row of ex-PoWs, and I was immediately arrested and sent to Bangan prison on the outskirts of Bangkok. To my surprise, I was put in a building for those accused of serious crimes.

The Koreans were on the ground floor while the Japanese were on the first floor, and the passage between us was locked. The Koreans were full of complaints against their former bosses. When a guard forgot to lock the door, some angry Koreans went upstairs to their former camp commander and made accusations such as 'What happened to our retirement allowance? Is it true that you said that you would not pay us a penny? Don't deny that you gave orders to us that a PoW who violated the rules should be punished on the spot!' Then they beat up the commander saying 'We have been wrongly accused because of you! You are the one who deserves to be treated like this!' They were very fearful for their future, as they were being treated as guilty of crimes for which their Japanese bosses should have been made responsible, especially those who had driven them hard at the PoW camps.

In the latter part of April 1946, I was transferred to Changi prison in Singapore. The food given to us at Changi was very meagre. I felt hungry all the time and was reduced to a walking skeleton. Despite the poor meals, we were forced to do gymnastics every day, and those who did not do them punctiliously were forced to run around for a long time. Gymnastics were a severe torture to us. I became so weak that I did not mind what happened to me when the investigation started in August. So far 60 per cent of those who had been put on trial had been sentenced to death. I thought that the trials were being conducted simply for revenge. In such a critical situation many men tried to shift the responsibility on to others, insisting that 'I did not order that' or 'He did it on his own initiative' and so on, passing the blame on to each other. In such adverse circumstances I could see the true nature of a human being. I really respect, and thank for his human kindness, my former camp commander at Hintok, Lieutenant Usuki, who volunteered to testify for me despite the fact that he could expect the death penalty for doing so. Even though I could not see him in the segregated prison, I got a verbal message from him conveyed through others that 'Hiromura is not responsible for anything he is being accused of. I, as the commander of the detachment, bear the responsibility for everything. Don't worry! Fight your way through. You will live a long life!'

I was prosecuted on the following charges, which were based on four affidavits by ex-PoWs:

1. I forced them to live in poor facilities with poor provisions;
2. I forced sick men to work;
3. I did not stop the violent acts of the guards who were under my command.

Some of the affidavits called me a camp commander, which was a mistake as I was the same rank as the other guards and no one was under my command. So charge no. 3 was unreasonable. As for no. 2, Lieutenant Usuki must have made it clear that he was responsible for ordering me to pull out slightly sick men and set them to work. No. 1 was the responsibility of the PoW camp administration, not of us, the lowest-ranking persons at the camp.

On 24 October 1946 I was released on the grounds that the indictment had been rejected, thanks to Lieutenant Usuki, and was transferred to Juron camp for those awaiting a ship for Japan. In January 1947 I got on a repatriation boat with many Japanese and a few Koreans. After five days the boat arrived at Hong Kong where a British officer came to the boat looking for a Hiramuro. As a civilian working for the Japanese army, I used the Japanese name Hiromura. Though the captain insisted that there was no such person on board, he could not continue to resist as he was told that the boat was to stay there until the suspect was found. So he called me and asked me to go with the officer. I was arrested again and was put in Star prison in Hong Kong where there were a hundred Japanese imprisoned. After staying there three weeks I suffered the miserable fate of being sent back to Changi prison in Singapore. I heard that Lieutenant Usuki, my respected former commander, had been hanged.

At the end of February I was given a charge sheet which stated that I had killed many PoWs by forcing sick men to work, charges which were supported by the affidavits of nine Australian ex-PoWs, though I had never been investigated personally. On 18 and 20 March 1947 my trial was held in the Australian military court at a temporary facility in Changi prison. It was a short trial and the Japanese defence lawyer, who was assigned to me as a matter of form, refused to look for the witnesses that I requested, and nobody appeared as a witness. On the second day I was sentenced to death, though I did not know why, and was handcuffed and transferred to the hall for convicted prisoners.

There were about 15 men in the hall, Japanese and Koreans together. They seemed not to be melancholy or miserable though everyone there was sentenced to death. Everyone used to spend his days busily engaged in something, or perhaps he was making himself busy intentionally. However about once every two months an Indian captain came in the evening with a notice of execution, while we sat in deep silence wondering who would receive it. Those who were notified were to be hanged at 9 o'clock the following morning.

The faces of those who received the notice turned pale even though they had been expecting to die. There was a dinner party for those notified, attended by a Buddhist priest. A modest Japanese meal and cigarettes were sent from the camp kitchen. The last meal! But many men could not eat anything. I attended such a last meal twice. A Korean friend to be executed said to me 'Mr Hiromura, I hope you will be granted a remission.' What could I say to him?

The condemned prisoners took a shower in the morning, and then paid their respects in worship to the home country far away, handcuffed as they were and cried out very loudly their last words to us, 'We are leaving now. We bid you farewell.' Soon afterwards the sound of steps climbing up the ladder and the shout, 'Long live the Emperor' or 'Hurrah for the Great Korean Country', were heard, as the execution platform was next to our hall. The foot boards were opened and a man was executed. What an unforgettable experience to hear them! We Koreans could understand the feelings of those being put to death. Their hearts were breaking, as they thought of the mental pain of their parents, to whom they could not give any convincing reason why they died. On the other hand a Japanese might be able to console himself with the thought that 'I am dying for the sake of my country. I did my best for my country when I forced the PoWs to work hard, and for that reason I am going to die, as unfortunately my country was defeated. My parents will regard me as an honourable man.'

Seven months passed. I still had not been executed. Suddenly I received a notice saying that my penalty had been reduced to 20 years' imprisonment. I had luckily avoided death. I was then confined as a prisoner in Changi. In October 1948 I was transferred to Autram prison in Singapore, and in August 1951 to Sugamo prison in Japan. I was paroled on 6 October 1956. I spent ten years of my valuable youth in prison. For what purpose?

Appendix

Lieutenant Eiji Hirota, the railway platoon leader, who employed the PoWs sent from the camp where Hiromura worked as a guard, was hanged on 21 January 1947. Hirota was one of the two officers from railway regiments who were executed. Hiromura's boss, Lieutenant Usuki, the commander of the 3rd section of the PoW camp, was hanged on 22 November 1946. A note left behind by him reads:

'I was sentenced to death in the war crimes court at Singapore on 25 August 1946, and have been kept in Changi prison. On 20 November I was told that I was to be executed on 22 November 1946. I was prosecuted on charges of maltreating PoWs and causing many of them to die in the construction of the great Thailand–Burma Railway. At that time I, as commander of 3rd section, 4th branch, Thailand PoW Administration Headquarters, supervised about five thousand British and Australian PoWs working on the construction of the railway, in a large trackless jungle in Thailand. In that place I was put in a very thankless situation. Firstly I was ordered to concentrate all my effort on the early completion of the railway and hence the maximum labour force of PoWs was required. Secondly the camps were completely surrounded by dense jungle, where the operation of transport was difficult, and where men fell sick one after another due to the hostile environment. Under these most adverse conditions, I proceeded to perform my duty with selfless devotion to my country, as well as doing my best to improve and rationalize the situation in the branch. It was not in my power to prevent many precious lives from being lost during the construction work because of such adverse conditions. It was in no way due to maltreatment on my part.

However heaven did not favour us and we were defeated, and I was summoned to Singapore as a suspected war criminal. As a result of the trial held from 16 to 22 August, I am now to fade away 'like the dew on the court'.

I am writing my last note with a serene mind. I always used powers delegated to me by the army code, faithfully from my heart. I want to die an honourable death by submitting my life to Heaven's will, and die on the scaffold like the fading dew. Yes I will end my life with a good grace. I thank you, my parents, for your love over the past twenty-eight years, which has been deeper than the sea and higher than the mountains. At the same time I deeply apologise for ending my life without requiting your love.

Mother! Please set your mind at rest as your son is going serenely to the land of the dead where Father awaits me, with the satisfaction that I used all my powers for the sake of the Japanese Empire and for the Emperor. Please mother, pay good attention to your health.

Dear brother-in-law and sister Tomie! Please excuse me for causing trouble to you while I was alive. I ask you to take good care of our old mother. I pray that you will live happily for a long time.

Dear sister Miyoshi! Please show great devotion to mother, adding my share too. I have not heard from you while I have been in the army and was concerned about how you have been.

The enclosed poems are expressions of my feelings in the jail. I will end my twenty-eight years of life wishing long life and happiness to Mother.

Farewell!'

Farewell Poem

What can I do as a defeated national,
When I have been blown on by a cold-hearted storm?
My faithful practice of doing my best has not changed
But a storm is blowing on my defeated body.
Even though my body has become thin and weak

My faith which is harder than steel has not changed.
From the blood of a brave Japanese man who is passing away
Fuchsias will bloom.
Keeping deep in my heart the many notes from my dear ones
I will pass away.

A poem left behind

The time when the violent storm will blow is not decided,
I have not been able to sleep expecting it every moment.
The war should have been won.
How miserable is the one who has been defeated,
Though the blood of a brave Japanese man was stirred
When I was put in the prison,
When the winning country judged me
My faithfulness could not be understood.
However much my body is tormented and wastes away
I shall still maintain the Japanese spirit.
I thank you for your efforts to defend me
Even though I may be defeated at the court.
As the evening lighting-up time comes close to the prison window
I pine all the more for the image of my mother.

Though I am in the country of eternal summer, as I am a prisoner
The wind blowing on me is chilly.
A year has passed since my country was defeated
From today my body will stand in the judgment court,
How miserable, as one of those in prison
I have no one to stand by my side.
In the streets on my way to the court
I see again the past Shonan* with nostalgia.
Though I give my fleeting life freely
My heart is pained when I think of my country.
Recollecting the image of my old mother
I go to the trial court tomorrow.
At daybreak I am reminded of the image of my fellow soldier
Who passed away leaving behind the cry of 'hurrah'.
As I am a human being
I am made to long for my mother by the singing of birds
     at the jail window.

---

* Singapore was called Shonan during the Japanese occupation

6.5   Sacrificed men (Chaplain at Changi prison)

(Buddhist) Prison Chaplain JSP Honryu Tanaka, Former Lieutenant,
Staff Section, Southern Air Force Headquarters

I graduated from Rissho University in Tokyo in 1940 and was ordained a Buddhist priest. Soon I was conscripted into the army. After training as an officer cadet (*eao*) I was attached to the headquarters of the army air force in Singapore. I was a senior lieutenant when the war ended. Then I was transferred to Malaya and was engaged in administrative duties, such as the transfer of weapons, ammunition and fuel to the Allied forces and the demobilisation of our men. About the end of 1945 a fellow staff officer committed suicide and I wanted to recite a sutra for him as I could do nothing else for him. But I could recite only half of the sutra which the believers of the Nichiren sect should remember. I had been reduced to being an unpriestly person while I was in the army. I continued my administrative duties until December 1946, when all the work was finished and I expected to go home. Then my boss, a former officer, told me that he had been asked to transfer me to the post of chaplain at Changi prison. I said that I did not want to go; I wanted to get on the next boat to Japan. The former officer said to me 'I cannot force you to be the resident priest. You yourself must decide yes or no.' Later I learnt that a person who had recently gone to Changi as a priest had come back within a few days, sick and with a high temperature. So my boss knew that it was such a hard job that he could not force me to go.

Having been told to decide the matter by myself, I spent some days in the palm-leaf barracks. One day, the wall newspaper was renewed and I read casually some *tanka* (Japanese 31-syllable poems) included in the mimeograph copy on rough paper pasted on the wall. On reading them, I was deeply impressed and stood stock still, and when I left, my mind was set on the new job. The poems were written by a student soldier, Mr Hisao Kimura, who was hanged in Changi.

I think of my homeland while sipping my morning porridge.
Mother! Do not lament. Father! Excuse me.
Listening to the sutra for the passing of a friend
I await my day counting on my fingers.
I have used up all my sorrow, tears and anger,
I shall die in this miserable solitude.

Up to that time I had been thinking only of myself, and wanting to get back to my homeland, but I realised that there were people who had to die leaving behind such inconsolable poems. The last part of his will read as follows:

Now I am going to die as one of the symbols to all the human beings on earth. I have never done any evil for which I deserve to be put to death. But in my case, the truth could not be found and I could not be vindicated. In the eyes of the outside world I am a Japanese. There is no room for complaint other than that I was unfortunate in being noticed by them. I can never meet death calmly if I feel that I have become a scapegoat for the Japanese army. However if I think that I die bearing all the sins of all the Japanese nationals, I shall not be angry and I can die smiling.

Without fear and sorrow, I go to the execution platform
With the smiling face of Mother in my mind.

This was his last poem written the night before execution.

I made up my mind and went to Changi prison on the last day of 1946 – a day I shall never forget. When I arrived at the prison it was possible for a person about to be executed to be given a pencil and paper and to write his will, his last message to his family. But the enemy had the will burnt after the execution, probably because they did not want some of the information to get into the hands of those awaiting trial, as the search for war criminals was still going on. As it was strictly forbidden to take papers outside, I received a man's will secretly at the time of giving him the final rites just before the execution, and then took it outside avoiding the eyes of the jailers and gatekeepers.

When I came back to my lodging, I hand-copied all the wills on sheets of paper and hid them in separate places, as I was afraid that they might be confiscated. I wept while copying them. Sometimes my tears dropped continuously on the paper and I could not continue writing.

The poems and will made by Mr Hisao Kimura, mentioned above, were written on the blank pages of a book, an outline of philosophy by Dr Gen Tanabe. At that time, those sentenced to death (who were in P hall) were not allowed to write except just before the execution, but they were allowed to read books. Mr Kimura had written his will in the book using a pencil he had secretly hidden. And my predecessor as priest, Mr Ryokyo Sekiguchi, had managed to take the book out of the prison, and later his will was somehow released to the newspaper I had seen on the wall.

Mr Kimura was hanged on 23 May 1946 at the age of 28. He had been called up while he was a student at Kyoto University, and sent to the Nicobar Islands on the eastern side of the Indian Ocean, when he worked for the military government as a private. As he spoke English he went out among the local inhabitants, so his name was well known to them. He was ordered to investigate inhabitants suspected of spying. According to his colleague, Private Minoru Ono, who was sentenced to ten years' imprisonment, the death of a local person who had died of malaria was regarded as a result of torture by Mr Kimura, due to the false testimony of a local man. He was unfortunate in being known to the local people who were eager for revenge against the Japanese.

Mr Ono's imprisonment was reduced to five years and he arrived back in Japan in March 1950. He went to see the mother of Mr Kimura at Suita and explained to her in detail what had happened in the Nicobar Islands, and how Mr Kimura had come to be hanged. Mrs Kimura maintained a brave attitude during his long explanation and finally said, 'Thank you very much. I shall now build a tomb for Hisao.' Up to that time she had not been able to believe that her son was dead, so his room had been kept tidy, awaiting his return.

As priest I went to P hall in the prison once every two days to meet those sentenced to death. Their life in prison before and after the judgement must have been one of agony as a human being facing death. When I started visiting them, most of the men in P hall seemed to have attained enlightenment in the face of death, living every day as a good day, as they had been there for a long time. They talked cheerfully in a serene state of mind. Though they were in an uncomfortable jail, they were spiritually awakened. Although I had no background to my purpose in visiting them, they consoled me and clarified for me various aspects of my anxiety over their situation. What they talked about to me every time, with unclouded minds, was the future of Japan, with sincere wishes for her prosperity, their dear home villages and their beloved families.

When they were finally notified of the execution date, they received the notice without emotion, and furthermore thanked the notifying official for what had been done for them. And they said more cheerfully, with happy faces, 'I can now set my mind at rest.' By contrast, I, and those seeing them off, could do nothing, as our hearts were full of emotion.

On their last night I had dinner with them. They ate a good meal, the first for a long time, with great relish, and sincerely thanked the work party for the noodles, fish and tempura-fries that they had kindly squeezed out of their meagre rations.

Mr Wakamatsu (a former captain) was kind-hearted and had a strong affection for his men. He spoke feelingly about his memories, the troubles he had undergone over the Thailand–Burma railway, and Mr Omi, his subordinate, who was executed before him. He showed me the hair of the deceased Mr Omi saying, 'Tomorrow I go to join him.' He smiled as he talked with frequent pauses, about his boyhood in his beloved homeland, and about the wife and children he had left at home; I thought only a perfect philosopher could act like this. As I listened to his gentle, brotherly, calm and sacred words, almost without realising it, I felt a quiet genial feeling stealing over me, while my human discontent, that such a good man had to go, still gnawed at my heart.

After a while, when Mr Fukuda and Mr Shimojo sang the military funeral song 'When man goes to sea' and 'Auld lang syne' as a parting present to him, Mr Wakamatsu stood by the latticed window, listened to them motionlessly, and then thanked them saying 'Thank you everybody, I will go in good spirits'. And he himself sang the national anthem at the top of his voice. Then he turned to Mr Abe who was in the solitary cell and said, 'Mr Abe, thank you.'

I was deeply moved, listening with closed eyelids, by the beautiful friendship between those seeing him off and Mr Wakamatsu who was about to leave. There were no shades of gloom about him; he was just like an excited child. Looking at him and talking with him, I felt my human complaints creeping up in my heart.

Early next morning I chanted the lotus sutra together with him and bade him farewell. He left saying, 'I go in high spirits. Goodbye. I am much obliged to you for your kind assistance.' His attitude was a noble one to the end. 'Though my body dies, may my home country prosper for ever!' was what everyone who died had in their minds. Their sincere concern for their country until the last moment, indeed even after they died, could not fail to impress anyone.

Depending on the case, it took up to a year for a person to be executed after the death sentence had been passed. Though according to the rules of the Allied forces a retrial was not possible, a few men had their death sentences reduced to life imprisonment or term imprisonment. This possibility of survival affected those in P hall, especially those who believed they were innocent. Despite the apparent peace of mind of those sentenced to death, I realised later that they must have been worried about family and other obligations. Lieutenant-Colonel Kazuo Masugi had been a staff officer with the Java army and was hanged on

25 May 1947, one of the 33 men I saw off during the eight months I was chaplain. Mr Masugi was 44 years old and had four children. He was a decent man who died without involving his subordinates in the case. When I copied his diary I came across a poem:

> 'I read a letter from my wife,
> A small child cried and cried, asking for its father and its meal,
> At long last it went to sleep.'

I felt his hidden feelings in having to die leaving behind such a young child and wanting to ask his wife to take care of the children though it would not be easy. However his wife had died, as was reported in a letter from his 13-year old daughter addressed to the Japanese staff of the defence attorney section, which had been set up virtually as a formality. It was a touching letter which said, 'I think that my father would be disturbed by knowing that mother had died, please don't tell him. If you judge that he would not, please convey this to him as you think fit.' This was about a month before his death.

I could not make up my mind for some time. But as he had never mentioned his family to me, and I did not know then that he had written such a poem, I finally made up my mind to tell him in the belief that he had a good sense of religion. Though he was told about the death of his wife, he did not show any sign of distress to me or to the men around him. I felt he was a man in a serene state of mind, as I had expected.

The night before his execution a supper party was held in the hall, attended by ten condemned men and me. A note left by a Korean interpreter/guard, Mr Hirahara, described the atmosphere at the party until a few minutes before he was hanged. Mr Masugi was smiling in a carefree attitude at the party. I felt at that time that he had no lingering attachment to this world and must be in a mental state like that of the Buddha. But afterwards, in copying his diary, I was awakened to the fact that I had seen only the outside surface of his mind. In fact, he died with a strong link to his family deep in his mind. This man who did not seem to be distressed when told of the death of his wife left the following poem in his diary.

> 'A letter came,
> my dear wife had passed away
> and my four children are waiting for their father.'

And I came across another which mentioned two old proverbs,

'Tears flow out as I think of my children,
a peacock in a burning field saves its children despite the risk to itself,
a crane in the cold night covers its chicks wholly with its wings.'

In this poem Mr. Masugi expressed his heart-rending parental sorrow and grief.

It was only for eight months that I was the prison chaplain, but during this period I learned much about the life of a priest, and received rigorous training for the priesthood. I am now the chief priest of Shoei-in Temple in Tokyo. In a corner of the Temple grounds stands the Cenotaph for the martyrs at Changi, Singapore, which was built by donations from those who were jailed at Changi, veterans of the war and the war-bereaved. It stands on a hill covered with cherry trees, from which the sacred Mount Fuji can be seen.

On the back of the memorial tower the following inscription (written by Mr Wakamatsu) is written:

After the end of World War II, one hundred and forty six former members of the armed forces and military employees were executed by the Allied forces as war criminals. However, unfortunately an unjust fate befell most of them, as mistaken victims of the war. Moreover these people had been forsaken by their mother country, were forced to face an unnatural death and suffering, and finally died a glorious death with their last cries 'May I be a human sacrifice for the reconstruction of my motherland, which may also lead to the peace of all mankind in the world.'

We shed copious tears when we think of the sentiments of those martyrs at that time, and swear that such a tragedy shall never be repeated.

Now we dedicate the ground here to let their souls rest in peace, and erect this cenotaph to pray for the repose of their souls.'

6.6   Petition asking for a reduced penalty (1 March 1952)

Former medical major Masaki Mori, former senior medical officer, Thailand PoW Accommodation Headquarters

I was the senior medical officer of the Thailand PoW Accommodation Headquarters from June 1943 to November 1944. My job included the guidance of the medical officers who were stationed at the branches, including Captain Tomizo Higuchi of the 3rd branch. The 3rd branch had about nine thousand PoWs dispersed in more than ten detachments which moved as the construction proceeded along the 120 kilometres of the railway from Thanbyuzayat to the Thai–Burma border. In the branch the PoWs were supervised by nine officers, 17 non-commissioned officers, 30 military employees in administration and 100 guards. After the end of the war, Mr Higuchi was prosecuted as a war criminal and was sentenced to life imprisonment at Singapore. He was transferred from the Changi prison to Sugamo prison in Tokyo in August 1951 where he was to be held for life.

I hereby submit a petition to the supreme commander of the allied forces asking for the reduction of his penalty on grounds which are summarised as follows:

Statement

Tomozo Higuchi was pronounced guilty on the basis of the following findings:

1. He moved many PoWs in the Thailand-Burma border area and had them engage in the construction of the railway.
2. He tortured PoWs by giving them poor meals, clothing and lodgings.
3. There was a shortage of medical supplies.
4. Methods of transporting sick PoWs were poor.
5. He forcibly diagnosed sick PoWs as fit for work.

I would like to explain the situation at that time as follows:

Clarification on item 1

'Use the PoWs in the railway construction work in the Thailand–Burma border area' was the operational orders of the commander of the southern army. Higuchi, being a low-ranking doctor in a peripheral location, was not in a position to affect the decisions or give guidance on such an important operation. Also the movement of PoWs in the border area was carried out under the operational orders of the commander, 3rd branch, which were issued at the request of the working party depending on the progress of the railway construction work, concerning which Higuchi as the doctor attached to the branch had no discretionary powers.

Clarification on item 2

According to the duties of the various branches of the former Japanese army, the quartermaster was in charge of the feeding, clothing and lodging, and the medical doctor was only able to advise him or his commander on a point of hygiene. The supply of materials and food to the border area was often stopped or disturbed by transport difficulties caused by heavy rain and a shortage of facilities. Even the Japanese soldiers, who were innured to poor meals, hardship and privations, suffered more as a result of the poor food, clothing and lodging facilities than as a result of the construction work. So it was natural that such conditions should be intolerable for the white men who had never been materially deprived and had been used to a high standard of living. But the PoWs were treated in the same way as the Japanese soldiers without discrimination.

Higuchi together with the quartermaster sent earnest and repeated requests to army headquarters, trying to get things for the PoWs, but the answer was always that the army had no stocks or the warehouse was empty.

Clarification on item 3

Medical supplies were delivered to the PoW camps from the freight depot under orders from the army, but the quantity was very small. Higuchi often asked the Moulmein depot for supplies, and sometimes went to the army headquarters at Rangoon and did everything he could, but he got only a very little as the army as a whole had only very limited stocks. I remember that I had written in the monthly medical report submitted to the Southern army as follows:

> The number of the sick has been increasing month by month due to the poor environment and continued overwork. However the medical supplies available to us are only a fraction of what is needed. Do not condemn my request as an astronomical figure. If things go on as they are, almost all the Japanese soldiers and PoWs will be wiped out when the railway is completed.

Medical supplies were seriously deficient in all the units of the southern army. Sadly, the case was as the Japanese proverb says: 'Nothing comes out of the sack but what was in it.'

Clarification on item 4

The transportation officer of the branch was in charge of moving both healthy and sick PoWs. In some cases they were moved by the work units. The method of transportation, which was carried out under the principle of 'do things expeditiously' might have been unacceptable under peacetime conditions. However it was essential to move sick men as quickly as possible from the depths of the jungle, as keeping them there one hour longer meant they got one hour nearer death. There were no ambulance cars in the branch even though Higuchi put in a request for them many times. Higuchi gave detailed advice to the transportation officer on the movement of patients by truck, which was the only available means. After the completion of the railway, patients were moved by rail, but the condition of the rail track was poor with frequent derailments and it was also under constant air attack by the Allied forces. So it was not possible to transport them under satisfactory conditions.

Clarification on item 5

About nine thousand PoWs in the branch were dispersed in detachment camps along the 120 kilometres from Thanbyuzayat in the west to the Thailand–Burma border in the east. Many of the camps were directly controlled by the branch staff while some of the camps were in the barracks of the working units. PoW medical staff were attached to all the detachments, and were in charge of medical matters. Whether to send sick PoWs to hospital, allow them to stay in bed, or let them do minor work in the camp was left to the PoW medical staff, who were under the control of the branch commander.

Higuchi was posted at the branch headquarters as the only doctor, and his responsibilities included treating Japanese soldiers; applying to his superior for the issue of medical supplies and receiving them; writing reports, and sending out the notices on disease prevention to everybody in the branch; and liaison with the working units. And when possible he went around all the camps and treated the Japanese staff, and interviewed the PoW medical staff to hear their requests, which he tried hard to fulfil.

As it took a week for Higuchi to go around the camps, many Japanese patients were treated by PoW doctors as he was not available during the tour. So it is clear that the statement 'Higuchi saw the PoW patients every day and diagnosed them as being fit for work' is not correct, considering the time and freedom of movement available to one person.

There had always been disagreement between the work units and the PoW camps, as the former were determined to complete the railway early by rushing the work at any cost, while the policy of the latter was to protect the lives of the PoWs. Some work units openly criticised Higuchi as a person who did not co-operate with the operations or as an undesirable military man, as he insisted on taking good care of the PoWs and treating the patients favourably from the hygiene point of view.

Petition

Hygiene is the key point in the success of operations in southern latitides as is clearly shown by the sad failure of the construction of the Benget road and by the success of Italy's Ethiopian operations which were carried out with full attention to hygiene under the guidance of an authority on tropical medicine. Looking back on the history of Thailand, troops of the Burmese kingdom from Rangoon tried to attack Thailand and failed three times as they lost more than a half of their members at the border, probably due to the plague. This had happened in the area where the Japanese built the railway.

It was really reckless to attempt to send a large number of troops to an area with such histories of failure. That kind of reckless attempt should be punished, but the constant efforts of Higuchi who tried to improve the situation of the PoWs under the strong pressure of the operations, does not deserve punishment.

Many PoWs died and their torture was great. I as his senior medical officer testified at the court that I could not guide or help him sufficiently due to my lack of ability and I believed that he should not to be blamed. I praised him for his contribution in having reduced the losses to such a degree when total annihilation was feared under such indescribable conditions. I sympathise with Higuchi who was once called an odious man on the side of the PoWs by the Japanese operating units, and later imprisoned for life as a war criminal.

I cannot stand the mental torture of myself not being imprisoned, as I was in a superior position with little contact with the PoWs, while Higuchi, who did his best under terrible conditions, is in prison for life.

I plead your special consideration of granting him parole.

Note

Mr Higuchi was paroled on August 1957 together with other Japanese and Korean war criminals, and subsequently practised medicine in Tokyo.

6.7   The British View: 'March to the Scaffold'

Editorial, Straits Times (published in Singapore 6 February 1947, retranslated from the Japanese)

The terrible march to the scaffold from Changi prison is still continuing, giving a demonic thrill to some people every time the footboard drops.

So far 153 Japanese have been hanged in Southeast Asia, most of them executed in Changi, and 27 men are awaiting their deaths. The war in Asia ended 17 months ago. But many men are experiencing at first hand the rigours of living in Changi prison, and those who, thankfully, were granted the freedom to live wish that matters relating to the war crimes should be cleared up as soon as possible.

There are only a few people among those who lived in Malaya during the Japanese occupation, either inside or outside of prisons, who do not have any doubts about the war-crimes courts. Today also in our homeland a similar feeling is spreading, as has been expressed in the letters from readers of this paper.

One reader wrote that it is necessary to carefully re-examine the methods of judgement and court procedures, because of the widespread and deeply rooted doubts regarding the Singapore court. Another reader who had been interned in a Japanese camp in Siam wrote, 'Many of us have deep doubts about parts of the published detailed testimonies.' And he continued:

For us it seems that the penalties become severer, the lower the ranks of the Japanese, on the assumption that those on the lowest rung of the society are the most cruel. The Japanese guards are the most severely punished. To take one example, Sergeant Shimojo, who was notorious for beating and bullying, was sentenced to death by hanging for malicious actions though they did not result in any deaths.

Lieutenant-Colonel Yanagida, commander of the 2nd Branch, who had been remembered by many prisoners of war as relatively humane, was sentenced to 20 years' imprisonment on the charge of shooting to death four runaways in the camp under orders from his superior, Colonel Sugazawa, the supreme commander of the camps in Siam, who was arrogant and insensitive as we saw when he inspected the camp, and said that we PoWs were being very well treated, and who got 12 years. The colonel was the direct superior of Lt-Colonel Yanagida. And finally Lt-General Ishida, the supreme commander of all the railways in 1943 and the highest political and military administrator, got only ten years.

What we would like to hear is, by what standard they judge the Japanese. Is there nobody in Singapore who can act as an adviser to the prisoners, who honestly intends to help the military court, who will not go along with the charges against those being prosecuted, and who can testify to the facts as we know them, and who is a legally learned man with a balanced judgement? Take the case of a man convicted by the military court of being a war criminal, who was tried again at a civilian court in Singapore.

It is the case of a Malay man, who had been hired as an interpreter, and was sentenced to 15 years' imprisonment by the military court on a charge of injuring several men. After the judgement, the Malay was found to be a British subject and the sentence was cancelled by the supreme commander. He was then tried at a second local court under Judge Russell, who sentenced him to 15 months' imprisonment. 'From 15 years to 15 months!'

Turning to American opinion on the war-crimes courts, we find a high-minded and brave expression of views which must be a high point of the tradition of Anglo-American laws. In the judgement passed in the US Supreme Court on the appeal of General Yamashita against the sentence of the American military court in Manila, the judge Murphy expressed a minority opinion as follows:

> Yamashita was put on trial hurriedly without time to prepare a proper defence, prosecuted inappropriately, and sentenced to death by hanging. In this prosecution which was carried out mean-spiritedly and in haste, there was no definite attempt to prove that the defendant Yamashita had violated laws of the war. To force an unjustified court on the enemy, and to mete out a punishment which had not been approved, and to do this in the heat of the desire for revenge, can only inflame hostile feelings in an enemy national and damage the mutual understanding which is needed for the building of world peace.

We in Singapore do know everything about Yamashita, and even if he had not been hanged in Manila, he would have been sentenced to death in Singapore for his bloody abuse of at least four thousand Chinese. However, setting aside the rights and wrongs of Mr Murphy's comments, it is certain that they present an important warning to the military courts who are judging the defeated enemy.

So-called malicious acts, which were testified to by PoWs or detainees after their release, were exaggerated by biased minds, and in most of the cases full investigations were not carried out. There are many points that need the greatest attention paid to them when it comes to sending a Japanese war criminal to the gallows. Most of the men prosecuted acted on orders from their superiors. They had been trained more strictly than those in any other foreign countries to obey orders passively and without questioning. Their statements, that they could not get the necessary food or medicine from their superiors as they were in short supply in the camp, must be the plain truth. They belong to an army whose harsh standards of military discipline are quite different from those of the British army.

The military war-crimes courts in Singapore have a very difficult duty, which is also a disagreeable form of service. Recently the courts have been handing out more reasonable sentences than before. These days there are no cases of a group of six to eight Japanese being sentenced to death at the same time.

In Southeast Asia a total of 181 men have been sentenced to death compared to 348 men given terms of imprisonment. The key facts of the case are the difficulty of deciding the true individual responsibility for the crimes being considered in the courts, the lack of the right to appeal to a higher court composed of professional judges, and the other considerations described above. These facts make it more important in the war-crimes courts than in general courts to temper British justice with mercy, even if the Japanese do not plead for their lives.

Appendix 1　The Influence of *Bushido*: Why Japanese officers drove PoWs to work unreasonably hard

Bushido, developed in feudal Japan, still had a strong influence on Japanese officers during World War II. *Bushido* demanded absolute loyalty and exacted the penalty of suicide (by self-immolation or disembowelment) for a dishonourable result. All the railway officers realised how important the Burma–Thailand Railway was for the survival of the Japanese army in Burma. So they knew if the completion of the railway were delayed and put the Burma army in danger, their regimental commander was sure to commit suicide for the dishonour, and the officer who did not do his part on time and caused the delay should also commit suicide, according to *Bushido*. This is the main factor which drove the officers to force PoWs to complete the daily quota of their work by all means, as the daily quota was based on the minimum required to complete the railway on time. Thus PoWs were forced to work over the standard work time even in miserable conditions.

In the Japanese army, orders are seen as absolute. Lower-ranking officers were not allowed to refuse the order to attack an enemy position. However the orders on engineering projects were flexible because of the nature of the work. The officer who did not complete the work on time might be demoted or at worst fired, never put to death. As an example, the railway regiment commanders did not accept the order to bring forward the completion of the Burma–Thailand Railway by two months, though this could cause demerit in their career.

The Japanese soldiers also understood the spirit of *Bushido* and co-operated with their officers in the construction work.

Bushido in its origin was based on Buddhism. However from the Meiji era Buddhism gradually lost its influence on the Japanese people, though they were registered as the flock of a Buddhist temple just for the sake of their funeral service. This had worsened the default of *Bushido*, as seen in the treatment of PoWs.

During the war with Russia (1904–5), Japanese army had about eight war Buddhist priests in a Division. However in World War II, there was no religious position in the Japanese army which was comparable to the pastors (chaplains) in British or American armies. Thus teachings of Buddhism such as benevolence to the weak or the vanquished were being lost from the practice of *Bushido*.

Japan had been renowned for the good treatment of PoWs until World War I. What caused the change was the declining influence of Buddhism on the Japanese people, together with the notorious army instruction of 1941, 'Die rather than be captured', which caused contempt towards PoWs among the Japanese.

There was another side to the overtime work. PoWs tried to do as little work as possible, as they also realised the importance of the railway to Japan. In accordance with the code of soldiers when they were captured, they were unwilling to work on the construction which was beneficial to enemy. However this resulted in the unsatisfactory progress of the task for which Japanese officers forced them to do overtime work. PoWs tried bravely and patiently to resist the Japanese despite the torture of being forced to do hard overtime work.

The following extract is from *Bushido* by Nitobe Inazo, a well-known educator/scholar/internationalist who later served as Under-Secretary General of the League of Nations. The book was written in English and published in 1900 by the Leeds & Biddle Co., Philadelphia, USA.

Bu-shi-do means literally Military-Knight-Ways – the way that fighting nobles should observe in their daily life as well as in their vocation; in a word 'Precept of Knighthood,' or the *noblesse oblige* of the warrior class.

It was an organic growth of decades and centuries of military career. It, perhaps, fills the same position in the history of ethics that the English Constitution does in political history.

Buddhism furnished a sense of calm trust in Fate, a quiet submission to the inevitable, the stoic composure in sight of danger or calamity, that disdain of life and friendliness with death.

Such loyalty to the sovereign, such reverence for ancestral memory, and such filial piety as are not taught by any other creed, were inculcated by the Shinto doctrines, imparting passivity to the otherwise arrogant character of the Samurai.

The high estimate placed upon honour was ample excuse with many for taking one's own life. How many acquiesced in the sentiment expressed by Garth,

> 'When honour is lost, it's a relief to die;
> Death's but a sure retreat from infamy,'

The physical endurance, fortitude, and bravery that 'the little Jap' possesses, were sufficiently proved in the Chino–Japanese war. 'Is there any nation more loyal and patriotic?' is a question asked by many; and for the proud answer, 'There is not,' we must thank the Precept of Knighthood.

On the other hand, it is fair to recognise that for the very faults and defects of our character, *Bushido* is largely responsible.

Unformulated, *Bushido* is still the animating spirit, the motor force of our country.

Appendix 2 Treatment of Japanese Surrendered Personnel (JSP)

The Japanese army and navy had never experienced national surrender, hence they had little idea what its outcome would be. They initially felt relieved to be made JSP rather than dishonourable and shameful prisoners of war (PoWs). This system was convenient and economical for the South East Asia Command, consisting mostly of British forces, in controlling the large number of surrendered Japanese soldiers and civilians – 783,000 men in Southeast Asia.

Though Japan had not ratified the Geneva Convention of 1929, the Japanese should have been treated as PoWs under the Hague Regulations of 1907, and should have had the basic human rights conferred upon PoWs. In Europe, German troops had been treated as 'surrendered enemy personnel' (SEP), who were similar to JSP. But the situation was different, as the German capitulation was both political, involving the dissolution of the government, and military, whereas the Japanese capitulation was only military. Moreover, disarmed Japanese were permitted to return to their homes under the Potsdam Proclamation, dated 28 July, issued by USA, Great Britain and China.

The disadvantages of having been JSP compared with the privilege of PoWs were as follows:

1. The JSP camps were located mostly in jungles or remote areas where there were no water and electricity services. The inadequate facilities were responsible for ruining the health of the Japanese. The occurrence of infectious diseases such as malaria, tuberculosis and amoebic dysentery was 21 per cent among JSP, double that in the Japanese army during the war. The death toll of JSP was more than 8,931. A total of 141,500 JSP were sent to the barren Rempang Island and about 60,000 of them were in a critical condition due to starvation as food was not sent to them in the initial two months.
2. JSP were fed 1,600 calories per day despite being forced to do hard work, whereas the British field ration was 3,300 calories (the amount which should have been fed to PoWs), and that of the Japanese army had been 3,600 calories.
3. JSP were forced to do unhealthy and dangerous work. At first many JSP worked without any time off.
4. Officers received no pay and other ranks, although compelled to do hard work, received no pay either, until May 1947. After that date, a token wage was paid in Japan.
5. JSP were rearmed and most were put on peace-keeping duties, mainly suppressing the independence activities of the local people. Approximately 167 JSPs died in combat in Indo-China, 627 in Java and 244 in Sumatra while on peace-keeping duties.

6. JSP had their personal property impounded without any receipt being given. Their money was also impounded.
7. No clothing and daily necessaries were given to JSP until May 1946.
8. Though JSP were promised an early return to Japan under the Potsdam Proclamation, 106,000 men were retained as working parties after June 1946, to carry out miscellaneous hard labour tasks. They were sent home by December 1947.

The Japanese felt that they were confined as JSP for the sake of revenge and as punishment for what they had done to Allied PoWs during the war. Japanese soldiers who surrendered to US armed forces by 1 September 1945, by contrast, were treated as PoWs and were repatriated earlier than the JSP under British control.

References

This appendix and the references given below were based on the survey carried out by the JSP Research Group, Tokyo.

Yoshito Kita, 'Koufuku-tekikokugunjin no Houteki-ichi wo meguru Shomondai' ('Problems concerning the legal status of Surrendered Enemy Personnel') in *Buryoku Funnsou no Kokusaihou* (International Law in Armed Conflict) (Toshindo, Tokyo, 2004).

Sadao Oba (ex-JSP), 'JSP wo tsuikyu site' ('Investing in JSP'), in *Yu Yu*, no.11, (Kigyou OB Pen Club, Tokyo, 2004).

Index

NB Asian place-names have been given in the English form used during the Second World War, with modern forms in brackets where appropriate. Illustrations are indexed in *italic* type.